"Former Navy SEAL Scott Taylor brings a critical perspective to the public policy debate. He speaks from the experience that he and his brothers in arms have gained in dangerous corners of the world where only strength and resolve keep the world's bad actors at bay. And he understands that American power—especially when you consider the alternatives—is good not just for Americans, but for the world. In *Trust Betrayed* Taylor exposes the Obama administration leaks that have endangered our special forces, and he makes the case for a foreign policy based on U.S. national interests, not grandiose ambitions or wishful thinking. This is an important book."

—**John Bolton**, former U.S. ambassador to the United Nations

"As Barack Obama has moved the US ever farther away from a foreign policy that actually safeguarded US national security, it has become increasingly difficult for patriotic politicians—and ordinary Americans—to see what can and must be done to get us out of this current mess, and restore America's strength and security before it's too late. But in *Trust Betrayed*, former Navy SEAL Scott Taylor analyzes the contemporary situation with the keen eye of a man who has seen the disastrous effects of Obama's policies up close, and provides a reasonable and realistic path back to national sanity. Not only should all candidates for national office be required to read this book—they should be required to report on it, and explain how they intend to implement its recommendations."

—**Robert Spencer**, author of the *New York Times* bestsellers *The Politically Incorrect Guide to Islam® (and the Crusades)* and *The Truth About Muhammad*

"Former Navy SEAL Scott Taylor does his country another valuable service. *Trust Betrayed* brings the valuable perspective of a boots-on-the-ground veteran to the foreign policy disasters under Obama and Secretary of State Hillary Clinton, from America's botched response to the Egyptian Revolution, to Benghazi, to the 'red line' debacle in Syria, to the renewed war in Iraq. Read this book to learn how America's role in the world has been jeopardized—and what can be done to restore it."

> —**Erick Stakelbeck**, host of CBN's *The Watchman with Erick Stakelbeck* and author of *The Terrorist Next Door*, *The Brotherhood*, and *Inside ISIS*

"*Trust Betrayed* is must reading. Former Navy SEAL Scott Taylor lays out in gripping detail exactly how the Obama administration has abused our Special Operations Forces for political gain. Taylor dishes out the blame the politicians richly deserve for appropriating the heroism of those who serve—and then leaking classified information that puts them and their families at risk. And if you didn't already know exactly why a Hillary Clinton presidency would be a disaster for America, you'll find out in this book."

> —**Bill Cowan**, Lieutenant Colonel (Ret.), U.S. Marine Corps, former Intelligence Support Activity operative, and expert in counterterrorism and hostage rescue

TRUST BETRAYED

TRUST BETRAYED

BARACK OBAMA, HILLARY CLINTON, AND THE SELLING OUT OF AMERICA'S NATIONAL SECURITY

FORMER U.S. NAVY SEAL

SCOTT TAYLOR

REGNERY
PUBLISHING
A Salem Communications Company

Regnery® is a registered trademark of Salem Communications Holding Corporation

Library of Congress Cataloging-in-Publication data

Taylor, Scott, 1979-
  Trust betrayed : Barack Obama, Hillary Clinton, and the selling out of America's national security / Scott Taylor.
     pages cm
   ISBN 978-1-62157-327-2 (hardback)
1. Obama, Barack. 2. Clinton, Hillary Rodham. 3. National security--United States. 4. Leaks (Disclosure of information)--United States. 5. Leaks (Disclosure of information)--Political aspects--United States. I. Title.
   E907.T38 2015
   355'.033073--dc23
                              2014047750

Published in the United States by
Regnery Publishing
A Salem Communications Company
300 New Jersey Ave NW
Washington, DC 20001
www.Regnery.com

Manufactured in the United States of America

10 9 8 7 6 5 4 3 2 1

Books are available in quantity for promotional or premium use. For information on discounts and terms, please visit our website: www.Regnery.com.

Distributed to the trade by
Perseus Distribution
250 West 57th Street
New York, NY 10107

This book is dedicated to the men of Naval Special Warfare, some of the greatest I will ever know. It is for those who no longer stand among us, those few courageous souls who dared to go forward on behalf of our flag, for the love of their brothers, their families, and their country. I will see you again, but not just yet.

"Greater love hath no man than this, that a man lay down his life for his friends." —John 15:13

CONTENTS

CHAPTER ONE

The Service

Some people join the military because it runs in their families. Some do it to pay for college. Some feel a patriotic calling. Some are inspired by events, such as the 9/11 attacks. Some feel the need for discipline in their lives. Some just need a job.

And sure, some people do it for the wrong reasons, and then suddenly realize they're likely to spend a lot more time performing tedious menial tasks than they ever will fighting pitched battles against an enemy. As a newly minted Navy SEAL, I cleaned my share of toilets.

But whatever the motive that brings you to the United States Armed Forces, everyone who serves honorably helps their country. You may never even understand how much of a difference your small contribution made, but everyone plays a role—one team, one fight.

And you aren't serving only the United States, but also often-ungrateful nations that would otherwise be suffering under someone else's yoke. This is why Ronald Reagan once described America as the world's "last best hope." It's an extremely appropriate phrase, thought out carefully for the occasion of a speech given when the world faced domination by Soviet communism.

Ideally, the United States government pursues national interests that benefit Americans, either directly or indirectly. But in practice, the world also depends upon us safeguarding our own interests. Our main goal—to minimize the risk of another major shooting war between the world's great powers—is one every reasonable person shares, including even some of our enemies.

That leaves us like the titan Atlas in Greek mythology, reluctantly holding the world on our shoulders. Whether we like it or not, we are the glue that holds a very messy world together—at times barely. And the military plays a huge role in this task, even in peacetime. The American soldier is the guy who puts the "strength" in "peace through strength."

That's not to condone every war we have fought, or every official stance we have taken. Quite the contrary—America has made many mistakes, and will make even more. We are not perfect, but for the rest of the world, every alternative to America's power is a worse alternative, involving greater suffering and pain and more death.

Liberals often criticize our role in the world as stifling the aspirations of smaller, weaker, and poorer nations. This simply isn't so. The critics fail to recognize two important realities. First, our yoke is light. We do not plunder our allies, or those we vanquish; to the contrary, we nearly always send our money to them. That is how it has been since the Marshall Plan. As Colin Powell once said, "We have gone forth from our shores repeatedly over the last hundred years...and put wonderful young men and women at risk, many of whom have lost their lives, and we have asked for nothing except enough ground to bury them in...."

Second, the alternative to American dominance has never been all nations minding their own business. Oh, that it could be as simple as that utopian vision! In reality, wherever our sphere of influence shrinks, someone else's sphere expands—and it's usually not a very nice someone else.

This should be especially obvious in 2015, when we've just seen Vladimir Putin flex his muscles in Ukraine and threaten to cut off

Europe's supply of natural gas. It should be obvious in the post–Iraq War period, as Iran extends its influence westward into Iraq, Syria, and Lebanon, and as the Islamic State rises up in the same region, committing mass atrocities against many different groups, including the Shiites sympathetic to Iran.

Wherever we retreat—and I don't mean that just in the literal battlefield sense of the word—we leave a vacuum that bad actors are sure to exploit. To put it another way, America is the teacher on the playground. When our authority disappears, anything can happen, but most likely that's when the bullies will go into action. The acknowledgment of this is the beginning of realism.

As you might have noticed, the world's bullies are starting to look very busy at the moment. This book takes a close look at many of the defects of President Barack Obama's foreign policy and the failures of Secretary of State Hillary Clinton on the world stage, and prescribes a better way forward.

But these defects are not what prompted me or my brothers in arms to become involved in the 2012 election, in a high-profile role that drew plenty of attention our way and even earned us a rebuke from the president himself.

Our motive was simpler and more concrete: We were upset because President Obama's White House and members of his administration were leaking sensitive information that could damage America's interests, make it harder for our military operations to succeed, and even get some of our people hurt or killed. And they were doing it in order to improve the president's political standing. Sure, they have prosecuted more leakers than any other administration in our history, but those were low-level leakers who spoke out mostly in opposition to the administration. The leakers at the highest levels of the administration—who were doing by far the most damage, all for short-term political gain—were all protected.

As I will describe in these pages, it was this culture of leaks, and not just some disagreement over policy, which brought together so many of us in the group we called OPSEC. OPSEC is short for "Operational Security," which is a fancy military term for keeping your mouth shut—that is, carefully guarding military plans and secrets so as to keep the advantage in the field.

Our group would have been much smaller and merited far less attention if we had been motivated by political disagreements with a politician.

No, it was the leaks coming out of the administration that inspired righteous anger among many in the Special Forces and intelligence communities. This included many active service members, who secretly voiced their support but knew better than to participate directly. But those of us who founded OPSEC were all retired or honorably separated from the service, having been there and done that. We understood how much damage a lack of official discretion can cause. And we viewed ourselves as the only ones able to speak out for the active servicemen and women, who in the course of serving their country under arms are rightly forbidden from speaking out publicly on political matters.

I was already quite politically active by the time OPSEC came together. After a few years working as a security consultant in Yemen, I had run for Congress in the Virginia Beach area in 2010 (I lost the Republican primary). I would later be elected to serve in Virginia's legislature.

Politics became my new skill set after my life as a SEAL was over. I had often been invited to appear on national news shows to speak about foreign policy, national security, and military issues. So naturally I was often asked to take interviews on behalf of OPSEC.

Even though I had already been involved in politics, many of OPSEC's founding members had never been politically involved in their lives. Some had rarely or never voted before. Others had even voted for Obama in 2008. However, in the early years of the new decade, they began to pay attention.

Everything changed for them when they saw how much potential damage the administration was doing. As the president used back channels to broadcast to the world his claim to this or that accomplishment, he was decreasing the chances of success for our covert military and intelligence operatives in the field. In attempting to increase his chances of reelection, he was creating huge new problems, and acting for reasons completely divorced from the interests of our country.

OPSEC wasn't just about Obama, though. We came together in 2012 to put pressure on all politicians to stop endangering our troops in harm's way for the purpose of advancing themselves politically. We wanted to make sure that anyone who thus endangered our national security would be held accountable in the only way politicians understand—they would face the fire when election time rolled around.

For those of us in OPSEC—including those among us who had voted for President Obama the first time around—it all goes back to the realities of military service and intelligence work. Once you've been there, you understand how hard the job is, and how much harder careless politicians can make it. Many of us still have friends serving. We had kept our oath to "support and defend the Constitution of the United States against all enemies, foreign and domestic," and now we set out to make the most of our rights under the First Amendment to that Constitution.

■ ■ ■

I was raised by a single mother and without much focus on academics. My family's lack of money and my mediocre grades made the military my best chance to get out of my hometown of Hebron, on Maryland's Eastern Shore—a small town without so much as a stop light.

I loved growing up in Hebron. I loved the freedom a small town provided. But I wanted more.

The fact is, I really did not have a strong opinion on the service aspect of joining the military. That would come later. For me, the desire to serve in the military was based strictly on the challenge, at least at first. I was young and a bit cocky, and I wanted to tackle the hardest thing anyone could throw at me. It may not have been the best motive to serve, but I'm glad it drove me to do what I did. (I'm guessing there are a lot of other SEALs who would say the same thing.)

Initially, I thought that meant becoming a Marine infantryman. Back in those days, the Marines' marketing campaign was a bit less politically correct than it is now: "We're looking for a few good men." But then my older brother mentioned the Navy SEALs. I listened to him more than he probably knows—he had been one of the main reasons I decided to wrestle in school rather than play basketball.

And so I looked into it. After watching the cheesy Charlie Sheen movie about the SEALs and reading Dick Marcinko's *Rogue Warrior*, I was completely sold. These guys were crazy-tough!

I'd found my challenge.

So I began my swim training with some impromptu breaststroke lessons from a wrestling competitor who was also a lifeguard at the YMCA. Back then, you couldn't just Google "how to prepare for BUD/S" or "what you need to know about SEAL training." There were no Discovery Channel documentaries about SEAL training available on YouTube. I had no idea how to prepare myself, so I just tried to do everything I thought might help. I did a massive amount of running and swimming, a huge number of push-ups, pull-ups, and sit-ups. It couldn't hurt, could it?

When I arrived at boot camp, the first thing I was asked to do was to become the laundry officer. This, more than any of the shouting or physical exertion, made me wonder for a moment whether I had made a mistake. Was I going to spend the next several weeks—or years— scrubbing skid stains out of other men's underwear?

But I kept my mouth shut and followed my orders as best I could. I wanted to do this. I'd realized later that the disappointment of being a small cog in a big machine is part of military training. If you can't obey orders, how can you be trusted to give them?

A couple of days later, I was made leader of my division of eighty-five men. That probably sounds good, especially considering I was awarded the next rank for it after boot camp, but it turns out that's a lot worse than laundry duty.

Boot camp was an intense indoctrination into military life. It was stressful, and my duties as leader of the division made it a lot worse.

(Guess who gets the blame whenever anything goes wrong?) Boot camp wasn't nearly as physically demanding as SEAL training—not even close—but I still found the latter less stressful.

I was also at a very specific disadvantage in boot camp. I had broken my wrist in high school wrestling that year, but out of a desire to continue through to the state finals, I had simply taped it up instead of getting a cast right away, like I should have done. As a result, by the time I'd gotten the cast removed, my wrist was still bad. It caused me to fail my entrance exam at boot camp, because I couldn't do push-ups with perfect form.

I was devastated and thought I would have to remain in the Navy for at least a couple years before I'd get another opportunity to take the entrance exam. Lucky for me, there was a Chief Petty Officer SEAL taking a break on shore duty in Pensacola, Florida, where I went after boot camp. I worked out with him every day until I had properly stretched out my wrist. I got another chance, and passed the test. That chief was then instrumental in getting me orders to SEAL training, known as BUD/S (Basic Underwater Demolition/SEAL), and simply pronounced "buds."

I will never forget one of the first things they said to us: "Look to the man on your right, your left, behind you, and in front of you," instructor Buchanan roared at us with his high brow and a mouth full of Copenhagen. He announced that if any of us were still there at graduation, none of the people immediately adjacent to us would be.

He was right, at least from a statistical perspective. Of the roughly 165 of us in the classroom that day, only twenty original men would be there on graduation day.

All of BUD/S is challenging—both physically and mentally taxing—but nothing was quite as intense as Hell Week. It's probably one of the least valuable parts of SEAL training in terms of tactics and real-world operational experience, but it remains the most important determination of character and a crucial rite of passage for every SEAL.

It's hard to explain this aspect of SEAL training to people. They often just assume you're exaggerating when you describe the physical miseries involved in this ordeal.

I'll just put it this way: You've never really felt the cold until, lying in the icy ocean surf for what feels like the hundredth time in a single night, you've prayed you could only get enough of a bladder up to pee in your pants, just for the momentary and fleeting warmth. You've never shivered until, when you finally get the chance to eat something, you are shaking so badly that just chewing your food is a challenge, even though you're starving. You've never felt tired until, after days without sleep, you are grateful when your boat team is permitted by the instructor to close your eyes for a few moments—a standing nap—as a reward for a task well done.

But the physical pain, the cold, the hunger, the lack of sleep, and the extreme soreness that goes hand in hand with suffering all those things for days on end are incidental to the real point. Hell Week is a lesson in free will. You and the instructors discover whether you really want to be there or not. That's all there is to it. That's why the strongest guys, the best swimmers, the fastest runners, are often the first to drop out. No matter how strong you are, you can't make it if you don't *really, really* want it. You must have the strongest mind and the most powerful will.

You might ask, why would you go to SEAL training if you didn't want to be there? Believe me, it's something you can know for sure only when you're pushed to the absolute edge of your tolerance for pain. That's why the attrition rate at BUD/S is so high.

And as a method of training, it makes a lot of sense. First, SEALs have to be ready for the enormous demands that will be placed upon them—you can't send a man into the field who is a weak link for his team. Second, the Navy invests considerable time, effort, and money training SEALs after Hell Week is over. It doesn't want to waste its resources on the half-hearted, or for that matter on those who are only 90 percent willing to go the distance.

I have to say, there were many moments during Hell Week when I didn't think I was going to make it through this first phase of training.

When you get to that place, a lot of doubts arise. Your mind begins to wander. Everything becomes a potential excuse to quit—and you can quit any time you like. The instructors are more than happy to accommodate you with a hot shower or some coffee. No matter how much you thought you wanted to be a SEAL, you suddenly start wondering whether you really belong there at all. Amid all the mind-numbing pain, you think as deeply about your life and its direction as you ever will.

I'm sure that the psychological experience is unique for everyone who has ever made it through the first phase of training. For me, each time I even thought about giving up, I first looked to those around me, who were somehow hanging tough. That was encouraging, but then a lot of them dropped out.

That was when I thought about Hebron. There was no way I was going back there, where I'd have to explain to each individual person I knew that I had quit—that I had rung the bell three times, according to the custom, and shipped out. For me, that was the pain and torture I feared most. They would have to kill me first.

And so I made it through Hell Week with a handful of other men who really wanted to be there. After that, the psychological torture ended, and the physical pain would never be quite as severe again. But the training only became more challenging, and it was relentless.

The goals became harder, the learning quicker, the swimming and running times faster. Diving drills and tests; shooting drills and tests; close combat; high explosives. These are not things you can afford to screw up in the field, nor even in a contained training environment. Even our diving method—pure oxygen diving, using a rebreather—is dangerous in itself. If you know a bit about it, you know that a lack of attention to detail can cost you your life in just a few feet of water in a common swimming pool.

The technical training was a lengthy and slow burn. Sleep was still scarce and always welcome. I was so exhausted that I developed the ability to lie down on the concrete, shut my eyes, and instantly take a power nap of a minute or two while waiting to head to the next iteration. But throughout, the sense of brotherhood with the men around you continues to grow, as the SEAL culture is driven home. At graduation, I knew I'd accomplished something few others ever will, and I knew I had not done it alone—I'd done it as part of a team.

In those days, each SEAL Team covered one part of the world, and I was given the chance to choose my preferred assignment. As much as I had wanted to be a SEAL, I had never held a strong opinion on this question. But then the representative for SEAL Team Four made his pitch, and it spoke to me: "South and Central America is like the Wild, Wild West." In high school, I had read more than sixty Louis L'Amour Westerns. I was sold.

For the next five years, I would be with SEAL Team Four. It was the late 1990s, and America was at peace, but I was constantly either training for war or on a deployment south of the border. We conducted counter-drug operations and FID (Foreign Internal Defense). We taught tactics to allied militaries. From the jungles of Panama to the mountains of Chile and everywhere in between, we roamed, learning a lot about the local cultures and interacting with host-nation counterparts.

I remember well the morning of September 11, 2001. I had returned from a deployment one month earlier. My girlfriend woke me up after the first plane hit. We sat glued to the television when the second plane hit the second tower. It was surreal.

The military base was on lockdown. We had made plans earlier to find a place to live that day, and we really did need a place, so we kept them. But it was strange to do anything that day. We kept the news on the radio all day long. A couple of months later, I would re-enlist early. I was eager to go and fight.

Unfortunately, you don't just get to do whatever you want in the military—not even if you're a SEAL. The SEAL Teams were still organized at that time in a way that was specific to an area of operation. Someone had to cover our commitments in South America until a large reorganization took place.

I was disappointed not to be heading for Afghanistan, but it proved providential, because if I'd deployed immediately, I would have missed the next big step in my training. That year, I attended SEAL sniper school. This was probably the most rigorous training I ever received. It was designed to up your game as an operator. We had hours upon hours upon hours of shooting practice in all types of weather. One day there was an ice storm, and we just kept on shooting—right up until our gun turrets froze! At least we got some idea of how quickly that would happen, and how to deal with it. It might come in handy some day.

We learned to stalk our prey in the field with maximum stealth. Instructors would sit at elevated positions, watching through binoculars as we inched toward them from the ground, trying not to show the slightest movement.

A few years later, I would go back to our training department to teach our platoons. After serving in another platoon as a sniper, I checked in to our training command to teach marksmanship and reconnaissance. It was then that I almost got my chance to go to Afghanistan. My war bags were packed, my deployment training was all current, and they eventually agreed to let me join up on a sniper trip that was being planned.

But then the whole trip got canceled. I never made it to Afghanistan.

I did, however, head to Iraq as a sniper in 2005. This assignment was a happy one for me. Not only was I going toward the shooting, but I was also reunited with several of my good friends from training.

Upon my arrival, I quickly jumped on a direct action mission with them. Their chief asked me to lead the external security unit. Our group went to a known bomb-maker's house to capture or kill him. He lived on the second floor of his building. It was a relatively simple job. One of our groups blew the first door and entered up the stairway. As they did that, my group, using explosives taped to long sticks, blew out the second-floor windows, just to discombobulate the men inside as our guys ran up the stairs.

The mission went off flawlessly, and we even captured the targets alive. We returned home with a couple of bomb-makers in tow.

■ ■ ■

Over the next few months, I would spend my time in Baghdad and later Ramadi, going on convoys to look for sniper hideouts and then heading out on missions.

It all came to an end one night in June 2005, when I got myself injured in what I consider the dumbest way possible.

We had received the go-ahead for a mission that would require several sniper pairs to suit up and be inserted into a vacant building. We were to stay in that location for three days, identifying and eliminating, from our position in the building, any threats to coalition forces. On these missions, we were guardian angels for the men in the field. It was necessary work—and if you were unlucky, it could get very exciting.

Before leaving our station for this mission, we headed up to the rooftop of our sniper house, where we had a makeshift gun range, to make sure our sniper rifles were dialed in. We had to keep low—a few guys had been shot at from positions across the river. Our place was called Shark Base, situated on the Euphrates River and at the edge of the daily-mortared base of Junction City in Ramadi. It was the same place that the late Chris Kyle, the most lethal sniper in American history, would later make famous.

With rifles calibrated, and having turned off the episode of 24 that we had been enjoying, off we went into the city in the middle of the night. Our night-vision goggles were on, our heads on a swivel. It was an uneventful drive and patrol, but you never knew where the bullets might come from.

We made our way to what was to be our home for the next three days. The building was supposed to be vacant, but you can't just walk in blind like you're coming home from vacation. You still have to take the building down as though you expect to find an enemy inside. Who knows? It's Iraq. There might well be an enemy inside.

Quietly entering, night vision goggles still on, we cleared the building, methodically entering each room and moving up, floor by floor. On the second floor landing in the stairwell, I pivoted, turning to hold security on the stairs leading up. My plant foot hit air. I fell right through a cut-out in the middle of the floor and fell twenty feet or so to the concrete below.

I was instantly unconscious. My teammates continued to clear the building—which is exactly what you're supposed to do in that situation—you have to win the fight before you tend to the wounded. Then our medic, Stout, came straight over to me and realized I wasn't breathing. As he explained to me years later, he first stabilized my back and then inserted a J-tube into my throat, clearing my airway and probably saving my life. He called in the Marine Humvees and the helicopter to extract me. Stout would ride with the Marines.

From what I remember, between the helicopter and us was a long road, typically filled with improvised explosive devices. I believe we lost eleven Marines on that road in that year alone. Stout didn't mind the risk—he would make sure I made it back safely, and then he would rejoin the team.

By the time I woke up, I was already in the helicopter, strapped in tight so I couldn't move. I couldn't feel anything because of the morphine Stout had given me. My first thought was that I'd been paralyzed. I passed out again.

The next time I awoke I was in a tent hospital in Balad, Iraq. I could move! I immediately grabbed for my legs—still there!—and then my package between them. "Thank you, God!"

Melanie, my nurse from Chicago, took good care of me. I still owe her a coffee. I had a pneumothorax, a bruised lung, and I had to use a breathing device to help cure it. Additionally, I would find out that I had been concussed. I had six broken ribs down my spine, and a torn PCL tendon in my knee.

That was the end of my vacation time in Iraq. I was sent off to the USA via Germany. I had no one to blame but myself—and perhaps some poor craftsmanship by Iraqi builders.

But then again, I had to keep things in perspective. While I was in the hospital, one of my teammates and best friends emailed me, informing me about the largest loss of SEAL life we had suffered in Afghanistan up until that date. He knew at that point that one of two helicopters had gone down, and his brother (both of his brothers are SEALs) was in one of them. He wasn't sure at the time if his brother was alive. Fortunately, he was. Just a day or so earlier, I had received an email from his brother, making fun of my sure footing and letting me know all the guys in Afghanistan were asking after me.

There was also one guy missing on the ground—this turned out to be Marcus Luttrell, later the author of *Lone Survivor*, who would be played by Mark Wahlberg in a 2013 feature film.

Suddenly, my injuries didn't seem like such a big deal. It turned out that several of my friends had been on the helicopter that went down—one of whom, Jacques Fontan, I had a very special bond with, as he had been in my boat crew during Hell Week. They were not the first friends I lost in these wars, nor would they be the last.

But I will never regret anything about serving; in fact, it has been a profound honor to serve with some of the best warriors that this world has ever known—better men than I am.

■   ■   ■

In the field, every tactical advantage is crucial. Any small piece of knowledge—whether in your hands or in those of your enemy—can be the difference between a successful operation and a catastrophic failure that wipes out your entire unit.

That's why operational security is such a big deal. It's something you appreciate a lot more when you've been out on an operation.

This book tells the story of how and why our group, OPSEC, came together. It also offers a broader look at what's wrong with American foreign policy in the age of Obama, and how we can do better as a nation.

Some politicians—and President Obama specifically—have in very important ways subordinated America's national interests to far less important and more parochial political considerations. That's a fact that troubles many of those who have served, and many of those still serving. The leaks that have emanated from the White House are a symptom of a broader problem that explains much of why so many of the world's longstanding issues are currently getting so badly out of hand.

Too much of our policy in recent years has been determined by a desire to produce political accomplishments, or by ideological theories of international relations that have nothing to do with keeping Americans safe or advancing American interests. And we're all paying the price—but no one more than the men and women currently in harm's way.

The result is what we see today in so many parts of the world. We are weakening our traditional allies and emboldening our enemies to become more aggressive. That makes the whole world a more dangerous and less predictable place—not just for Americans, but for all people of good will.

CHAPTER TWO

Dishonorable Disclosures

Have you ever had a boss who used everything you did to promote himself—even if it made your job harder?

President Obama is the commander-in-chief of the United States Armed Forces. He was never my boss—I was out of active service by the time he was inaugurated—but he is boss to many of my Navy SEAL brothers and other Special Operations and covert intelligence officials. If he valued their contribution more, he would blab a lot less about what they do.

As I and several of my old Special Operations comrades began to notice during Obama's first term, he doesn't keep this sort of thing to himself—at least not when there's something in it that might make him look good.

We noticed that wherever there was an opportunity for Obama to promote himself and his reelection in 2012—or even just to downplay public fears that maybe he wasn't a tough enough leader—the covert operations of U.S. Special Forces and intelligence had a tendency to become not so covert anymore.

Potentially compromising information started getting out. And this wasn't just one incident, but a pattern. The White House kept springing politically helpful leaks that undermined operational security.

And of course no one was punished for these leaks. They were unofficially-officially sanctioned leaks deployed for political benefit, with information in numerous news articles attributed to unnamed high-ranking administration officials.

Just because you have a top secret security clearance does not mean you have access to all top secret information. At the top level, everything is highly compartmentalized and available only on a need-to-know basis. Clearly, what was happening here was not the work of some disgruntled government employee. These leaks were not only unprecedented and purposeful; they were also coordinated at the highest levels of the Obama administration.

Sometimes the inappropriate leaks were crucial to the political goals of Obama's reelection campaign. For instance, when Obama was taking heavy criticism for his weak stance with Iran, U.S. and Israeli involvement in creating the Stuxnet computer virus conveniently became a public story, showing that covert (again, the key word) action had been authorized against Iran.

Sometimes, it was just that too much information came out by accident, because political hacks were doing too much bragging and said more than they should have—after all, politicians aren't known for their discretion.

David Axelrod, one of the president's top political operatives, was rumored to be at the Tuesday terror meetings, where highly classified information was discussed. As David Sanger of the *New York Times* put it, "But over the course of 2009, more and more people inside the Obama White House were being 'read into' the cyber program, even those not directly involved." Why do you suppose a political operative would be attending these meetings?

And so the leaks kept coming, and it was obvious where they were coming from.

It was during World War II that the famous adage became popular: "Loose lips sink ships." The phrase appeared on posters and in leaflets to remind Americans not to divulge too many details about matters that could clue in enemy spies. The point was that any piece of knowledge—even something as mundane as where someone's husband was headed in the Pacific, or a few details about local factories or the whereabouts of one ship or another—could ruin months of military planning or, even worse, cause American servicemen to die or American forces to lose battles.

In the Obama White House, this old and fundamental rule didn't seem to apply. This is just one of many ways Obama's administration has subordinated important national security goals to political considerations. But it is also probably the most outrageous. It is what motivated my comrades and me, in the Special Operations Forces groups and the intelligence community, to get involved during the 2012 election.

Perhaps Obama is wrong on certain foreign policy issues because of principles he holds dear. We will look at some of those issues in later chapters. But that isn't the case here. These leaks were all about political expediency. They were all about Obama.

■   ■   ■

Shortly before midnight on May 1, 2011, two MH-60 Black Hawk helicopters carrying twenty-three Navy SEALs and a Pakistani-American translator crossed from eastern Afghanistan into northern Pakistan with a mission as clear as the night's cloudless sky: to kill Osama bin Laden.

Bin Laden had been America's most wanted man since he claimed responsibility for the attacks of September 11, 2001, which took the lives of nearly three thousand people in New York, Washington, D.C., and Pennsylvania. Bin Laden had eluded justice for nearly a decade.

About ninety minutes after entering Pakistani airspace, the helicopters arrived at bin Laden's one-acre compound in Abbottabad, a small city located thirty-five miles north of the Pakistani capital of Islamabad.

Within fifteen minutes, the Special Operations Forces team had descended upon the hideout and killed bin Laden (along with four other adults). After another twenty-five minutes, they disappeared with bin Laden's corpse and a large collection of documents and computer hardware. With that, one of the longest and costliest manhunts in American history was over.

Codenamed Operation Neptune Spear, the raid was the successful culmination of nearly a decade of intelligence work by thousands of Americans in the Central Intelligence Agency (CIA), Department of Defense, Joint Special Operations Command (JSOC), Naval Special Warfare Development Group (SEAL Team Six), and numerous other departments, agencies, and units.

We know all of these details because someone leaked them.

President Obama deserves some credit for authorizing this risky mission. President Bill Clinton had had the opportunity to kill bin Laden in 1998 (at the time, bin Laden was wanted for his role in the 1998 bombings of U.S. embassies in Tanzania and Kenya), but didn't even try.[1]

I remember very vividly when I got the news about bin Laden's death. I was in Sana'a, Yemen, sleeping, when my phone rang with an international incoming call. It was the press. My phone blew up with calls, as did my inbox with emails containing requests from media ranging from CNN to a Jacksonville TV news affiliate.

I lay there groggy, in bin Laden's ancestral homeland, very proud of the men and women who had sacrificed much over the years to achieve American justice. Responding to CNN and the Daily Caller's request for a statement, I released this one:

> The just death of Osama Bin Laden is a significant, symbolic, and moral victory for America and the world. We must remain vigilant in combating terrorism in whatever corner of the globe and brace for potential retaliation. As Americans we must stand behind those brave men and women in harm's way who protect us while we sleep at night. We must never forget those who selflessly paid the ultimate sacrifice,

ensuring our way of life. While this act does not right the
wrongs committed, those families who have given so much
for this country can proudly stand with some peace knowing, in the end, justice came with an impact of an American
bullet.

Obama had authorized the successful strike over the reservations
of many of his top advisors (and also his vice president).[2] Earlier, he
had reinvigorated the mission to hunt down bin Laden, directing CIA
head Leon Panetta to create a detailed plan for locating bin Laden
and bringing him to justice.[3] And once bin Laden was finally located,
Obama chose not to involve or even notify the Pakistani authorities
of the mission—a decision that risked a military confrontation with
an ally.[4]

Still, most of the credit belonged to the intelligence specialists
who had spent years tracking bin Laden—to say nothing of the SEALs
and helicopter crews who risked their lives bringing him to justice
that night.

Three days after bin Laden's death, Obama appropriately pledged
not to call undue attention to his role or use the killing to score political points. "You know, we don't trot out this stuff as trophies," Obama
said in a CBS interview about his decision not to release photos of bin
Laden's corpse.[5] The president noted that doing so might "create a
national security risk.... Americans and people around the world are
glad that he's gone. But we don't need to spike the football."[6]

But those were just words—just promises that Obama apparently
didn't feel compelled to abide by in an election year. Over the next
year and a half, Obama would do exactly the opposite of what he had
said. He would do the very thing that he had said might "create a
national security risk."

It's not just that the president and his surrogates behaved boorishly
as they repeatedly dramatized his role in bin Laden's death. It isn't just
that he demeaned his own office and the hard work of others in a
transparent effort to blunt criticism of him as weak or indecisive on

national security issues, or unprepared for the 3 a.m. phone call about a world crisis.

The bigger problem is that in the process of glorifying Obama and paving the way to his reelection, political officials in his administration leaked intelligence that put American lives in danger and made American forces less effective.

In announcing bin Laden's death to the world, Obama gave thanks to "the countless intelligence and counterterrorism professionals who've worked tirelessly to achieve this outcome." He also used a series of self-referential phrases—"I determined," "at my direction," "I met repeatedly"—that seemed designed to exaggerate his own role in the operation.[7]

No serviceman or veteran likes to hear this sort of thing, but we all know it's inevitable. We do the work, and some politician takes the credit. It got more irritating, though, as Obama began to incorporate the boast into his reelection campaign.

"Nine days after American commandos killed Osama bin Laden, President Obama has added the event to the rundown of administration achievements in his political stump speech," New York Times reporter Jackie Calmes noted. "While Mr. Obama gave credit to others, his implicit share in that credit now seems likely to be a staple of his political message into the 2012 election season. Since Bin Laden's death, Mr. Obama previously had spoken of it, also in patriotic and national security terms, in public events at ground zero in Lower Manhattan and to troops at Fort Campbell, Ky."[8]

However irritating, at least this sort of boastfulness was relatively harmless. It even came with some appropriate respect for the troops. The disrespect began with the leaks of sensitive information.

Immediately after the killing of bin Laden, the Obama administration correctly refused to identify any details about the military unit that had participated in the raid. In his bin Laden announcement, Obama referred to the commandos simply as "a small team of Americans."[9]

Yet today, we know it was SEAL Team Six. That's because, two days later, Obama's notoriously chatty vice president gave the game away. This is what Joe Biden said before a national audience: "Let me briefly acknowledge tonight's distinguished honorees. Admiral James Stavridis is a—is the real deal. He can tell you more about and understands the incredible, the phenomenal, the just almost unbelievable capacity of his Navy SEALs and what they did last Sunday."[10]

Then, later that evening, Biden repeated the gaffe: "Folks, I'd be remiss also if I didn't say an extra word about the incredible events, extraordinary events of this past Sunday. As Vice President of the United States, as an American, I was in absolute awe of the capacity and dedication of the entire team, both the intelligence community, the CIA, the SEALs. It just was extraordinary."[11]

Reporters quickly identified the unit responsible: SEAL Team Six. From there, it didn't take long for other details of the raid to emerge, from the number of team members to the types of aircraft involved, the tactics used, and even the name of the bomb-sniffing dog taken along.

Biden's disclosure may seem minor to civilians. But it wasn't—certainly not for the SEALs and their families. It was foolish and dangerous.

As far back as 2009, the first year of Obama's presidency, several SEAL wives had sent me messages about the administration's tightening of the Afghanistan rules of engagement—worried the new rules would get their husbands killed. Now, messages came fast and furiously. SEALs' wives were upset that the administration had publicly put their families at risk. By identifying the killers of bin Laden as SEALs, Vice President Biden had made it easier for al Qaeda or an al Qaeda sympathizer to come after them and their families. If a terrorist knew which unit was involved, it would not be hard to figure out in what area their families were located, where their children went to school, and perhaps even the address where they lived. There were countless people across the globe who might have wanted to avenge bin Laden's death and no good reason at all to reveal information that could help them do just that.

And of course, someone could also go after the wrong group of SEALs or their families, too. By revealing the force responsible for his death, Biden had put the lives of every SEAL and every SEAL's family in danger.

When the press called and emailed, there were numerous questions I had to politely but firmly decline to comment on. CNN asked, "Do you know any of the members of SEAL Team 6 who were on the operation?" I didn't blame the media for prying, trying to get all the details for a hungry public—that's their job. It wasn't their fault that our political leaders had undermined our security in this way.

It doesn't take a genius to tell you that this information in the enemy's hands puts our boys and girls at risk and hinders future operations. Bottom line, there was no need to know, despite a public audience full of inquiring minds. This is real life, where the stakes are potentially American lives, not an episode of *Homeland*.

Senior administration officials also began telling reporters what they had found in the trove of at least one hundred flash drives and DVDs, ten cell phones, five computer hard drives, journals, and other documents recovered from bin Laden's lair. One administration official called the haul "the single largest collection of material from a senior terrorist ever."[12]

Many observers felt the disclosures were inappropriate. "Instead of broadcasting the intelligence grab," Peter Brookes, a national security expert at the Heritage Foundation, said at the time, "we might've waited a while—so we could more fully exploit some of the windfall before alerting al Qaeda operatives to take defensive measures."[13] Compromising our ability to take advantage of actionable intelligence was an amateur move that made many of the men and women who put their lives on the line for such information cringe.

Obama's own Defense Secretary, Bob Gates, was disturbed by the leaks. "My concern is that there were too many people in too many places talking too much about this operation," Gates told reporters at a Pentagon briefing two weeks after the raid. "And we [had] reached agreement that we would not talk about the operational details. I am very concerned about this, because we want to retain the capability to carry out these kinds of operations in the future."[14]

And that's the real concern—all of this politically beneficial leaking was not harmless. It was revealing too much about U.S. methods and capabilities, and potentially causing enemies to take new precautions that would hurt us next time we went after them.

Gates reportedly approached national security advisor Tom Donilon and suggested a new strategic communications approach: "Shut the f--- up."[15] But of course, that would have defeated the purpose. These leaks were part of a political strategy with little respect for operational or military priorities.

On the anniversary of the raid, the Obama administration declassified numerous documents found in the bin Laden compound, an act the *Washington Post* described as coinciding "with new efforts by President Obama to make the administration's counterterrorism achievements a central part of his reelection campaign."[16] There were no other reasons to do it—or rather, no *good* reasons.

Think about it for a second. Just one year after the operation, with people still in the field in ongoing operations, the president decides to declassify bin Laden compound documents. That's quite an expedited declassification schedule. By way of comparison, there are still thousands of documents about JFK's assassination that remain classified![17]

But the bin Laden raid was Obama's signature first-term foreign policy achievement—something the campaign wanted voters to remember as Election Day approached.

For this—just for a few good talking points—the Obama administration may have failed to exploit valuable intelligence by letting what we had out of the bag prematurely.

One could argue that the Obama White House's leakiness was just a really bad solution to a critical problem the administration had. Obama and his political base were averse to open military action or the appearance thereof. Thus the president has relied heavily on covert operations and drone strikes, both of which are largely invisible to American voters.

Such operations can produce terrific results at times, but it's hard to claim credit for them. Hence the need for leaks. The administration chose to undermine our national security apparatus for the benefit of talking points that shore up the president's shaky credibility on military and foreign policy.

BARACK OBAMA, COMIC BOOK HERO

In the year following bin Laden's death, numerous publications ran feature articles about the raid, quoting senior administration officials anonymously. Some of the accounts discussed classified information and included quotes from the president and other information that only those involved in the highest-level meetings could have known. In short, the White House was feeding all kinds of sensitive information to journalists.

And of course, journalists tend to reward those who give them access. The stories portrayed Obama in almost ridiculously glowing terms. One journalist—liberal Obama-skeptic Glenn Greenwald— observed wryly that a *New Yorker* piece about the bin Laden raid "made Barack Obama look like a mix of Superman, Rambo, and Clint Eastwood."[18] I would love to see the reaction of operators in a Special Operations team room if this quote were read out loud there.

At least three films were made about the raid. *Targeting bin Laden*, the History Channel account that appeared on the tenth anniversary of 9/11, included interviews with key national security advisors and the president himself. It highlighted Obama's decision to approve the raid over the reservations of some senior White House officials. Obama is depicted as thoughtful yet decisive, and other administration officials interviewed sing his praises.[19]

No one doubts that the president deserves some credit for killing bin Laden. But he had all the pieces to the puzzle—an amazingly talented unit, verified intelligence, and the logistical means to take out the world's most wanted man. That fact makes all the slobbering more than a little excessive.

Members of our armed forces had been making raids into Pakistan for years, as the president and his administration were fully aware.

George W. Bush's green-lighting of those raids had been reported on back in 2008.[20] The decision to go after bin Laden was probably easier than many of the decisions about those missions, which carried all of the same risks but much smaller potential rewards.

Hollywood filmmakers got unprecedented access to the people who planned the raid.[21] In May 2012, the watchdog group Judicial Watch filed a Freedom of Information Act lawsuit demanding the release of hundreds of Department of Defense and CIA communications on this subject.[22] The documents Judicial Watch obtained contained emails revealing that in June 2011, Mark Boal and Kathryn Bigelow, the producer and director of the Academy Award–winning movie *Zero Dark Thirty*, were granted interviews with people intimately involved in the mission.[23]

They were given a briefing by undersecretary of Defense Mike Vickers and had access to a Navy SEAL who was the "planner, operator, and commander of SEAL Team Six."[24] The filmmakers also met with John Brennan, the president's chief counterterrorism advisor, and Denis McDonough, his deputy national security advisor.[25] Documents also showed that Boal visited with acting CIA director Michael Morrell and saw a model of bin Laden's Abbottabad compound inside CIA headquarters.

These revelations provoked a strong response from lawmakers. "After reviewing these emails, I am even more concerned about the possible exposure of classified information to these filmmakers, who as far as I know, do not possess security clearances," House Homeland Security Committee Chairman Peter King, a New York Republican, said in a statement. "The email messages indicate that the filmmakers were allowed an unprecedented visit to a classified facility so secret that its name is redacted in the released email. If this facility is so secret that the name cannot even be seen by the public, then why in the world would the Obama Administration allow filmmakers to tour it?"[26]

That was a good question, but the answer was obvious. The film, which was originally scheduled to hit theaters just before the

2012 election, could be expected to bolster the president's image just days before what many political pundits believed would be a tight election.[27]

THE LONGEST VICTORY LAP

As the 2012 campaign season swung into full force, the catch-phrases of the Obama campaign began to take shape:

"I promised to go after al Qaeda and bin Laden, and we did it."

"Bin Laden is dead, GM is alive."

These became staples on the campaign trail for Obama, Biden, and their surrogates.

At one point Biden even portrayed his boss's decision to go after bin Laden as the boldest stroke in modern military history, going back nearly to the Turkish capture of Constantinople. "You can go back 500 years," Biden said at a New Jersey fundraiser in March 2012. "You cannot find a more audacious plan. Never knowing for certain. We never had more than a 48 percent probability that he was there."[28]

It was an absurd claim. Where did Biden come up with those numbers? Forty-eight percent, and not just forty-seven? And was it really more audacious than George Washington's Christmas attack on Trenton, or the launch of Operation Overlord on D-Day?

But the absurdity of the claim apparently didn't matter. The point was to exploit the SEALs' mission for political gain, and in the comfortable confines of the posh home of a big fundraiser, this Biden line probably did the trick on a group whose only concern was how many zeros to put on their next check to an Obama-supporting SuperPAC. Neither Biden nor the Democrats' donors would ever have to kit up, put their helmets on, adjust the night-vision goggles, and step out into the night—having made their peace with the fact that it might be the last night they ever experience.

On May 2, 2012, the anniversary of the bin Laden raid, Obama visited Bagram Air Base in Afghanistan, where the Navy SEALs had launched their mission one year earlier. In a speech delivered to more than three thousand military personnel, Obama thanked the troops, but also took some time to gloat a little. "Slowly and systematically, we have been able to decimate the ranks of al Qaeda," Obama said. "And a year ago, we were able to finally bring Osama bin Laden to justice."[29]

Later that day, in a primetime televised address, Obama presented his plan to end the war in Afghanistan, and said, "The goal that I set—to defeat al Qaeda, and deny it a chance to rebuild—is within reach."[30] How ridiculous does that boast sound in 2015? *The New York Post* referred to the trip as Obama's 14,000-mile victory lap.

The same day, NBC's *Rock Center with Brian Williams* broadcast a special featuring interviews with senior administration officials who had been involved in the mission. The show included an exclusive interview with the president from the Situation Room, for which the network was given unprecedented access to the most secret and secure part of the White House.[31]

Williams also interviewed Admiral Mike Mullen, who was chairman of the Joint Chiefs of Staff during the bin Laden raid. Before we go into what Mullen said, let me say that I believe Mullen is a man who truly cares about his troops. In August 2011, I sat at Dover Air Force Base with the crying family of one of my very best friends as we waited for his body and the remains of thirty other soldiers who had perished in the Extortion 17 operation. The president, secretary of Defense, secretary of the Navy, and Admiral Mullen came to speak with the surviving family of the deceased. Out of all of them, Mullen and his wife really seemed to feel the pain of the families. (I will never forget how one of the widows told me that the president seemed the most uncomfortable and least compassionate among them.)

By the time of the interview with Williams, Mullen had left the administration, so he could speak candidly. He expressed concern that the raid would be politically "spun" during the election, telling Williams, "Well, I worry about it, just because it's the political season.... I do worry a great deal that this time of year that somehow this gets spun into election politics. I can assure you that those individuals who risk their lives—the last thing in the world that they want is to be spun into that. So I'm hoping that that doesn't happen."[32]

But it *was* happening. Perhaps the most egregious example of spinning Osama's corpse was an Obama campaign ad titled "One Chance." Narrated by former president Bill Clinton, "One Chance" had been released a couple of days before the bin Laden raid anniversary.

In "One Chance," Clinton asserts that Obama took "the harder and the more honorable path" in ordering the takedown of bin Laden. Then the ad asks, "Which path would Mitt Romney have taken?"[33] In 2007, Romney had expressed reservations about the wisdom of sending troops in to find bin Laden. "It's not worth moving heaven and earth, spending billions of dollars just trying to catch one person," Romney told reporters back then.[34]

Romney amended that statement a few days later, saying in a Republican presidential debate, "We'll move everything to get him. But I don't want to buy into the Democratic pitch that this is all about one person. Because after we get him, there's going to be another and another.... It's more than Osama bin Laden. But he is going to pay, and he will die."[35]

Besides attacking Romney in the ad, Clinton also extolled Obama's leadership and pondered the political implications for Obama had the raid failed. "Suppose the Navy SEALs had gone in there and it hadn't been bin Laden. Suppose they had been captured or killed," Clinton says. "The downside would have been horrible for him."[36] Clinton's remarks echoed an earlier comment by Joe Biden, who had speculated at a fundraiser, "If [Obama] was wrong [about his decision to send in the SEALs], his presidency was done. Over."

Funny how neither Clinton nor Biden dwelt much on the fact that, had the operation failed, Navy SEALs, pilots, and crewmen probably would have lost their lives. This crass preoccupation with the political risks of the raid was not lost on political commentators, even some on the Left.[37] Outspoken liberal Arianna Huffington told *CBS News,* "To turn [the bin Laden killing] into a campaign ad is one of the most despicable things you can do."[38]

When a reporter asked Obama whether the White House's attention to the anniversary might constitute "excessive celebration," Obama denied it, but then proceeded to pat himself on the back one more time: "I said that I would go after Bin Laden if we had a clear shot at him—and I did."[39]

Obama explicitly acknowledged how crucial the bin Laden raid was to his reelection hopes on at least one occasion. At the annual Alfred E. Smith Memorial Foundation Dinner just a few weeks before the election, Obama gave the comic speech traditional to the occasion. Part of his joke was what he called a preview of what he would emphasize in his third and final debate with Republican Mitt Romney, which was to focus on foreign affairs: "Spoiler alert: We got bin Laden," Obama said, to hearty applause.[40]

On Election Day itself, Obama made one last attempt to remind voters of his bin Laden triumph, this time via social media. Obama's Twitter account displayed a large photo of the president with big block lettering underneath it that said, "President Obama: Brought Justice to Osama Bin Laden." Above the photo, it said, "President Obama ordered the raid on Osama bin Laden's compound, eliminating the man responsible for the 9/11 attacks."[41]

In retrospect, as new terrorist groups form and attack Americans in places like Libya, and as ISIS, an al Qaeda spinoff, achieves al Qaeda's strategic goals in Iraq, that boast seems particularly hollow. But even at the time, people in the Special Operations community, especially its veterans, were very upset by the use of the raid for political gain. I do not speak for everyone, I readily admit, but many people in our community were, to put it baldly, pissed off at being abused by self-aggrandizing politicians. This is not how our minds operate. We sacrifice for the greater good, for the team, and we expect the same from our leadership.

AN ACHIEVEMENT BUILT ON "TORTURE"

Left unsaid amid all of the self-congratulation was the fact that the hunt for bin Laden predated Obama's administration. Much of the groundwork had been laid by his predecessor, George W. Bush, and the pursuit involved the extraordinary efforts of numerous individuals risking life and limb, or working tediously over the years.

After bin Laden's death, the Associated Press reported, "Current and former U.S. officials said that Khalid Sheikh Mohammed, the mastermind of the Sept. 11, 2001, terrorist attacks, provided the *nom de guerre* of one of bin Laden's most trusted aides. The CIA got similar information from Mohammed's successor, Abu Faraj al-Libi. Both were subjected to harsh interrogation tactics inside CIA prisons, in Poland and Romania."[42] The pseudonym of the "trusted" aide was Abu Ahmed al-Kuwaiti. But the U.S. didn't know how important al-Kuwaiti was until it interrogated another terrorist, Hassan Ghul, being held in a secret prison in Pakistan.

In 2004, Ghul was captured in Iraq and told the CIA that al-Kuwaiti was bin Laden's courier. For providing this information, one U.S. official dubbed Ghul "the linchpin" in the search for bin Laden. The courier eventually led U.S. authorities to bin Laden's lair.[43]

Clearly, intelligence received from the harsh interrogation of terrorists in "black site" CIA prisons was crucial to finding bin Laden. "We got beat up for it, but those efforts led to this great day," Marty Martin, a retired CIA officer who for years led the hunt for bin Laden, told the Associated Press.[44] It was ironic that the president now taking credit for that "great day" had gotten elected partly by running against the so-called "torture" by which the Bush administration had uncovered the original leads in the search for the terrorist mastermind.

George W. Bush stayed mostly silent when bin Laden was killed. But it reportedly irked him to see Obama hogging all the credit while condemning the methods by which the information that made the entire mission possible was obtained. "Obama gave no credit whatsoever to the intelligence infrastructure the Bush administration set up that is being hailed from the left and right as setting in motion the operation that got Bin Laden," a source close to the former president told *New York Daily News*. "It rubbed Bush the wrong way."[45]

All of Obama's boasting, however unseemly, did help shape public opinion in his favor. Several polls showed that killing bin Laden helped the president's image with voters. A *New York Times*/CBS poll found that approval of Obama's handling of foreign policy got a thirteen-point bump to 52 percent after bin Laden's death, and that the president's overall approval shot up eleven points to 57 percent.[46]

Obama's bin Laden bounce was still evident on Election Day. Most polls in the months leading up to the 2012 election showed that more Americans approved than disapproved of Obama on foreign policy— a rather sharp contrast with 2008.[47] Exit polls from the 2012 election found that among voters for whom foreign affairs was their top issue, 56 percent voted for Obama, while just 33 percent voted for Romney.[48]

Just as SEAL Teams use smoke grenades to mask their movements, the president successfully deployed his smoke screen, and the American people fell for it. In fact, he may be the most successful president in the history of the United States at fooling tens of millions of people on a multitude of fundamental issues—twice.

How great a role did the bin Laden killing play in Americans' perceptions of Obama's foreign policy? That's debatable. What is not debatable is that by 2014, with the Middle East again in flames and Russia on the prowl, the successful bin Laden raid was a distant memory for most Americans. In August 2014, Obama's approval-disapproval spread stood at a dismal negative eighteen (36 percent approve, 54 percent disapprove).[49]

THE PRESIDENT'S KILL LIST

The bin Laden disclosures were just the first droplets in what would become a cascade of politically motivated national security leaks. Over time, a pattern emerged of leaks that put America's national security at risk while bolstering the president's reelection chances.

In late May 2012, the *New York Times* and *Newsweek* both published stories detailing the process by which President Obama decides which terrorists to kill via drone strikes in Pakistan, Somalia, and Yemen. In the *Times* piece, reporters Jo Becker and Scott Shane wrote that Obama personally approves drone targets from a "kill list." "Several were Americans," they reported. "Two were teenagers, including a girl who looked even younger than her 17 years."[50] Becker and Shane reported that Obama kept official counts of civilian casualties low by effectively counting all military-age men in a strike zone as combatants.

The *Times* article drew on interviews from "three dozen of [Obama's] current and former advisors."[51] The piece included numerous anonymous quotes, but also some on-the-record interviews with national security advisor Thomas E. Donilon and counterterrorism advisor John Brennan. The story describes a meeting in the Situation Room in which Obama studies a chart of potential targets that looks like a "high school yearbook."[52]

The president was said to take great care to avoid killing civilians. "Many times," General James Jones, Obama's national security advisor from 2009 to 2010, told the *Times*, "at the 11th hour we waved off a mission simply because the target had people around them and we were able to loiter on station until they didn't."

The *Times* piece made Obama seem thoughtful and circumspect as he presided over a shadow war against al Qaeda. The president's advisors described him as "[a] student of writings on war by Augustine and Thomas Aquinas [who] believes that he should take moral responsibility for such actions."[53]

But despite this genuflection to Obama's image as an intellectual critic of America's military adventures, both articles seemed ultimately designed to reassure voters that their commander-in-chief would do whatever it took to fight terrorism and keep Americans safe. When the *Times* reporters asked Donilon what surprised him most about the president, he "answered immediately: 'He's a president who is quite comfortable with the use of force on behalf of the United States.'"[54]

The *Times* piece noted the paradox: "Mr. Obama is the liberal law professor who campaigned against the Iraq war and torture, and then insisted on approving every new name on an expanding 'kill list,' poring over terrorist suspects' biographies on what one officials calls the macabre 'baseball cards' of an unconventional war. When a rare opportunity for a drone strike at a top terrorist arises—but his family is with him—it is the president who has reserved to himself the final moral calculation."[55]

Here was another example of Obama's preferred use of clandestine tactics that are less likely to draw the ire of his liberal base. But that meant that—as with Special Operations Forces missions—he could claim political credit only by strategically leaking details to journalists hungry to be in the circle of trust.

Politically speaking, discussing Obama's "kill list" meetings with reporters must have seemed like a no-brainer to the White House. Polls showed that Americans overwhelmingly supported the use of drone strikes. A February 2012 ABC News/*Washington Post* poll found that 83 percent of Americans approved of the policy.[56] But it was probably tactically helpful to the terrorists to have some of the criteria he uses spelled out for them in the *New York Times*, and helpful to them from a recruiting perspective because it helped highlight the number of attacks.

PLAUSIBLE DENIABILITY

Three days after the revelations about Obama's "kill list" deliberations, the *Times* ran another story that included top-secret intelligence leaks. This one exposed America's efforts to thwart the nuclear plans of America's longtime adversary, the Islamic Republic of Iran.

Iran has long maintained that its nuclear program is for peaceful civilian energy purposes. But the United States, Israel, and other governments believe the Islamic Republic has been enriching uranium to develop nuclear weapons for military use.

In June 2010, Iran acknowledged publicly for the first time that the uranium-enrichment program at the nuclear plant in the city of Natanz had been infected by a computer virus.[57] The virus took over the controls of roughly one thousand centrifuges, reportedly a fifth of Iran's stockpile at Natanz, causing them to spin out of control and shatter. The virus was so sophisticated that it was able to trick machine technicians at the plant into thinking the centrifuges were operating normally until it was too late.[58]

At the time, Israel and the U.S. were suspected of having conducted this act of cyberwarfare. But nobody knew for sure—both nations had what is known in the diplomatic world as "plausible deniability." Even if it was obvious, no one could directly connect either nation to the virus.

But that plausible deniability ended on June 1, 2012, because of another damaging Obama leak. The *New York Times* published an article by reporter David E. Sanger exposing the program, codenamed "Operation Olympic Games," and providing classified details about it and the computer virus "Stuxnet."[59]

Initiated by the Bush administration and expanded under Obama, Operation Olympic Games was seen by American officials as the best way to obviate any need for a conventional strike by Israel on Iran's nuclear facilities. Sanger's story in the *Times* was adapted from his book *Confront and Conceal: Obama's Secret Wars and Surprising Use of American Power*, which debuted the same month as his *Times* article was published. He detailed Obama's decision-making process in approving the cyber-attacks.

Sanger's reporting included information that could only have come from Obama's national security inner circle. At one point, he describes the atmosphere surrounding a high-level meeting in the Situation Room: "At a tense meeting in the White House Situation Room within days of the worm's 'escape,' Mr. Obama, Vice President Joseph R. Biden Jr. and the director of the Central Intelligence Agency at the time, Leon E. Panetta, considered whether America's most ambitious attempt to slow the progress of Iran's nuclear efforts had been fatally compromised.

"'Should we shut this thing down?' Mr. Obama asked, according to members of the president's national security team who were in the room."[60]

In *Confront and Conceal*, Sanger even thanked the Obama administration for its willingness to talk to him so openly, and specifically the press team for "setting up interviews with all levels of the White House staff." Sanger also boasted that "almost every senior member of the president's national security team was generous enough to sit down and talk through their experiences, some more than once."[61]

Not only did Sanger discuss Stuxnet with many high-level Obama administration officials, but he also later acknowledged that the administration never discouraged him from revealing most of the program's details. "No government agency formally requested that I not publish the story," Sanger told Gawker's John Cook.[62] In fact, Sanger acknowledged that the Obama administration probably enjoyed seeing the details in print. "I'm sure the political side of the White House probably likes reading about the president acting with drones and cyber and so forth," he told CBS's *Face the Nation* on June 3, 2012.[63]

The leaks prompted calls for an investigation, and the U.S. House and Senate Intelligence Committees began reviewing legislation to strengthen safeguards against leaks of classified information.[64] Meanwhile, the administration reacted to charges of politically convenient leaks with outrage. White House Press Secretary Jay Carney said, "This administration takes all appropriate and necessary steps to prevent leaks of classified information or sensitive information that could risk ongoing counterterrorism or intelligence operations.... Any suggestion that this administration has authorized intentional leaks of classified information for political gain is grossly irresponsible."[65]

But no one was ever punished for this leak, so it's rather difficult to avoid the conclusion that that "grossly irresponsible" suggestion was the plain truth. It's pretty clear that Carney was simply instructed to tell a transparent lie and that the administration leaked the intelligence on purpose to reassure people that President Obama was doing something about Iran.

Politifact, a Pulitzer-Prize-winning fact-checking program associated with the *Tampa Bay Times* newspaper, found that the Obama administration did in fact leak details about Stuxnet. "[I]t's clear that the Obama administration provided details—including a quote from Obama himself in a meeting—to the *New York Times*," the fact-checkers concluded. "So the administration—broadly defined—confirmed its operational role in the creation of the worm."[66]

What makes this amateur move so careless is the fact that the White House itself had earlier called cyberattacks an act of war[67] and

threatened to retaliate: "When warranted, the United States will respond
to hostile acts in cyberspace as we would to any other threat to our
country. We reserve the right to use all necessary means—diplomatic,
informational, military, and economic—as appropriate and consistent
with applicable international law, in order to defend our Nation, our
allies, our partners, and our interests. In so doing, we will exhaust all
options before military force whenever we can; will carefully weigh
the costs and risks of action against the costs of inaction; and will act
in a way that reflects our values and strengthens our legitimacy, seeking broad international support whenever possible."[68]

Perhaps the president and his National Security team forgot about
that during the reelection season.

THE AWLAKI LEAK

The Stuxnet and "kill list" leaks were by no means the only leaks
that threatened America's national security and damaged our relationships with our allies.

When American-born Muslim cleric Anwar al-Awlaki was killed
by a U.S. drone strike in Yemen in 2011, legal experts and members
of Congress demanded that the administration release a declassified
copy of the Justice Department memo providing the legal rationale for
killing an American citizen without trial.[69]

Instead of simply releasing the memo, the administration leaked
portions of it to—you guessed it—the *New York Times*.[70] The resulting piece discussed the names of the lawyers who drafted the memo,
where it was drafted, and which agencies were involved.

The administration had argued that Awlaki, who had been linked
to the attempted bombing of a Detroit-bound plane on Christmas Day
2009, was a leader of al Qaeda in the Arabian Peninsula (AQAP).
Because Awlaki was aligned with al Qaeda, the Justice Department
had concluded that his death could be authorized under the use of
military force against al Qaeda passed by Congress and signed by
President Bush a week after the 9/11 attacks. The memo also justified

a drone strike against Awlaki on the grounds that it was not feasible to capture him alive.[71]

The *Times* reporter to whom the memo was leaked, Charlie Savage, noted the paradox of the administration releasing the documents while simultaneously refusing to officially acknowledge having killed an American citizen without trial. "The Obama administration has refused to acknowledge or discuss its role in the drone strike that killed Mr. Awlaki last month and that technically remains a covert operation. The government has also resisted growing calls that it provide a detailed public explanation of why officials deemed it lawful to kill an American citizen, setting a precedent that scholars, rights activists and others say has raised concerns about the rule of law and civil liberties," wrote Savage, "But the document that laid out the administration's justification—a roughly fifty-page memorandum by the Justice Department's Office of Legal Counsel, completed around June 2010—was described on the condition of anonymity by people who have read it."[72]

This leak prompted Harvard law professor Jack Goldsmith to accuse the administration of trying to "have its cake (not talking about the [drone] program to serve diplomatic interests and perhaps deflect scrutiny) and eat it too (leaking to get credit for the operation and portray it as lawful)."[73]

In 2014, the administration finally made public a redacted version of the Awlaki memo as a result of Freedom of Information Act lawsuits filed by the American Civil Liberties Union and the *New York Times*.[74]

WHAT'S SO BAD ABOUT BRAGGING?

President Obama's overreliance on unconventional, secretive tools and methods of warfare (computer viruses, Special Operations Forces, and drone strikes) has left him very vulnerable from a public relations perspective. Americans are far more likely to hear about the civilian casualties that result from such attacks than they are to hear about the positive accomplishments.

And in many cases, the accomplishments are more meaningful if they are *not* widely shared or bragged about. Obama bragged about them anyway, and his administration shared extensive, sensitive information about them. After all, his political life was at stake. There's the priority list: short-term personal goals over long term American interests.

Take the Stuxnet virus, for example. Its introduction into Iran's nuclear program was brilliant—a relatively safe and inexpensive way to disrupt Iran's nuclear programs without the risk of loss of life or the full commitment to a shooting war with Iran. But in revealing the covert sabotage, which Iran could plausibly consider an act of war, the administration gave up the advantages of secrecy and hindered its own future diplomatic efforts. As journalists Richard Silverstein and Muhammad Sahimi have pointed out, "Can we imagine how the US would react if a competing power engaged in such acts of terror against us? In fact, we don't need to: the *Wall Street Journal* reported a year ago that the Pentagon determined that computer sabotage may constitute an 'act of war' against the United States, to which we might respond militarily. So, in effect, we are doing to Iran precisely what we've said we might attack another country for doing to us."[75]

Also, as Silverstein noted, it's an open question whether the cyberattacks did very much damage. Stuxnet destroyed just 20 percent of Iran's centrifuges. That delayed its nuclear program probably for just a few months.[76]

The president, however, had thrown another smoke grenade to look like he was actually stopping Iran from getting the bomb. At the time of this writing the president's strategies (or lack thereof) had led to Iranian ally Bashar al-Assad's position becoming stronger; a takeover of Yemen's government by Iranian proxies (the Houthis); and Iranian domination of the parts of Iraq not dominated by the Islamic State. Thus, Iran began its 2014 nuclear talks with the U.S. from a stronger position as a result of Obama's decisions. Iran has become the regional hegemon in the Middle East, and the Islamic Republic is closer than ever before to getting an atomic bomb.

White House leaks to the media about details of the CIA's use of drone strikes, and in particular Barack Obama's direct involvement in the vetting and choosing of targets, is also problematic. It can be damaging to America's national security when the media report that the president sometimes authorizes the assassination of people "based on patterns of behavior" instead of after a rigorous review of a person's terrorist activities and a determination of guilt. It also damages our prestige and trustworthiness when a news source reveals, as NBC News did, that "the CIA did not always know who it was targeting and killing in drone strikes."[77] And what message does it send when America's commander-in-chief is quoted bragging that he is "really good at killing people," as Obama was in Mark Halperin and John Heilemann's book *Double Down: Game Change 2012?*[78]

Such disclosures are damaging. What's worse, they don't accomplish anything valuable—except perhaps politically. At best, they increase hatred of America and sympathy with or allegiance to terrorist groups such as al Qaeda and ISIS. As a congressional letter of inquiry notes, drones are "faceless ambassadors that cause civilian deaths.... They can generate powerful and enduring anti-American sentiment."[79]

Drone strikes often result in "collateral damage"—that is, civilian casualties. In fact, according to a study by the New America Foundation, one in five drone strike casualties are civilians.[80] And again, that number may actually be low, because the Obama administration "in effect counts all military-age males in a strike zone as combatants."[81]

According to the Bureau of Investigative Journalism, in Pakistan alone between 416 and 951 civilians, including 168 to 200 children, have been killed.[82]

According to a large study by the Pew Research Global Attitudes Project, the use of drones has damaged America's image abroad. "In 39 of 44 countries surveyed," Pew found in 2014, "majorities or pluralities oppose U.S. drone strikes targeting extremists in countries such as Pakistan, Yemen and Somalia. Moreover, opposition to drone attacks has increased in many nations since last year. Israel, Kenya and the U.S. are the only nations polled where at least half of the public supports drone strikes."[83]

None of this is to say that drone strikes or computer viruses should never be used. But if they are going to be part of America's national security apparatus, it seems unwise to broadcast details of how and when we use them. Plus, the overuse of drones in places such as Yemen has done more to promote anti-American perceptions and recruit terrorists than Guantanamo Bay ever did.

What's worse, the administration's own leaks show how it is undermining not just operational security, but international security as well. Drones are not too difficult to produce, and several countries either have or are close to having armed drones. The administration's careless leaks are making the dangerous future use of armed drones by other countries more likely.

STILL LEAKING

In 2013, the Libyan government gave the U.S. tacit permission to conduct a Special Operations raid in the Libyan capital of Tripoli, and in the raid U.S. forces captured senior al Qaeda official Abu Anas al-Libi. Libi was wanted for playing a role in 1998 bombings of U.S. embassies in Africa that killed hundreds of people.

The Libyan government officially denied being aware of the U.S. mission. But its involvement became public when the Obama administration leaked Libya's involvement to the *New York Times*.[84] "U.S. Officials Say Libya Approved Commando Raid," the piece's title blared. "After months of lobbying by American officials, the Libyans consented 'some time ago'—weeks or perhaps even months—to the operations."

Once again, the *Times* had what seemed like unlimited access to Obama administration insiders and sensitive and possibly even classified information. The reporters spoke with "more than half a dozen American diplomatic, military, law enforcement, intelligence and other administration officials."[85]

These leaks were damaging in at least two ways. First, and worst, al Qaeda briefly kidnapped Libyan Prime Minister Ali Zeidan in retaliation for the Libyan government's cooperation with the U.S.[86] If that isn't a direct and obvious blowback, it's hard to see what would be.[87] In fact, it wouldn't be long after this story was published that the Libyan government would be forced to flee the capitol, as Islamist militias took over.

Second, the leaks also revealed plans for another raid—to capture Abu Ahmed Khattala, one of the terrorists responsible for the attacks on the U.S. diplomatic facility in Benghazi on September 11, 2012, which killed four Americans, including U.S. Ambassador to Libya Christopher Stevens.

The *Times* reported that Khattala was living "his life normally in eastern Libya...."[88] As Marc Thiessen pointed out in the *Washington Post*, this leak at the very least alerted Khattala to the fact that he was vulnerable to capture. Khattala was captured the following summer, but leaks like this one have the potential to make future missions much more difficult—in some cases, impossible. Imagine how much harder Special Operations' job would have been if bin Laden had known in advance they were coming.

This is why our government keeps secrets about operational measures. Secrets preserve America's advantage. They make future missions easier because the bad guys don't know what we are doing or even what we know. The element of surprise is a very important component of a successful mission.

Fast-forward to 2014 and the ISIS threat. The group, by that time calling itself the Islamic State, had kidnapped an unknown number of Western journalists and aid workers. These barbarians revealed in a grisly video that they had two American journalists—James Foley and Steven Sotloff. They beheaded Foley on camera and announced that Sotloff would be next if the United States continued to conduct air strikes against their forces in Iraq.

Obama's reaction to this horror was truly disgraceful—and I'm not referring to his decision to keep his tee time and let himself be

photographed in a gleeful game of golf just minutes after acknowledging the situation on camera. Days after the beheading video was released,
the Obama administration told reporters that there had been a failed
rescue mission to save Foley—the 160th Special Operations Aviation
Regiment had successfully infiltrated ISIS-held territory and found the
spot where they believed Foley was. They killed several ISIS fighters.
Unfortunately, Foley was no longer being held there.[89]

Now, why on earth would Obama authorize a release like this one
at a time when he knew that the enemy still held and was threatening
to kill at least one other American? Reporting on the very conference
call in which these beans were spilled, the *New York Times* noted that
the White House "had kept the mission secret in an attempt to 'preserve
future opportunities' to conduct another one."[90]

Yet they released the information anyway, and with far too many
details—specifics, for example, about the helicopters and weapons
used, the tactics, the branch of Special Operations Forces involved—all
things ISIS might not have known, even if it knew it had been attacked
by us.

The brass at the Pentagon were justifiably infuriated: "Two Defense
Department officials, who spoke separately on the condition of anonymity because of the operation's delicate nature, expressed anger at
the administration for revealing the mission.... [one] official said, the
conference call on Wednesday revealed new details that ISIS is not
likely to have known. 'This only makes our job harder,' the official
said. 'I'm very disappointed this was released. We knew any second
operation would be a lot harder.'"[91] And now it would be harder still.

The White House pleaded that it didn't want to release this information, but felt compelled to because reporters were already asking questions about the story. But even assuming the White House itself wasn't
already those reporters' primary source, most responsible newspapers
are willing to withhold publication under such circumstances—when it
could potentially cost an American (in this case, a journalist) his life.

Instead, the White House just spilled the beans to everyone, giving
out far too much information, as the anonymous Pentagon officials

noted. Why? Perhaps one reason is that Obama had looked so bad playing golf moments after expressing his outrage about Foley's death. The leak helped convey the impression that Obama had been more engaged in the situation, and more decisive in trying to save Americans, than his behavior on the day of Foley's death suggested.

I shudder to think that this face-saving, ass-covering leak changed plans at the Pentagon—especially that any mission in the works to save Sotloff (who later was also beheaded on camera) or any other ISIS hostage was negatively affected.

This last incident occurred long after Obama had been reelected, and long after my friends and I had formed OPSEC. But it was precisely this kind of careless, self-promoting chatter by the Obama administration that brought me together with a number of other retired Special Operations Forces and intelligence officers during the 2012 election.

As the next chapter explains, I was already a politician at that point, but many of the others with whom I worked had never been involved in politics. What we had in common is that we saw what Obama was doing, and we were fed up.

The problem with smoke grenades is that the smoke only lasts so long.

CHAPTER THREE

Call of Duty

I n 2008, Barack Obama's lack of experience in international affairs was one of the reasons he ultimately chose Joe Biden as his running mate. Biden had decades of foreign policy experience in the U.S. Senate, including several terms as chairman of the Senate Foreign Relations Committee.

In the general election, Obama faced Republican John McCain. McCain had spent twenty-three years in the U.S. Navy, including two years in solitary confinement in a North Vietnamese prison during the Vietnam War. In his nearly thirty years in Congress, McCain had been a leading voice for a strong national defense and a hawkish, interventionist foreign policy.

Leading up to the election, polls showed McCain with large advantages over Obama on questions asking voters which candidate could better "handle the responsibilities of commander-in-chief," and which "would do a good job on the terrorism issue."[1]

On Election Day, exit polls showed that 86 percent of voters who named terrorism as their top issue voted for McCain. Fortunately for Obama, in the midst of an economic meltdown, those voters constituted barely one-tenth of the electorate.[2]

Once in office, Obama quickly signaled that he was breaking from George W. Bush's foreign policy and national security agenda, both in substance and in tone. On his second day in office, Obama signed executive orders ending the CIA's use of secret prisons, calling for the closure of the Guantanamo Bay detention camp within one year, and banning waterboarding and other enhanced interrogation techniques.

In his inaugural address, Obama invited "the Muslim world" to "a new way forward, based on mutual interest and mutual respect." He also announced that the U.S. would "extend a hand" to those "who cling to power through corruption and deceit" if they "are willing to unclench" their fists.[3]

A few months into Obama's term, Attorney General Holder announced plans to give accused September 11 mastermind Khalid Sheikh Mohammed a civilian trial in New York City—a decision that ignited weeks of sharp criticism from members of Congress and family members of 9/11 victims.

It was an extremely controversial decision, not least because Mohammed and his lawyers would have had access to national security information.[4] The Obama administration later dropped the plan, citing what the *New York Times* called "almost unanimous pressure from New York officials and business leaders."[5]

It was against this backdrop, it appears, that the Obama administration—and then the Obama reelection campaign—recognized a constant need to reassure the public that even though their commander-in-chief had embraced a national security and foreign policy agenda more conciliatory toward some of America's traditional foes (such as Iran and Russia), he was still doing everything in his power to keep Americans safe from terrorists.

And this, it seems, is the reason the Obama administration became as leaky as it did. A president who embraces the "dove" banner can stick to his principles when accused of weakness and trust voters to reward him, or he can constantly feed the press with information reassuring the public that, behind the scenes, he is in fact breaking things and killing people, and doing whatever it takes to keep Americans safe. The Obama administration chose the latter path, often compromising important information along the way.

THE BACKLASH

The leaks provoked bipartisan outrage on Capitol Hill and beyond. The response by members of Congress was perhaps best captured in the lead sentence of a newspaper article published soon after the Stuxnet and "kill list" leaks occurred. "Democrats and Republicans on Capitol Hill don't agree on much these days," *Politico*'s Reid J. Epstein noted on June 7, 2012, "but they agree that the Obama administration has a serious problem with leaking classified information."[6] This newfound bipartisanship spoke not only to the number of national security–related leaks that were happening but also to how overtly political and potentially damaging the leaks were.

"It has to be for re-election," Republican Representative Peter King of New York told *Politico*. "[The administration] can deny it all they want. But it would require a suspension of disbelief to believe it's not being done for political purposes."[7] "I don't think you have to be Sherlock Holmes to figure out what is going on here," Republican Senator Lindsey Graham of South Carolina said. "You've had three leaks of intelligence that paint the president as a strong leader."[8] Senator John McCain, the ranking Republican on the Senate Armed Services Committee, was just as upset: "Let me be clear: I am fully in favor of transparency in government. I have spent my entire career in Congress furthering that principle. But what separates these sorts of leaks from, say, the whistle-blowing that fosters open government or a free press is that these leaks expose no violations of law, abuses of authority, or threats to public health or safety. They are merely gratuitous and utterly self-serving." Earlier, McCain had called the leaks "unconscionable" and accused the administration of "intentionally leaking information to enhance President Obama's image as a tough guy for the elections."[9]

Opinion columnists across the political spectrum also weighed in. On the Right, syndicated columnist Charles Krauthammer called the *Times*'s "kill list" piece "a White House press release." "A rather strange ethics. You go around the world preening about how America has turned a new moral page by electing a president profoundly offended by George W. Bush's belligerence and prisoner maltreatment, and now you're ostentatiously telling the world that you personally play judge, jury and executioner to unseen combatants of your choosing and whatever innocents happen to be in their company."[10]

On the Left, *Washington Post* columnist Richard Cohen wrote that the number of officials the Obama administration made available to reporters "suggests the sort of mass law-breaking not seen since Richard Nixon took out after commies, liberals, conservationists, antiwar protesters, Jews and, of course, leakers."

"The leak that troubles me concerns the killing of suspected or actual terrorists," Cohen wrote. "The triumphalist tone of the leaks—the Tarzan-like chest-beating of various leakers—not only is in poor taste but also shreds a long-standing convention that, in these matters, the president has deniability. The president of the United States is not the Godfather."[11]

Some former intelligence officials spoke out against the administration's actions. Former CIA spokesman Bill Harlow told columnist Debra Saunders that the *New York Times*' Stuxnet and "kill list" pieces "left a trail that Helen Keller could follow" to "a small universe of people."[12]

Law professor Kenneth Anderson accused the administration of "conducting the foreign policy of the U.S. by leaked journalism."[13] And the editorial page of *Investor's Business Daily* quipped that "[u]nder this president, our enemies don't need spies."[14]

In Congress, it wasn't just Republicans who saw the danger—some Democrats were just as outraged. Representative Dutch Ruppersberger, the top Democrat on the House Intelligence Committee, said, "I've

been on this committee close to ten years. This is one of the most serious breaches in the last couple articles that have come out that I have
seen. It puts us at risk. It puts lives at risk."[15]

Senator Joe Lieberman, the chairman of Senate Homeland Security and Governmental Affairs Committee who had been Al Gore's
vice presidential running mate, said, "The recent series of leaks are
the worst in a long time."[16]

In calling for an investigation of the leaks, Senate Intelligence
Committee Chairwoman Dianne Feinstein, California Democrat, told
CNN's Wolf Blitzer, "I think what we're seeing, Wolf, is an avalanche
of leaks and it is very, very disturbing. It's dismayed our allies. It puts
American lives in jeopardy. It puts our nation's security in jeopardy."[17]
Feinstein told columnist Debra Saunders that after reading half of
David Sanger's *Confront and Conceal*, "You learn more from the book
than I did as chairman of the intelligence committee, and that's very
disturbing to me."[18] Later, in a speech to the World Affairs Council,
Feinstein said, "I think the White House has to understand that some
of this is coming from its ranks. I don't know specifically where, but
there—I think they have to begin to understand that and do something
about it."[19]

Senator John Kerry, the Massachusetts Democrat who was then
chairman of the Senate Foreign Relations Committee and would later
become Obama's Secretary of State, wondered aloud whether the *New
York Times* had put American security at risk by publishing the "kill
list" and Stuxnet stories. "I personally think there is a serious question
whether or not [the articles] served our interest and whether the public had to know," Kerry told reporters. "To me it was such a nitty-gritty
fundamental national security issue. And I don't see how the public
interest is well served by it. I do see how other interests outside the
United States are well served by it."[20]

By mid-summer 2012, both the Senate and House Intelligence
Committees had authorized bills to crack down on national security
leaks. Among the provisions included in the 2013 Intelligence Authorization Act was one that called for reducing the number of people at

intelligence agencies permitted to speak to reporters, and another that would have required that anyone seeking to disclose intelligence information first give notice to the Senate and House Intelligence Committees. A third provision would have allowed the government to take away the pensions of intelligence officers who illegally disclosed classified information.[21] All three measures were later stripped from the bill before passage.[22]

The Obama administration pushed back on accusations that it was purposefully leaking intelligence. "The notion that my White House would purposely release classified national security information is offensive. It's wrong," President Obama said during a press briefing on June 8, 2012. "And people, I think, need to have a better sense of how I approach this office and how the people around me here approach this office."[23]

But Obama had it backwards. Republicans and Democrats alike were accusing him of leaking sensitive national security intelligence for political purposes. And it was not because they didn't understand his approach to the presidency, but rather because they had come to understand his approach all too well. He had been caught red-handed. One could say that he no longer had "plausible deniability" about leaking sensitive information that could help him politically.

At this point, Obama began assuring the public that he had "zero tolerance" for leaks and that those responsible would "suffer consequences."[24] Attorney General Eric Holder used similar language. "The unauthorized disclosure of classified information can compromise the security of this country and all Americans, and it will not be tolerated," he said.[25] Soon, Republicans were calling on Obama and Holder to appoint a special prosecutor to probe the leaks. In a letter to Holder, thirty-one GOP senators wrote that a special prosecutor would ensure an investigation free of political influence.[26]

During the Bush administration, a special prosecutor had been named to investigate national security leaks that led to the disclosure of the identity of a CIA operative. Ultimately Vice President Dick Cheney's chief of staff, Lewis Libby, was charged with and convicted

of perjury. Back then, Senator Obama urged the use of a special prosecutor.[27]

But things were different now that it was the Obama administration doing the leaking. Instead of naming a special prosecutor independent of Obama's Justice Department, Holder appointed two U.S.
attorneys, Ronald Machen Jr. of the District of Columbia and Rod
Rosenstein of Maryland, to investigate the leaks. They reported directly
to Holder and Obama.

It was soon discovered that Machen, an Obama appointee, had
donated $4,350 to Obama's campaigns over the years and even helped
Obama's 2008 campaign vet potential running mates.[28] This was a
political investigation—just as the leaks had been political leaks.

HOW LEAKS HURT

While the White House intelligence leaks probably helped Obama
win reelection, they did so at the expense of the national security of
the U.S. and its allies.

No wonder the leaks deeply frustrated many members of the Special Operations Forces and intelligence communities. As Jaime Wil-
liamson, a retired Special Operations colonel, said of the bin Laden
leaks, "To hear the secrets that I've spent over 25 years protecting—
cover name of a unit, the actual name of a special mission unit and
the location of a special mission unit—all reported within the same
sentence—not only did they identify the special mission unit, we had
tactics, techniques, procedures that were compromised. We even knew
the name of the dog that was on the operation."[29]

Leaks can compromise intelligence sources that take years or
decades to develop. As former FBI Director Robert Mueller has said,
"Leaks…threaten ongoing operations, puts at risk the lives of sources,
makes it much more difficult to recruit sources, and damages our
relationships with our foreign partners."[30]

The moment the Obama administration announced that the SEALs
had hauled away a large collection of al Qaeda documents and other

materials from bin Laden's hide-out, the information lost much of its value, because terrorists in the al Qaeda network were tipped off and could alter their plans if necessary. They could pop right out of their rabbit holes and into new rabbit holes we didn't know about. The instant President Obama announced the successful Osama bin Laden raid, he was giving the bad guys the opportunity to change their tactics and patterns of behavior. Why didn't he, at a minimum, wait forty-eight hours?

And later revelations—for example, the details shared with the makers of the movie *Zero Dark Thirty*—may have had even more deadly consequences. Rowan Scarborough has reported in the *Washington Times* about the possible link between leaked information and the failures of several special operations missions, including recent hostage rescue attempts: "Special operations forces' three most recent attempts to rescue American hostages failed. Last year, SEALs attempted a beach insertion to capture a terrorist leader in Somalia but were spotted and repelled. There was also the horrific loss of SEALs in a helicopter shoot-down that some family members believe was an ambush." As Scarborough reports, "In the secretive special operations community, officials are debating whether to tweak tactics for daring and risky missions involving hostage rescue and terrorist targeting that have been compromised by years of detailed news accounts and Hollywood portrayals. Some believe Islamic extremists have gone to school on special operations forces. The classroom is the U.S. media."[31]

Defense Secretary Robert Gates had warned the administration of precisely this risk after the bin Laden raid: "I reminded everyone that the techniques, tactics, and procedures the SEALs had used in the Bin Laden operation were used every night in Afghanistan and elsewhere in hunting down terrorists and other enemies.... It was therefore essential that we agree not to release any operational details of the raid. That we killed him, I said, is all we needed to say. Everybody in that room agreed to keep mum on details. That commitment lasted about five hours. The initial leaks came from the White House and CIA. They just couldn't wait to brag and to claim credit."[32]

I'm not naïve. I realize that every administration leaks some intelligence to the press. I also realize that sometimes it can be hard to distinguish between leaks and good, in-depth journalism. There are times when sources really do slip up and accidentally divulge information they shouldn't—and it's clear that has happened during Obama's administration, too. Sometimes government officials mistakenly reveal information that leads a talented reporter—who may be equally or better informed about a topic than his source—to confirm a suspicion or connect crucial dots himself.

I also understand that America's national security apparatus is large—perhaps too large. There are nearly five million government employees and contractors who hold security clearances. As Elizabeth Goitein of the New York University law school told the *New York Times*, "That's not a recipe for keeping secrets."[33]

All that said, no administration has ever leaked national security intelligence with the regularity that the Obama administration has, or for a purpose that was so transparently political—never in the history of this nation. American voters may have been the intended audience for the leaks; but the terrorists and our enemies were also watching carefully.

Each piece of information about how the U.S. operates its foreign policy and national security that becomes public can potentially help terrorists avoid detection or counter such operations.

All military operations rely on intelligence. No one commits troops in the field blindly. Intelligence is crucial to get authorization to conduct even the most minor operation. In many cases, good intelligence is the difference between losing lives on a pointless mission and achieving a crucial goal to the exact specifications ordered.

And the best intelligence is human intelligence, because it can provide a window into the thinking of the enemy's leadership. All the technical intelligence in the world can't replace that knowledge. Things are just different on the ground—the perspective, the smells, the angles, and the relationships.

The process of protecting intelligence is called operational security, or OPSEC. Put simply, OPSEC means never letting the enemy know your intentions. Maintaining OPSEC can mean the difference between a success and failure. And when OPSEC is violated, our enemies gain the upper hand. Once the enemy knows what we're doing, he can change tactics, directions, locations—anything—and the good guys end up flying blind.

OPSEC

The Special Operations OPSEC Education Fund, Inc., a.k.a. OPSEC, was launched in the summer of 2012. OPSEC is a non-partisan grassroots advocacy group whose purpose is to provide a voice to the many former members of the CIA and Special Operations Forces who have grown frustrated with the misuse of information and the politicization of intelligence.

Our main mission was to stop politicians—and sadly, that especially meant the sitting president—from exploiting U.S. national security operations and secrets for political gain. Another part of our mission was to help Americans understand the cost of intelligence leaks.

To that end, on August 15, 2012, we released a twenty-two-minute documentary video called *Dishonorable Disclosures*.[34] The video featured many former Special Operations and intelligence officers, including myself. Our message was simple. As former Navy SEAL Ben Smith put it so emotionally in the video, "Mr. President, you did not kill Osama bin Laden, America did. The work that the American military has done killed Osama bin Laden. You did not. As a citizen, it is my civic duty to tell the president to stop leaking information to the enemy. It will get Americans killed."

The film clearly hit a nerve. It was viewed more than 5.2 million times on YouTube, and OPSEC began to receive a lot of attention in the media, winning a strong spot in the national news cycle for a week. We received enough attention to get multiple rebukes from the Obama administration—and even one from the president himself.

When Obama campaign spokesman Ben LaBolt was asked about OPSEC, he didn't take us on directly; instead, he used the film to attack Obama's general election opponent, Republican Mitt Romney. LaBolt accused "Republicans" of "resorting to Swift Boat tactics because when it comes to foreign policy and national security, Mitt Romney has offered nothing but reckless rhetoric."[35] It was a strange leap for LaBolt to try to link a video by an independent group of former military and intelligence men to Governor Romney's presidential campaign. And the reference to "reckless rhetoric" is ironic.

Stranger still was LaBolt's mention of "Swift Boat tactics," a reference to a campaign by the Swift Boat Veterans for Truth to discredit John Kerry's Navy service during his 2004 presidential campaign. It was an inapt comparison, to say the least. The Swift Boat Veterans' narrow purpose was to expose and debate Kerry's war record. Our goals were far less personal to Barack Obama and also pertained to a much more current and pressing issue. The politicization of the Navy SEALs and the CIA was and is still a current event, not something that had happened decades earlier. Members of all parties had noticed and called the Obama administration out for it. Unlike the Swift Boat Veterans, we were not discussing disputed events that had occurred in the Vietnam War.

What's more, we did not intend to stop pursuing our mission once the election ended, no matter who won or lost.

Predictably, the Obama administration deployed John Kerry to attack us. Kerry also used the "Swift Boat" line of attack, saying, "Seeing the new outrageous attacks made against President Obama from a shadowy Republican-allied veterans group called OPSEC, which take issue with the mission to kill Osama bin Laden, remind [sic] me all too well of the notorious 'Swift Boat' attacks I faced in the 2004 campaign."[36]

Kerry's comments exposed him as a hypocrite. Only a couple of months before he attacked us, Kerry, as chairman of the Senate Foreign Relations Committee, had himself criticized the very same Obama administration leaks we were criticizing, expressing sentiments almost identical to ours: "A number of those leaks, and others in the last months about drone activities and other activities, are frankly all against national-security interests. I think they're dangerous, damaging, and whoever is doing that is not acting in the interest of the United States of America."[37]

But by August, Kerry had apparently set aside his concerns for the "interest of the United States of America," and begun working for the interests of the Obama reelection campaign—and for the next step in his career.

What could have changed Kerry's mind in those two months? Only he knows for sure. But less than seven months later, Kerry was named Obama's Secretary of State, a position he had reportedly coveted for years.

OBAMA ATTACKS

Even President Obama himself lashed out at us—which I took as a clear sign that we had at least accomplished something.

"I don't take these folks too seriously," the president told the *Virginian-Pilot* newspaper. "One of their members is a birther who denies I was born here, despite evidence to the contrary. You've got another who was a tea party candidate in a recent election. This kind of stuff springs up before election time."[38]

Obama's birther comment actually applied not to us, but to another group of ex–Special Operations members that had organized a political group to oppose his candidacy. I assume his "tea party candidate" comment was a reference to me. Because yes, at that point, I had run for U.S. Congress—not as a tea party candidate, but as a Republican—in a Virginia primary. (I got clobbered.)

Even so, neither fact made our arguments any less credible or legitimate. Our nation has a long history of former military figures continuing to serve the country through political activism. In fact, 109 members of the current Congress have served in various capacities in the military.[39] John Kerry was not the first politician to come from this background—you might call General George Washington an early adopter.

And although many members of OPSEC would call themselves conservatives (the military tends to be conservative, both culturally and politically), it is a non-partisan organization, and some members are Democrats. At least one of our inner circle had even donated to Obama's 2008 presidential campaign. Others had voted for him. These were convenient things for Obama to ignore.

Most of OPSEC's members were not particularly political at all—as is the case with many in the military and many veterans as well. What brought us together and united us was not our politics, but our alarm at what the Obama administration was doing, and our common belief that we had to become involved in the political process to do all we could to stop the exploitation of our brothers in arms and our nation's military secrets for political gain. And our only effective way of getting involved was going to be participation in an election-year campaign of our own. Politicians, after all, only listen when their political lives are at stake.

While our respective Special Operations Forces groups are close-knit, there is also some overlap among the different branches. E-mails were certainly flying around the Special Ops community as the Obama White House's leak problem became more evident. In my view, President Obama had no one to blame but himself for the indignation within our community.

We viewed our task as a mission. Tremendous planning and detail went into our process. Tasks were divided up. We knew it would be necessary to raise money and hire a top-notch communications firm that had access to television producers and could react to media inquiries.

Our documentary launched to huge fanfare. I believe we were quoted or talked about in just about every major American publication in August 2012. I even fielded calls from publications overseas. We held documentary showings in several states. In Virginia Beach, our screening drew an audience of over a hundred people. Because of the launch sensitivity (again, OPSEC), we gave them only two days' notice ahead of the showing; even so, two local news stations covered it. This is the same documentary that has now been viewed more than 5 million times on YouTube.

Our organization was set up so that donors did not have to be disclosed. This is a choice that's controversial to some people, but we wanted to ensure that those who helped us get our message out would not suffer retaliation for doing what is right. We also needed large donors to get our effort off the ground, even though we were able to raise a significant amount from the tens of thousands of private citizens on our email list.

I was the politician, the chairman, and the main spokesperson for our group, and so the task of dealing with large donors fell largely to me. I remember flying to Dallas to meet with one prospective donor. Armed with a strong issue and statistics about our group's exceptional performance in our brief existence, I sat across the table to sell our mission. The donor was very respectful and asked several probing questions before propping his feet up on the table in a very Texas type of way.

"Hold on a second. Let me make a couple calls," he said.

"Yes sir," I responded.

He proceeded to call and talk to a buddy who was tapped out, having already spent tens of millions in politics that year. Then he placed another call, and within about thirty seconds, looked at me and asked, "Can you get to Houston by 10 a.m. tomorrow?" We were in Dallas, recall, and it was almost 5:00 p.m.

"Yes sir," I responded.

"Good. I want you to meet my buddy and see what he says."

I arrived, on time, in Houston the next day, where I met another potential donor. My presentation this time was even shorter.

"Can you step out of the office? I'm gonna call my friend in Dallas and we are gonna see," he said.

"Yes sir," I responded. Five minutes later he comes out and says, "He wants you in Dallas, can you be there by 3 p.m.?"

"Yes sir," I responded. This was getting ridiculous.

At 3:00 p.m. I was sitting on an office couch, back in Dallas once again. I didn't have much time before I had to catch my own flight back to Virginia; I had a War Memorial Board of Trustees appointment early the next day. The Virginia governor had appointed me to the board, and I didn't want to miss the meeting. Ten minutes went by before I saw the governor of Florida walk in past me with his crew.

Knowing my meeting would be bumped, I went to the secretary and let her know I had to leave to catch a flight, and to tell the donor that I truly appreciated his time. I wasn't sure if I would ever hear back from him or his office again.

A week later, two $250,000 checks arrived for us. We were up and running again. We would be able to headline more events, conduct more screenings, and participate in numerous media interviews because someone had given back to his community and his country—someone who cared deeply about the contribution of the men and women in the field.

In September, the Benghazi attack occurred. Given our experience, we knew instinctively that it was a terrorist attack. To paraphrase Senator John McCain, you don't take a mortar to a spontaneous demonstration. Naturally, we stepped up to the plate to call out Hillary Clinton, Susan Rice, and President Obama for the cover-up and the lies they told—when the consulate was still smoldering. I penned an op-ed for the *Washington Times* on how Obama was putting his personal politics above our nation's security. Benghazi was another—and this time a truly horrific—example of the problem we had originally formed OPSEC to counter: American national security, and the safety of those who serve, being subordinated to political gain.

Our group would later run television ads in three critical swing states—again, realizing that politicians only pay attention when their political lives are in jeopardy. It's a shame they were not paying attention when others' lives were in jeopardy for real in Benghazi.

The criticism also kept pouring in. General Martin Dempsey, chairman of the Joint Chiefs of Staff, also attacked our group. "One of the things that marks us as a profession in a democracy is, it's most important we remain apolitical," he said, chiding OPSEC's members for getting political. "That's how we maintain our trust with the American people. The American people don't want us to become another special-interest group. In fact, I think that confuses them.... If someone uses the uniform for partisan politics, I'm disappointed in that. I think it erodes that bond of trust we have with the American people."[40]

I respect General Dempsey very much, but he got this one dead wrong. Ironically, he was in uniform when he made this statement defending a politician from a group of veterans exercising their First Amendment rights. None of the Special Ops and intelligence community members who spoke out as part of OPSEC were active duty. As retired servicemen, we had the right—and, we felt, the obligation— to speak out on issues we felt passionately about. We were most concerned with protecting those still in uniform from being used or having their safety compromised for partisan political purposes.

Our group was able to offer a rebuttal of General Dempsey's comments in a Fox News segment, where I made our position very clear: "The Obama campaign continues to promote a highly partisan attack ad that used military footage and photographs from the White House Situation Room to support sharp criticism of the president's political opponent. The use of those in uniform and the work they do for partisan political purposes is not only unhelpful, as General Dempsey said, but is dishonorable, and the campaign should immediately remove the ad for good."

Internally, we at OPSEC were upset with General Dempsey. We knew that he could not publicly attack his Commander in Chief, but his attack on private citizens—veterans who were out of uniform—were unfortunate. We were merely objecting to an administration that was leaking classified intelligence and Special Operations missions, tactics, and capabilities when those leaks could get people killed.

What Dempsey had pointed out—that active duty members of the Armed Forces really cannot make their voice heard as we were able to—only made our task more urgent.

I remember receiving a message from a deployed SEAL brother in Afghanistan: "Scott, what can we do to help? This is bullsh*t." He, of course, could really do nothing, given that he was on active duty. But, here was an example of a friend in the fight, paying attention and pissed off at what was happening. He intimately understood the potential consequences. We had to speak out for his safety.

We were speaking openly about protecting those in uniform. The Obama administration had been leaking classified or sensitive intelligence about Special Operations missions, tactics, and capabilities, leaks that leaders of both parties had said have reached alarming levels under this administration.

President Obama, who has a very tough time taking responsibility for anything that goes wrong, preferred to blame a predecessor, his subordinates, and even our country. He had no interest in truly cracking down on these leaks. He obviously hoped to keep the information flowing through Election Day, and in the meantime to use his political might to silence critics like us.

I take this very personally—not for myself, but on behalf of the many years of honorable service to this nation that our group has given and continues to give. Many of us in OPSEC have lost friends and family members, or have been wounded in combat. One member was even burned in the Pentagon on 9/11.

This was exactly the right group to step up—veterans with the credibility to demand that the Obama White House stop selling out and undermining our safety and national security for its own political goals.

An editorial in *Investor's Business Daily* summed up the situation accurately, distinguishing what we were doing from what the Obama administration was up to: "Dempsey said the military remaining 'apolitical' is 'how we maintain our bond and trust with the American people.' But it's President Obama who politicized that bond. The self-named OPSEC ('operations security') objectors, through a YouTube short film, 'Dishonorable Disclosure,' are simply telling the truth."[41]

As the debate over OPSEC ramped up, we were the subject of numerous profiles in leading publications, including the *New York Times*, *Wall Street Journal*, Reuters, and CNN. I appeared several times on CNN, Fox News Channel, and other networks introducing the public to OPSEC and explaining our mission, as well as weighing in on other foreign policy-related topics as they surfaced during the campaign.

Some of the media attention was negative, but we also received a lot of support. When I appeared on *On the Record with Greta Van Susteren*, Greta and I discussed President Obama's and General

Dempsey's attacks. She offered some encouraging words that stick with me to this day: "In my wildest dreams, Scott, I can't imagine anyone saying in reference to Navy SEALs, 'I don't take these folks too seriously.' I can assure you that 99.9 percent of Americans are in great awe of the sacrifice of Navy SEALs and other intelligence officers, people who put their selves on the line for us. I suspect the president wasn't thinking when he said that because I know that—I mean, everybody does respect the Navy SEALs immensely, and the intelligence people."[42]

Greta was giving the president more of the benefit of the doubt than I would have, but I appreciated her kind words. As it turned out, she was not the only one who felt Obama was being too dismissive of our concerns. I was getting the same impression from many Americans I met—and even quiet thumbs-up from people in active service who knew not to speak publicly, for the very reasons Dempsey had outlined. They overwhelmingly supported the work the Navy SEALs had done, and they were aghast that it was being exploited for political gain.

A DOUBLE STANDARD

The Obama administration was happy to leak sensitive, classified information when it had a good story to tell the American people. But when leaked information embarrasses this administration, it vigorously prosecutes leakers. In fact, the U.S. government under Barack Obama has prosecuted eight people for alleged felony leaks of classified information—more than all previous American presidents combined.[43]

Six of the prosecuted leakers were mid-level bureaucrats or military personnel, while two others were government contractors. Meanwhile, high-level officials close to the White House have leaked with impunity. Steven Aftergood, who tracks classified information policy for the Federation of American Scientists, said of the Obama administration's double standard, "There has never been an agency head or an assistant secretary or senior agency official who has been prosecuted the way the mid-level and lower individuals have."[44]

Instead of prosecuting the high-level leakers of classified information, they were investigating whistleblowers or low-level violators, or even those who leaked information about the top-level leakers. For instance, after internal Pentagon and CIA investigations concluded that then–CIA Director Leon Panetta and Undersecretary of Defense for Intelligence Michael Vickers were responsible for disclosing sensitive information to the makers of the Hollywood film *Zero Dark Thirty*, it wasn't they who were held to account. Instead, the Pentagon's Inspector General's Office began investigating who might have leaked to reporters the fact that Panetta and Vickers were being investigated.[45]

"I'm concerned that the inspector general's office is barking up the wrong tree," Republican Senator Charles Grassley of Iowa told *McClatchy* in 2013. "There's no doubt they should look into the 'Zero Dark Thirty' fiasco, but they should focus on holding people accountable for leaking highly classified operational material instead of wasting time and money investigating who leaked the report."

And guys who have served in the field are punished, while the higher-ups or political advisors get a pass. When former SEAL Team Six member Matt Bissonnette published *No Easy Day*, his best-selling memoir about the bin Laden raid, the Obama administration moved swiftly to hold him accountable. The Pentagon threatened legal action against Bissonnette, who had participated in the mission that killed bin Laden, and anyone "acting in concert" with him for material breach of non-disclosure agreements.[46]

The Obama administration even disciplined a group of Navy SEALs for dereliction of duty for disclosing classified information to the makers of a military video game. Bissonnette had recruited seven SEALs to work as paid consultants in the production of a video game called *Medal of Honor: Warfighter*.[47]

None of the seven had notified their commanding officers about their actions, which included disclosing inappropriate information—including showing some of their equipment to the game's producers. All the SEALs received a letter of reprimand, sometimes called a "career killer" because it may foreclose any future promotions. They also lost two months of pay.

Bissonnette certainly should have submitted the manuscript to the Department of Defense for review, as is standard practice, especially for such a fresh topic. Many in our community were upset with him. I believe Bissonnette (who published his book under the pseudonym "Mark Owen") and the other SEALs who consulted on the video game should have been held to the same standard as others who had divulged classified information.

But the administration was applying a dishonorable double-standard in threatening to prosecute Bissonnette, a five-time winner of the Bronze Star, while dragging its feet about identifying and charging numerous senior administration officials who purposely leaked classified information that put those serving on the front lines at risk. As I put it in an OPSEC press release at the time, "If President Obama is going to pursue an immediate and vigorous prosecution of American war heroes, he should hold his senior aides to the exact same standard."[48] Needless to say, nothing of the sort happened.

I believe that the SEALs were probably encouraged to disclose more than they should have by the pervasive culture of leaks in the Obama administration. Operation security protections apply to everyone in the chain of command. Leadership matters, as does its absence. When the people at the top don't follow the rules on critical matters, what do you expect from the people at the bottom? More recently, Robert O'Neill came out, if you will, as "the shooter" of Bin Laden, on a Fox News special. While I may disagree with how Robert went about it, this is a symptom of the root cause. I know Rob personally and he was a great SEAL. If anything I would trust Robert and Matt far more than a political actor in keeping national security secrets that could potentially harm the men they stood shoulder to shoulder with. Their stories seemed to be continuing the tale let loose at the highest levels. Some may be mad at the two for trying to earn money off their stories. While that is a judgment call I leave up to them, the movie *Zero Dark Thirty*, with help from the Obama administration just after the raid, grossed over $132,000,000 worldwide. This, of course, was with leaders giving secrets and collaboration, disregarding security clearances, for a film originally to be released just prior to the president's reelection. Is that fair? How much of that money has gone to veterans' causes?

Several other people involved in sensitive intelligence disclosures have been vigorously prosecuted or harassed with other legal action by the Obama administration:

Thomas Drake: In 2010, Thomas Drake, a senior executive at the National Security Agency (NSA), was indicted for divulging classified information about an NSA technology program called the Trailblazer Project to a reporter for the *Baltimore Sun*. Drake said he was motivated to contact the *Sun* by his frustration over the program's wasting of hundreds of millions of dollars—a classic whistleblower claim.

Drake was prosecuted on ten felony charges involving the mishandling of classified information and obstruction of justice. He was threatened with thirty-five years in prison. All ten charges were eventually dropped, and Drake pleaded guilty to one count of exceeding the authorized use of a government computer, a misdemeanor. He served no prison time because the government refused to provide information about the documents Drake was accused of leaking. Drake was sentenced to one year of probation and 240 hours of community service. Drake's sentencing judge called the Justice Department's conduct in the case "unconscionable."[49]

Bradley Manning: The Justice Department prosecuted Army intelligence analyst Bradley Manning (who subsequently asked to go by the name "Chelsea") on espionage charges for working with WikiLeaks to release the largest set of classified documents ever leaked to the public. Manning was convicted in July 2013 and sentenced to thirty-five years in a military prison with the possibility of parole after eight years, and was dishonorably discharged from the Army. The disclosures included U.S. diplomatic cables and videos of U.S. airstrikes in

Iraq. Joint Chiefs Chairman Admiral Mike Mullen said WikiLeaks "might already have on their hands the blood of some young soldier or that of an Afghan family."[50]

James Risen: In 2011, former CIA officer Jeffrey Sterling was arrested for leaking classified information to *New York Times* national security reporter James Risen about Operation Merlin, a Clinton- and Bush-era covert CIA operation to provide Iran with a faulty design for constructing a nuclear weapon in order to derail the Iranian government's nuclear program. Risen wrote about the operation in his 2006 book *State of War*. The administration has tried to force Risen to testify at Sterling's trial, threatening the reporter—who has called President Obama "the greatest enemy to press freedom in a generation"—with jail time if he doesn't give up his source.

Sterling may have broken non-disclosure agreements and his faith with the CIA, but Risen was just practicing journalism, not unlike other reporters who have received classified information. The Obama administration's double standard on national security leaks was captured in a tweet by Associated Press reporter Matt Apuzzo. "[*New York Times* foreign policy reporter David] Sanger writes on successful Iranian operation, gets wide access. Risen writes on botched Iranian operation, gets subpoenaed."[51]

James Rosen: In 2013, Fox News reporter James Rosen's phone logs and emails were secretly subpoenaed and seized in a Justice Department investigation. DOJ obtained two months of records to track Rosen's visits to the State Department and got a warrant to search his personal emails.

Rosen was described in one subpoena as "an aider, abettor and/or conspirator" of an indicted leak defendant for merely doing the job national security journalists do. The Rosen case provoked a backlash from conservative and liberal journalists alike. Liberal *Washington Post* columnist Dana Milbank wrote, "The Rosen affair is as flagrant an assault on civil liberties as anything done by George W. Bush's administration, and it uses technology to silence critics in a way Richard Nixon could only have dreamed of."[52]

Edward Snowden: In 2013, National Security Agency contractor Edward Snowden leaked documents exposing the NSA's program of widespread monitoring of phone and internet data of U.S. citizens who are not suspects in terrorism investigations. Snowden was charged with two counts of violating the Espionage Act and stealing government property, crimes punishable by up to thirty years in prison. He fled the country and is living under asylum in Russia.

I'm not defending the alleged or convicted leakers in any of these cases—quite the contrary, some of them probably did a lot of damage. And there are whistleblowing procedures that someone like Manning could follow without dumping thousands of sensitive documents for the entire world to see.

But what's striking is the Obama administration's stark double standard in investigating and prosecuting leakers. As Senator John McCain told *Politico* in 2012, "The fact that this administration would aggressively pursue leaks perpetrated by a twenty-two-year old Army private in the 'Wikileaks' matter and former CIA employees in other leaks cases, but apparently sanction leaks made by senior administration officials for political purposes, is simply unacceptable."[53]

There are very good reasons for prosecuting leakers. Those involved in OPSEC have been in on enough secret operations and intelligence briefings to understand just how important it is to keep one's mouth shut. The enemy can learn a lot more than you would think from even the most mundane disclosure.

The real question is one of hypocrisy. How can the Obama administration adopt the pretense of holding operational security in such high regard, zealously pursuing leakers, yet set the bar so low for its own political operators?

This was what drove our little campaign in 2012. It was simply about making the White House and the politicians accountable; to make them show some respect for the men and women who protect us all by putting their lives on the line. Sure, wars and military operations always end up having some kind of political angle, but politics should never be this acutely damaging to their effectiveness—especially when the only aim is to advance a personal agenda.

I hope we at least raised awareness of the issues involved. I'd like even more to be able to say that we shamed the Obama administration into exercising more discretion with respect to national secrets, but I'm afraid that isn't the case.

CHAPTER FOUR

"Leading from Behind"

The Obama administration's unprecedented and damaging leaks of classified information aren't the only way this White House has put the president's policy aims and political viability ahead of the safety of those who serve—and, ultimately, above the security of the American people.

President Obama's feckless and inconsistent foreign policy and his often counterproductive interventions abroad have come under sharp criticism from his Republican opponents, from foreign policy experts, and even from former Obama administration officials.

But those of us who have served in our nation's Special Operations Forces have a unique perspective on the debacles into which President Obama has led the U.S. on his watch. It's our brothers in arms who inevitably suffer the brunt of American foreign policy failures. It is they who look into the eyes of the enemy, and who will forever bear the scars of war. When U.S. policy runs into the buzzsaw of hostile world events, our military, and especially our Special Ops guys, are the ones who get chewed up. That principle is actually truer today under an administration that relies heavily on such resources as drones and Special Ops in an effort to leave only a "light footprint" on the world—i.e., to minimize U.S. commitments and political risk to the president.

You might say that the Special Ops community is the canary in the coalmine of U.S. foreign policy. If the U.S. government begins burning through resources at a dangerous rate, it's going to be our brothers in arms who suffer for it first. That's one reason the folks who have served in Special Ops have a useful perspective to share with the American people.

American citizens who serve in the Armed Forces are subject to the president's orders, and must pay him the respect he deserves as commander in chief. But those of us who no longer wear the uniform are American citizens who have the right, or perhaps I should say the obligation, to speak out in policy debates under the First Amendment. And perhaps we value our constitutional rights just a little more for having seen the cost of defending them.

Those of us who have served our country in military actions overseas (and in many cases have gone on, after our service, to work as security contractors in some of the most dangerous places in the world, where plots against America are often hatched) also bring valuable experience. We have fought against our nation's enemies and alongside our nation's allies. We have conducted life-or-death negotiations on the ground in places where the rules and the mindset differ dramatically from our own. We're intimately familiar with the fact that not everyone in the world shares Americans' assumptions, priorities, and worldview.

Some American politicians feel certain that "everyone" in the Middle East "wants freedom," that Muslims will be charmed by a president whose middle name is Hussein, or that "engagement" in talks is as valuable to the Iranians as it is to us. But those of us with Special Ops experience know first hand the reality that our adversaries, and even our allies, often hold values quite different from our own with respect to family honor, religious purity, tribal prestige, and freedom.

In many places, power is much more respected than anything like open-mindedness or a willingness to negotiate. And we've been there and seen the difference in action.

In short, we bring a dose of realism to national security and foreign policy questions. That realism could be an especially useful asset in an era of foreign policy developed in academic journals—or, as we shall see in chapter six regarding President Obama's position on the Israeli-Palestinian peace talks, undergraduate coursework.

The current administration's thinking on national security has too often been shaped by wishful thinking, personal political ambitions, or academic theories. But closing one's eyes to unpleasant realities can have disastrous consequences. If you don't believe that, let me give you an argument in one word: Benghazi.

What occurred in Benghazi, Libya, on September 11, 2012, was a tragic, unforgettable, and completely avoidable occurrence. Two American diplomats and two former Navy SEALs working for the CIA died that day. But Benghazi wasn't just a tragedy for four men, their families, and their buddies. It spilled over into a political discussion in the middle of a heated election, with the administration scrambling to brush reality under the rug at least until the election.

On September 11, 2012, Americans heard vague rumors of attacks on American embassies in several locations. In Cairo, relatively harmless Islamic protestors stormed the walls of our embassy. The attack there prompted a stream of craven messages sent out from the official Twitter feed of the U.S. embassy to Egypt. These tweets included apologies for a film that had been created by a Coptic immigrant to the United States, a film that had supposedly prompted the protests there.

The scene in Egypt was an embarrassment, but eight hundred miles to the west—in Libya, where Americans were more popular than in most Arab nations—there was another situation entirely. In Benghazi, terrorist groups were commemorating the anniversary of the 9/11 attacks by staging a well-planned and coordinated attack against the U.S. diplomatic compound.

It wasn't as if the Benghazi attack had come as a real surprise. The security situation in that city, once a focal point of the resistance against dictator Moammar Gadhafi, was already known to be shaky. The only thing that should have surprised anyone was how little U.S. officials had done to protect our personnel.

In April 2012, five months before the attack, terrorists had thrown an explosive device over the U.S. consulate's wall. Two months later, the British ambassador in Benghazi had survived an assassination attempt, and the Tunisian consulate there had also been attacked by one of the same groups that would be involved in the September 11 attack on our consulate.

Throughout 2012, Ambassador Christopher Stevens—who would lose his life that September in Benghazi—repeatedly asked for more security, only to have his requests denied again and again. The official Senate report on this question would suggest that Stevens had turned down offers for more security, but this suggestion was misleading. As former station chief Gregory Hicks has explained, Stevens persistently asked for more security personnel from the State Department (requests that were ignored or rejected), but at one point he had been obliged to turn down an offer of help from the Defense Department because his superior, Undersecretary of State Patrick Kennedy, had made the decision to decline the offer.[1]

Apparently the top brass at the State Department were more concerned with maintaining a "small footprint" in Libya than with adhering to their own Overseas Security Policy Board (OSPB) standards for diplomatic security, which had been strengthened after al Qaeda's bombing of U.S. embassies in Kenya and Tanzania in 1998.

Just how determined was Hillary Clinton's State Department to avoid following these rules in Libya? One trick they used to circumvent the OSPB standards was to classify the Benghazi facility as something that doesn't exist within their protocols. The Benghazi facility has been referred to as an "embassy" (which is clearly incorrect) and a "consulate," but its actual title was "Special Mission Compound." This title, Republican Representative Pete Roskam of Illinois noted in the first hearing of the Benghazi Select Committee, does not exist anywhere in statute or regulation—nor could Roskam's staff find it used at any time in the Lexis-Nexis news and legal database.

So just what is a "Special Mission Compound"? Roskam asked Todd Keil, a veteran diplomatic security expert, an Obama appointee in the Department of Homeland Security until 2012, and a member of the Independent Panel on Best Practices that was formed after the Benghazi attack. Keil's answer is revealing: "I don't know. To be honest, from our review, Under Secretary [Patrick] Kennedy, in authorizing that, made up that term in order to avoid the OSPB security standards."[2]

One of the most frustrating things about Washington is that this is how the bureaucracy operates. If you make them turn down the heat in the office, they wrap a wet towel around the thermostat. When you put safeguards in place to protect the lives of diplomatic personnel in "consulates," they rename the "consulates" something else so that they don't have to follow the rules.

The Benghazi attack occurred at a time when security was even lighter than usual. At State's insistence, the Special Operations Forces team that had protected U.S. personnel in Benghazi and Tripoli up to that point had been removed from that role. Meanwhile, the special "In-extremis" force intended to respond to serious emergencies in Africa (there are similar forces in other locations) was still being trained in the U.S. The Combatant Commanders In-extremis Force (CIF) in Europe, the CIF, was training in Croatia, and their planes and gear were with them. This force would have been able to respond.

Having been a part of a CIF, I couldn't imagine why they were not deployed. When we were on the CIF, all of our gear bags were packed, numbered, and ready to be grabbed and loaded at a moment's notice. Each man is equipped with a pager and, if paged, had to be back at the command and ready to be "wheels up" in an hour, no excuses for being late and no questions asked. Our team often trained while we waited, but our commitment was always there. I have no doubt that these boys in Europe were ready, willing, and able to get into the fight, if they had been called on in a timely manner.

Ambassador Stevens became an easy target in Benghazi when he visited that day from Tripoli for a meeting with a Turkish diplomat. There were only nine U.S. diplomatic security personnel in all of Libya on the day of the attacks—including those at the embassy back in Tripoli.

The belief in the White House, and at the top levels of Hillary Clinton's State Department, was that if we just closed our eyes to reality, no one would see us. This is what the "light footprint" strategy was all about.

Instead of well-trained and professional American personnel, cheap unarmed Libyan security guards were hired through a British firm to patrol the compound with flashlights and batons. Perhaps predictably, they vanished when the September 11 attack began.[3] It is important to note that most embassies around the world do have a local guard force. But given the well-documented threat in Benghazi, total dependence on such a light force made little sense.

The lax attitude toward security had been prompted at least in part by wishful thinking. The administration seemed to feel that providing Americans on the ground with adequate security would draw unwanted attention, and that it would be a tacit admission that Libya was unsafe and filled with terrorist threats—which, of course, it was and still is. The Obama administration was committed in principle to the idea that its "kinetic military action" in Libya had succeeded, and that the terrorists were on the run worldwide. This is one of the more subtle ways in which political ambitions can rise above national security.

The same head-in-the-sand behavior continued after the September 11 attacks in Benghazi began. The White House, for example, failed to convene the Counterterrorism Security Group (CSG), an action that would have amounted to an official acknowledgement that the mission was under a terrorist attack. That would have been awkward—just five days earlier, President Obama had declared at the Democratic National Convention that "al Qaeda is on the path to defeat, and Osama bin Laden is dead." In fact, as the report of the Senate Intelligence Committee would later confirm, at least two al Qaeda affiliates participated in the attack.[4]

The State Department failed to deploy its Foreign Emergency Support Team, which had been specifically designed to respond to terrorist attacks like this one.[5] When the team's head asked, he was told that the FEST had been ruled out early, on orders from the top.

Officials in Washington did not order deployment of any air cover—something the men who survived the ordeal would later remark upon. Even a few simple flyovers might have been enough to send the enemy running.

The team in Washington may not have realized when they made (or failed to make) the critical decisions, but their choices meant that a band of exhausted CIA contractors and diplomatic security agents would spend about thirteen hours largely fending for themselves. Imagine if you were those men, outnumbered, fighting for your life, and waiting in vain for the help dictated by protocols. How would you feel?

■　■　■

The attack on Benghazi was important. It bothered many people to see it happen, to see the White House go into typical "CYA" ("cover your ass") mode, and to see the nation's commander-in-chief gallop off to Las Vegas for a campaign event just a few hours after the firefight was over.

In fact, the American people still do not know what the president did the night of the attack. He may have been giving orders or doing handstands or even sleeping. Contrast this blackout with the revelations about the bin Laden raid, for which every conceivable piece of information was divulged—including photographs in the Situation Room—and then used in campaign commercials, dramatic news stories, and Hollywood movies.

OPSEC has done everything we can to make sure that the truth comes out, wherever it leads, and that justice is done. We helped former Congressman Frank Wolf find dozens of sponsors in support of the formation of the select committee on Benghazi, which is now investigating under the leadership of Republican Congressman Trey Gowdy.[6]

But Benghazi is only the most prominent symptom of a much larger problem in Clinton and Obama's foreign policy. The attack succeeded because American foreign policy was being run under the Obama doctrine, with U.S. interests coming a distant second or third to other considerations—primarily his reelection.

There is a bigger picture here that goes beyond lax diplomatic security in Libya, beyond the delays imposed upon the CIA contractors on the ground, and beyond the political rear-end-covering and the deceptions conveyed on the Sunday talk shows. Benghazi can only be understood by looking back to how Libya became the mess it was in September 2012, and how it has deteriorated since.

Just as the killings of four Americans on that fateful anniversary of terrorism were completely avoidable, so was the subsequent collapse of Libya as a nation—a monumental event nearly unnoticed in America. How did it happen? It's complicated, but America helped bring it about, on one man's decision.

Libya is now lost. And it was lost as a result of a badly conceived foreign policy, grounded in academic theories rather than American interests in the real world.

Obama's announcement of U.S. airstrikes and missile attacks on Libya came on March 19, 2011, on the eve of the eighth anniversary of the Iraq War. Speaking from Brasilia, he called the operation "an international effort to protect Libyan civilians" and cited a United Nations Resolution on Libya as his justification.[7] He also categorically ruled out placing "boots on the ground."

Why was he doing this? The rationale for the Libyan invasion fits a popular theory of military intervention—known as "the responsibility to protect"—to which several of Obama's advisors subscribe, most notably UN ambassadors Susan Rice and Samantha Powers. This principle seems to have been adopted in large part out of regret that the U.S. did not attempt to stop the Rwanda genocide under President Clinton. The basic idea behind this doctrine is that the United States can and should intervene militarily when possible in order to save people from their own leaders.

"The last decade was not, on any view, a proud one," wrote Gareth Evans, expounding the "responsibility to protect" theory in 2004. Evans, president of the International Crisis Group and co-chair of the International Commission on Intervention and State Sovereignty, described the aim of the theory as "to ensure, above all, that there are no more Rwandas."[8] The short version of Evans's thesis runs roughly as follows:

> The argument is that the responsibility to protect, whatever else it encompasses, implies above all else a responsibility to react to situations of compelling need for human protection. When preventive measures fail to resolve or contain the situation and when a state is unable or unwilling to redress the situation, then intervention by other members of the broader community of states may be necessary. Coercive measures may include political, economic, or judicial measures, and in extreme—but only extreme—cases, they may also include military action.

This sounds reasonable, because no one wants to see humanitarian crises unfold. And it is not the first time such thinking has been aired in public. One of the arguments offered for the Iraq War in 2002 and 2003 was that Saddam Hussein was an oppressor who had used chemical weapons against his own subjects, and that our invasion was for their own good.

But in Iraq, this was a secondary argument used to bolster the main arguments for war—arguments, no matter how flawed, that pertained to national interest. In the U.S.-NATO campaign in Libya, the "responsibility to protect" appears to have been the sole consideration.

And this is where the theory can become dangerous. When one's sole purpose in a military intervention is to stop a humanitarian crisis in progress, one tends to act in the now without much concern for the future. When a massacre is already afoot—as it was in Libya—

commonsense concerns about the aftermath of the intervention fade. And indeed, in Libya, such concerns were apparently even more remote from policy-making than they had been in Iraq, which partly explains how rapidly Libya has gone down the drain since our intervention.

The U.S. became involved in Libya despite lacking both a national interest in the country and an endgame for restoring stability after Gadhafi's downfall.

The Libyan operation was intended to tip the balance of the conflict there to the rebels against the Gadhafi government, but those rebels were untested, and their aims were poorly understood by the West. In fact, the groups involved in fighting Gadhafi were nearly as diverse as the foreign countries that had lined up against him. Arab countries in the region—most notably the United Arab Emirates and Qatar—supplied aid to rebels, but not to the same ones. Qatar, in particular, was putting its money behind Islamic radicals who, three years after the putative end of the Libyan Civil War, would still be fighting against the more secular groups.

Obama bragged about what he had accomplished in Libya in the October 22 presidential debate, comparing it to Iraq in a favorable light: "I and Americans took leadership in organizing an international coalition that made sure that we were able to—without putting troops on the ground, at the cost of less than what we spent in two weeks in Iraq—liberate a country that had been under the yoke of dictatorship for 40 years, got rid of a despot who had killed Americans.... This is an example of—of how we make choices, you know, when we went into Libya and we were able to immediately stop the massacre there.... Muammar Qaddafi had more American blood on his hands than any individual other than Osama bin Laden. And so we were going to make sure that we finished the job."[9]

Unfortunately, "finished the job" and "stop the massacre" were both overstatements.

President Obama's drive-by approach to the war in Libya gave the rebel forces the bump they needed to overthrow Gadhafi, but it wasn't enough to achieve peace. In fact, it was just enough to make a bad situation much, much worse. And then, without doing anything to ensure that the war led to a satisfying conclusion and a lasting peace, he left it to deteriorate from there.

WHAT'S HAPPENING IN LIBYA NOW?

If you were to ask the average American what has been happening in Libya since the Benghazi attack, he would honestly have no idea. For a variety of reasons—sympathy for Obama, lack of public interest in a backward part of the Sahara, or (perhaps the most likely explanation) the sad fact that most Americans probably could not find Libya on a map—the media have reported virtually nothing about the sorry state of post-Gadhafi Libya (setting aside the Benghazi attack itself) since late 2012. In fact, the violent environment in which the Benghazi disaster occurred has only become more chaotic since then.

Libya is now more unstable than it was under Gadhafi. One only needs to pull up the *Libyan Herald* online to see the chaos happening all over that country and certainly in Benghazi. As I was writing this, the *Herald* published an article announcing that ISIS is launching a television station in Libya.[10] You don't see that every day. And as this book was being prepared to go to press, CNN reported that the Islamic State had taken control of the Libyan town of Derna, population 100,000, on the Mediterranean coast "not far from the Egyptian border and just about 200 miles from the southern shores of the European Union."[11]

The warning signs about the nature of the Libyan opposition were there from very early on—even while Gadhafi was still massacring his people in a last-ditch attempt to cling to power.

For one thing, from the very beginning of the conflict, before the United States even became involved, Libyan rebels began lynching blacks, who were believed—in most cases unfairly—to be mercenaries helping Gadhafi. The BBC quoted one Turkish construction worker: "We had 70–80 people from Chad working for our company. They were cut dead with pruning shears and axes, attackers saying: 'You are providing troops for Gaddafi.' The Sudanese were also massacred. We saw it for ourselves."[12]

The *Wall Street Journal* reported in July 2011 about one town, Tawergha, where the mostly black population was perceived as loyal to Gadhafi and blamed for participating with his forces in raids on the neighboring city of Misrata.[13] By October, the city of thirty thousand had been abandoned as its residents fled in terror from a reprisal campaign of racist violence. Jihadist militiamen from Misrata made it clear that the Tawerghans were not welcome to return to their homes.

And the barbaric slaughter of black Libyans and foreigners, many of whom had come to the country simply to find work, would continue well after the U.S. became involved and in fact even after U.S. forces were long gone. The former inhabitants of Tawergha, for example, made the news again in August 2014, when ten thousand of them who had settled in a refugee camp in Tripoli were attacked by militias. Their plight was a sign of the misery that would beset many Libyans in the chaos that followed Gadhafi.[14]

The fragile situation of Libya's government after Gadhafi is another part of this story of disintegration.

Libya held its first post-Gadhafi election in July 2012, with reasonably high (60 percent) voter participation and much excitement. The resulting General National Congress was supposed to choose a prime minister, write a new constitution for the State of Libya, and organize elections for a new parliament.

This did not go smoothly. There were four prime ministers in quick succession. The first was kidnapped by gunmen in retaliation for his cooperation with the United States, because of the leak from the Obama administration that I mentioned in chapter two. He was released, but he was later removed from office for failing to bring the country's many warring militias to heel. At that point, he fled the country.

The second prime minister had served for just a couple of weeks when he abruptly quit the job—because gunmen had attacked his family. The selection of the third prime minister, an ally (though not a member) of the Muslim Brotherhood, was overruled days later by Libya's Supreme Court, which reinstated the second prime minister.

On June 25, 2014, Libyans elected a new parliament. In a sign of how disillusioned the population had become with the government's inability to govern, only 18 percent came out to vote this time, less than a third of the turnout in the first post-Gadhafi election.

Islamist parties did poorly in the election, but in the end it didn't matter. When they could not win with ballots, they took control with bullets. In July, attempts by the Libyan military to suppress Islamist militias were failing miserably. The militiamen began conducting offensives and seizing military bases, getting their hands on relatively sophisticated weaponry from the Gadhafi era.[15] Soon, they had control of most of Tripoli.

In August 2014, the newly elected, mostly secular parliament—the friend of U.S. interests, essentially—was forced to flee en masse to Tobruk, a port city in the country's far east. By September, this almost powerless parliament was reduced to holding sessions in a converted ferry-boat in the port—symbolic, though perhaps unwittingly, of the strong likelihood that they might have to flee the country at any time.

Meanwhile, in Tripoli, Islamic radicals illegally invalidated the June elections and established themselves as a rump parliament. They chose a fourth, unelected prime minister.

So in fall 2014, Libya had two rival governments, neither of which was really in charge of a country being overrun by various militias. With the world's attention focused on crises in Syria, Iraq, and Ukraine, the Libyan Civil War had started up again.

That September, the United Nations estimated that just from that summer's new fighting, 150,000 people had fled the country and another 100,000 had been displaced within it. Libya's population is only six million, so that's a pretty large displacement—a tragedy on roughly the same scale as the flight of Yazidis from ISIS in Iraq.

Obviously, nobody wants Gadhafi back. He was a psychopath who had shown his true colors in the last days of his reign. On a 2013 trip I made to Egypt with a high-level delegation with the Westminster Institute, a foreign policy think tank, I asked one of the assistant ministers of defense at a casual dinner who the craziest dictator in the region was. A smile beaming from his face, "Gadhafi!" he exclaimed. He explained to me, "That guy was insane; he would come to meetings with sunglasses, flamboyantly dressed, wanting to be called the leader of all Africa."

But just three years after Gadhafi's removal from power, Libya had become something straight out of a Mad Max movie, with militias battling each other in the desert over oil. It was a failed state—a governmental, economic, and humanitarian crisis all rolled into one.

While the "responsibility to protect" sounds good in theory, in practice acting on that principle—particularly without counting the costs and weighing the likely long-term consequences—may lead to more suffering than if we had not intervened. There are many parts of this world that are not peaceful. With finite resources, we must never take intervention in another country lightly. The first priority of the government Americans elect should be our national security and our specific interests. What is ironic is that President Obama had often railed against Bush for going into Iraq without a good reason and for not having a plan for the aftermath. Pot, meet kettle.

THE CLUELESS CRUSADER

So what went wrong in Libya? Everything. And unfortunately, Libya is the perfect representation of President Obama's grand strategy in foreign policy. Funny how Hillary Clinton is now trying to distance herself from his foreign policy, despite her having led the charge on Libya.

The guiding principle of President Obama's foreign policy, it appears, is to improve the world—not necessarily in a way that supports any particular American interests, but rather to step in and right wrongs whenever they become serious enough. And he prefers to pursue this goal on the cheap—to use small, surgical operations that are relatively painless for the public and have little chance of backfiring politically.

This preference, again, explains the president's over-reliance on Special Operations Forces and covert operations, as well as his reputation as the pioneering president in drone assassinations. But it betrays a profound weakness of conception. When the United States acts under President Obama's orders, it is unlikely to follow through—because following through requires too much investment of limited military resources—and, crucially, of the president's political capital. When forces unleashed by Obama's initially painless interventions get out of control, he has proven that he's not willing to make the lasting—and over time, almost certainly unpopular—commitment that would be required to contain the mess.

While I am partial to Special Operations, and many of my brothers still serve today, there are limits to Special Operations Forces' capabilities. Over-reliance on one percent of the military, which in turn makes up roughly one percent of our nation's population, is bound to backfire sometimes. As we have seen time and again, it has also had the noxious effect of encouraging Obama's political team to divulge too much information.

Obama's aversion to commitments that might make him unpopular helps explain why, as we shall see in chapter five, he was willing to acquiesce to Iraq's corrupt government and abandon the country without a Status of Forces Agreement, setting the scene for the rise of the Islamic State. As for putting boots on the ground to defeat ISIS—if he does it, it will be with extreme reluctance. Boots on the ground would be a huge step for a president who views even a large American "diplomatic footprint" as a potential problem. After all, Obama's State Department, under the orders of Secretary Hillary Clinton, had made a decision to lie low in Benghazi, and that meant low security.

I'm sure Clinton would not dare go to Benghazi or anywhere in Libya with relaxed security. I remember her visit to Yemen a few years ago. I was in the desert at the time as a civilian, but Clinton had a full Personal Security Detail (PSD) unit, which was a SEAL platoon, as she walked through the ancient market in Sana'a. The platoon chief was a BUD/S classmate of mine. Apparently it was quite a spectacle.

Libya's downward spiral should not have been unexpected. It was an admonitory example of where this kind of foreign policy leads. Libya is the untold story of how the United States intervened senselessly in a conflict where it had no national interest, created a power vacuum, and then moved on to other distractions as Libya gradually slid into the chaos of a failed state. The people of Libya, originally grateful for American intervention, suddenly found themselves in an even worse situation than they had been in before—they were on their way to becoming the new Somalia.

This chapter in the Obama-Clinton foreign policy story, nearly ignored by the American news media, affected more than just those unfortunate enough to live in Libya. It also cost the U.S. enormous prestige in our relationships across the region. If journalists had covered Libya with the vigor they covered Iraq, perhaps public opinion would have helped contain or shift the president's feckless foreign policy.

When I spoke to Egyptian general Abdel Fattah al-Sisi on the 2013 Westminster Institute trip, he expressed his fears about the security situation in post-Gadhafi Libya, his nation's neighbor. Al-Sisi specifically stated that arsenals of weapons were being smuggled from Libya into Egypt through the Sinai Peninsula. He believed that these weapons would destabilize his country, become a threat to Israel, and increase terrorism. I remembered this conversation later, at the point at which it became clear that al-Sisi had decided to stop listening to the United States.

By late 2014, al-Sisi—at that point the president of Egypt—had become so concerned about Libya that he did something unusual. His relationship with Obama already strained, al-Sisi essentially told the American president to take his international policy preferences and put them where the sun doesn't shine. In late August of that year, Egypt and the United Arab Emirates, two erstwhile U.S. allies, completely disregarded American wishes and worked together on a semi-secret bombing campaign against some of the jihadist militias fighting for control of Tripoli.[16] According to subsequent news accounts, the two countries had recieved a frosty response when they informed American diplomats of their intentions, but they didn't care anymore. When Washington told them not to do it, they did it anyway.

Perhaps their mission accomplished something positive in the grand scheme of things, but it was an indication of a disturbing trend: for many of our allies, America is becoming less relevant. Under Obama, we are a less reliable and less useful partner than we once were. As a result, the voice of the United States now carries much less weight among allies in the region than it used to.

Ironically, it was in Cairo that President Obama had delivered the speech that was supposed to be a positive turning point for our relations with the countries the Middle East. But those were just Obama's words. Because of his deeds—including his State Department's public support of the Muslim Brotherhood on Hillary Clinton's watch, which we will address in more detail in chapter seven below—we risk losing one of our most important Middle Eastern allies.

Obama has managed to produce an outcome that's precisely the opposite of what he promised when running for president in 2008— to restore U.S. relations with the world, which had supposedly been damaged under President George W. Bush. But the Egyptians and many others in the Middle East had no big problem with Bush. Now they no longer trust their American allies to look out for their interests—and have started seeing to matters themselves. And no wonder. Destabilized Libya is Egypt's neighbor and a threat to its own national security—much as Mexican cartels, extremists, and a porous border are threats to ours.

That's how Obama's "leadership from behind" is going over in the Arab world. It has made American interests irrelevant to their leaders.

A NIGHT IN BENGHAZI

On September 11, 2012, the day of the attacks on the diplomatic mission in Benghazi, CIA contractors were stationed at an annex just a mile away from the diplomatic compound. The word "contractor" may convey the wrong mental image. Don't think of the guy who rewires your house—think of Jack Bauer from *24* or Michael Westen from *Burn Notice*.

These CIA contractors were former Special Operations Forces fighters—a former Ranger, several ex-SEALs, and ex-Marines—bad-asses, like so many of the men I had the honor of serving with. They were not the type to run in any direction except toward the shooting, especially when they knew American lives were in danger. I've attended numerous funerals for men better than myself who ran to the fight in order to save those under fire. The presence of those contractors in Benghazi that fateful night probably prevented several additional American deaths among the diplomatic and security staff.

Two of them died that night in Benghazi, and five others have since co-authored a book, *13 Hours*, about what happened.[17] They fastidiously and appropriately avoid drawing political points from their experience, but they agree on this one conclusion: they could have gotten there in time to save the two non-combatants who died that night, Ambassador Christopher Stevens and Sean Smith.

What stopped them? Another bad decision, grounded once again in the irrational self-delusion that characterized American behavior in Libya: a severe aversion to any demonstration of American force. Upon learning there was trouble at the compound, the contractors raced to dress and arm themselves, but after their rush to deploy, they were then tragically ordered to wait.

Under orders, they wasted a critical twenty to twenty-five minutes sitting around, itching to get into the fight, while their base chief went through the pointless exercise of trying, unsuccessfully, to get a friendly local Libyan militia to do the job for them instead. They were told to "stand down" and that "we are going to have the local militia handle it."

The CIA contractors describe this order as coming from their base chief "Bob" (they don't give his name) on his own authority. But it would be wrong to make him a scapegoat. His order hewed closely to the principles that his superiors had established. It's clear that the modus operandi for American officials in post-Gadhafi Libya was to keep a small footprint, above all else. The mission was burning, civilian diplomats were in danger, and this wrongheaded and dangerous principle still took priority at the level where decisions were being made.

The last straw came when the contractors heard a diplomatic secu-rity official plead with them from the compound on the radio, "If you guys do not get here, we are going to die!" So, as they recount in *13 Hours*, they defied their orders and headed out anyway. They learned on the way that the building containing the safe haven was on fire. Ste-vens and Smith died in that fire. The contractors, by their account, were just minutes too late to save them.

The contractors made their entrance at the compound, repulsed some five dozen armed attackers, and helped the diplomatic staff and security make their withdrawal to the CIA annex with Sean Smith's body. They covered the rear and followed them back to the annex, knowing this would probably be only the beginning of their troubles.

When they arrived back at the annex, they found themselves under siege from the terrorists. They repulsed two assaults—a smaller one, then a larger one with dozens of armed attackers—that came hours apart. Before dawn, a seven-man detachment arrived from Tripoli to help them in the fight and evacuate the non-shooting personnel.

During the third wave of attacks, the bad guys, who had now properly adjusted their mortar fire, killed two former SEALs—Glen Doherty and Tyrone Woods—just before sunrise. This happened six hours after the original engagement began.

Again, no air cover ever showed up. "I was expecting at least some kind of air support, even if it was just a flyover by a jet, or whatever," John Tiegen, one of the CIA contractors who helped write the book, told Fox News's Bret Baier in a special aired September 2014. "Some-times that's all it takes," said his colleague, Kris Paronto. "It gets the bad guys down."[18]

Where I live in Virginia Beach, deafening jet noise can be heard on a daily basis. It's something we are accustomed to. But Kris certainly has a point. A low flying jet usually scares the you-know-what out of a bad guy in a Third World country. I spoke to a good buddy of mine, a former SEAL, now diplomatic security for the State Department. In discussing Hillary Clinton and the Obama administration he stated, "We are on our own when the bullets start flying."

Major General Darryl Roberson, Vice Director of Operations for the Joint Staff, would tell the Senate Intelligence Committee that no support had been possible:

> There were no ships available to provide any support that were anywhere close to the facility at Benghazi. The assets that we had available were Strike Eagles loaded with live weapons that could have responded, but they were located in Djibouti, which is the equivalent of the distance between here [Washington, D.C.] and Los Angeles. The other fighters that might have been available were located in Aviano, Italy. They were not loaded with weapons. They were not on an alert status.... Unfortunately, there was not a carrier in the Mediterranean that could have been able to support; the assets that we mobilized immediately were the only assets we had available to try to support.

This is intended as a reasonable excuse for what happened. Yet when you think about it, it doesn't make much sense. We had only just wound up our military involvement in Libya a few months earlier, and the country was already in chaos. Given the obviously dangerous situation there, and the minimal security on the ground, how is it there were no air assets available?

Was this the "small footprint" asserting itself once again? Could it be that Washington was simply unwilling to admit that it had a serious problem on its hands in this region of the world?

The five authors of *13 Hours*—two of whom go by pseudonyms—largely avoid taking sides in the political controversy over the Benghazi attack, which is mostly about its aftermath, including the rush to blame the violence on anger over a video about Muhammad. In Washington, administration officials scrambled to get their story straight for the Sunday talk shows. The White House and State Department would repeatedly deny that there had been any coordinated attack. President Obama avoided directly calling it a terrorist attack. In fact, when asked directly in a *60 Minutes* interview the very day after it happened, he bent over backwards in trying to avoid that term:

STEVE KROFT: Mr. President, this morning you went out of your way to avoid the use of the word terrorism in connection with the Libya attack, do you believe that this was a terrorism attack?

PRESIDENT OBAMA: Well, it's too early to tell exactly how this came about, what group was involved, but obviously it was an attack on Americans. And we are going to be working with the Libyan government to make sure that we bring these folks to justice, one way or the other.

This segment of the interview, by the way, famously never made it to television. Instead it was quietly released on the internet days before the election. That allowed Obama, in a crucial debate against Mitt Romney, and with unprecedented aid from debate moderator Candy Crowley, to keep up the appearance that he had never tried to downplay the involvement of organized terrorist groups.

Both Obama and Secretary Clinton would absurdly and confidently cite a YouTube video as the cause of the attack—a statement to this effect was actually issued while the two ex-SEALs were still alive. Never mind that the attack had happened on September 11. And never mind that it came one day after al Qaeda leader Ayman al-Zawahiri had called on Libyans to avenge the death of a Libyan al-Qaeda propagandist, Abu Yahya al-Libi, in a CIA drone strike in Pakistan.[19]

Clinton even blamed the video when trying to console Woods's father. "We're going to have that person arrested and prosecuted that did the video," she said upon meeting him, much to his annoyance.[20] The administration would, for a time, maintain falsely that the attack in Benghazi had started as a protest—until the facts overtook their fabrications.

The video was an implausible story from the beginning. But it has to be understood for what it was. As with so much of Obama's foreign policy, this had to do with putting politics before national security. Obviously, neither the president nor Secretary Clinton had ever wanted the attack to happen in the first place—and even less did they want to deal with the consequences.

First things first. It was election season, and all they had to do was run out the clock until Obama was locked in for another four years. If anyone still cared about the mistakes that had been made, and who had made them, and why this had happened, it could wait until Wednesday, November 7, 2012.

ADDENDUM on the House Intelligence Committee's Report on Benghazi

As this book was being prepared for the press, the House of Representatives' Intelligence Committee issued its report on Benghazi.[21] From the report—and especially from its introductory executive summary, which was bound to shape the story in the media[22]—you would think all the questions about the September 11, 2012, attack that killed two American diplomats, including the first U.S. ambassador to be murdered since 1979, and two ex–Navy SEALs had been answered. The House Intelligence Committee claims to have "conducted a comprehensive and exhaustive investigation" into Benghazi and says its report is "meant to serve as the definitive House statement on the Intelligence Community's activities before, during, and after the tragic events that caused the deaths of four Americans."

The report's findings are stated definitively: "the Committee finds that there was no intelligence failure prior to the attacks"; "the Committee found no evidence that there was either a stand down order or a denial of available air support"; and "the Committee found no evidence that any officer was wrongly intimidated, wrongly forced to sign a nondisclosure statement or otherwise kept from speaking to Congress, or polygraphed because of their presence in Benghazi."

"Benghazi Debunked," trumpeted the *Washington Post*,[23] and defenders of President Obama's feckless foreign policy—and supporters of Hillary Clinton's bid to be elected president so she can continue along the same lines—took heart. A Committee of the Republican House of Representatives had put to rest "a series of bizarre conspiracy theories intended to besmirch the Obama administration."[24]

But the report is grossly inaccurate, flatly contradicting the testimony of eyewitnesses. When former Ranger Kris "Tanto" Paronto and former Marine John "Tig" Tiegen, two of the CIA contractors, the men who actually defended American lives on the ground in Benghazi, saw what the report said, they knew they had to set the public record straight. So we at OPSEC helped them put out a statement.[25]

Why the whitewash by the House Intelligence Committee? It's a mystery. A few months before the report was issued, an article by Micah Morrison in the Daily Caller had pointed to the possible significance of a company named Aegis, "a private military contracting firm that until recently was run by his [Intelligence Committee Chairman Rogers's] wife, Kristi Rogers" and quoted the *Intelligence Online* newsletter's report "that thanks to Ms. Rogers' efforts, 'Aegis won several major contracts with the U.S. administration.'" When the report was released, Mollie Hemingway at the Federalist pointed out, "One of the most common criticisms levied against the intelligence oversight committees is that they're far too approving and accepting of what the intelligence community wants."[26] And at the *Weekly Standard*, Stephen F. Hayes and Thomas Joscelyn suggested that committee chairman Rogers may have been simply "sick of Benghazi" and put off by the "frenzy of conspiracy theorizing" of other Republicans; Hayes and Joscelyn quoted committee member Representative Peter King to the effect that "the best interpretation is that it [the report] was an attempt to be bipartisan."[27]

I certainly don't claim to have fathomed the inner workings of the Intelligence Committee. But whatever their motivations, they issued an erroneous report that was immediately rebutted by surviving brothers in arms of Tyrone Woods and Glen Doherty, the two ex–Navy SEALs who died in Benghazi.

The first inaccurate statement the contractors point out in the report may seem like a small thing. The Intelligence Committee claims that "Security Officers from the CIA's Benghazi Annex recalled hearing explosions from an unknown location around 9:40 a.m."[28] But the contractors explain that there was never anything "unknown" about the location of the explosions—they were aware from the beginning where they were coming from, and they testified to the committee that "the explosions and gunfire were known to be at what was known to us as the U.S. consulate, which per security requirements after the attack, was changed to the U.S. Special Mission and was then called the 'Temporary Mission Facility' by U.S. Department of State, and later in this report. Note that the location of all gunfire and explosions were known to those of us at the U.S. Annex. At no time did we state to the committee that we did not know the location of the gunfire or explosions. We had visited what we knew to be the U.S. Consulate on a weekly basis."[29]

Why does it matter whether the contractors knew from the start where the explosions and gunfire were happening? By the time they got to the diplomatic compound to rescue Ambassador Chris Stevens, it was too late. An American ambassador died. What caused the delay? The Intelligence Committee seems to want to suggest that the contractors were unclear about where the attack was, and thus about what or whom was being attacked. But the men who might have rescued Stevens maintain they knew about the attack right away and understood clearly from the start that it was the U.S. compound that was being attacked.

It matters, because this delay is at the heart of the Benghazi disaster. The CIA contractors who might have been able to rescue our diplomatic personnel have good reason to believe that they could have saved them if they had been able to leave the Annex and arrive at the mission compound in a timely manner. And here's where the House Intelligence Committee report really flies in the face of the true facts on the ground in Benghazi.

As the contractors explain, "Paronto stated to Mike Rogers and his committee, looking Rogers directly in the eye, that he was delayed and was told to wait twice. Paronto also stated to Mike Rogers and his committee that the '27' minute delay and his team waiting was a severe military tactical mistake made by leadership figures who had little to no military training or experience in combat operations, and the delay cost the lives of Ambassador Stevens and Sean Smith due to them dying of smoke inhalation—something that takes time."[30] And that initial delay was compounded by the way the attackers used the time it gave them: "The delay departing the Annex allowed Ansar Al Sharia to reinforce the avenues of approach to the Temporary Mission Facility with AK-47s and RPG's. This caused the GRS security contractors to dismount their vehicles to suppress enemy fire and tactically move the remaining 350–400 meters, approximately, on foot over several 8-foot concrete walls and backyards through 'dead space' adding an additional 20 minutes delay to the 27 minutes delay from the Annex."[31]

The Intelligence Committee, incredibly, concluded that "the Annex team left in a timely and appropriate manner."[32] This seems to be a case of airy speculations by people who were not on the ground in Benghazi trumping the eyewitness testimony of those who were there. The Intelligence Committee report quotes Deputy CIA Director Michael Morrell saying, "It has occurred to me that the Benghazi senior intelligence official sent them the moment they were ready at that 15 minute mark."[33] The committee found corroboration for this speculation in the fact that "Testimony from an Active CIA official who has personal experience in crisis situations provided a detailed validation of Morrell's assessment."[34] The contractors point out that here the Committee shows itself to prefer the opinion of "an outside source that was neither involved in the fighting in Benghazi or the decisions made that night into the following morning" to their eyewitness testimony of what actually happened.[35]

The Intelligence Committee Report claims that the "CIA security team chief in Benghazi, in consultation with the Chief of Base, made the decision to organize the rescue mission and to commence the operation" and that "no officer at CIA was ever told to stand down."[36] But the contractors—not CIA officers, but nonetheless working for the CIA—testified not only that they were repeatedly told to wait, but that they ultimately *defied their orders* to go to the aid of the U.S. personnel at the Mission compound. (They made the decision to disobey their superiors when they heard one of the Diplomatic Security officials pleading on the radio that "we are going to die" if the contractors could not come to their aid.)[37]

These are pretty basic facts the Intelligence Committee got wrong, and so it's no surprise the report's conclusions are erroneous. The committee heard from eyewitnesses and yet somehow managed to produce a report at odds with the true facts on the ground in Benghazi.

The contractors point out that the Intelligence Committee never asked Tiegen—the CIA contractor to whom "Bob," the CIA base chief at Benghazi said the literal words "stand down"—whether he had been told to "stand down" instead of immediately going to the aid of the U.S. personnel at the Mission compound. The committee called Tiegen to testify not with his fellow contractors but "alongside the CIA GRS staff team leader. This was a tactical maneuver by the Committee and the CIA since Tiegen was still employed by the CIA and scheduled to deploy shortly thereafter. This put immense pressure on Tiegen to testify in line with the CIA...."[38] Still, if the committee had asked Tiegen directly under oath about the "stand down" order, he would have had to testify that the CIA chief of base, "Bob," had indeed spoken those very words. But instead of asking Tiegen about the "stand down" order, the contractors point out, "That question was directed, by the committee, to the GRS staff team leader."[39]

In contrast, Kris Paranto, CIA contractor and former Army Ranger, was grilled at length by a committee staff member on his decision, along with the other contractors, to go to the rescue (after the more-than-twenty-minute delay) in defiance of orders. The committee member "asked Paronto about his military background and went on to continually ask for several minutes if it was normal for Rangers to disobey direct orders since it was not proper to disobey orders when he, the staff member, served in the Navy."[40] So the Committee's conclusion that "the CIA security team chief in Benghazi, in consultation with the Chief of Base, made the decision to organize the rescue mission and commence the operation"[41] is very strange; it contradicts facts that were known to the committee based on the questions asked. As the contractors point out, "If the Chief of Base 'Bob' and GRS Staff Team Leader commenced the rescue operation immediately, the exchange between Paronto and the committee staff member would never have occurred."[42]

The contractors also raise questions about another major issue—the lack of air cover. The Intelligence Committee report maintains, "Those officers who attended the emergency action committee meetings had discussed intimately what, if any, U.S. military resources were in the area. Those officers knew exactly what was and was not in the area, and they understood that there was no air support or any other assets in the general area."[43] And yet, as the contractors point out,

Paronto asked for an ISR (Drone) and an Ac-130 Specter Gunship at 9:37 p.m., again at approximately 12:00 a.m., and again at approximately 2:30 a.m. He did so via his personal ICOM radio, something that the entire Annex personnel team uses. He was told by the GRS staff team leader and GRS deputy Chief of Base over the ICOM radio system that they were "working on obtaining both." Paronto received no response at 2:30 a.m. from his base leadership. At no time did the Annex leadership state over the ICOM radio system that the Specter gunship or air assets were unavailable. This was told to Mike Rogers and his committee by the GRS security contractors.

What is unclear is who "those officers" were in Mike Rogers and the Committee's report and why this crucial information was not passed on to the GRS Security Team in Benghazi. If what these anonymous "officers" told the committee is true—and the way their testimony was represented in this report was accurate—then that would be an intelligence failure. It's unheard of for such crucial information to be withheld from a security team.[44]

For the complete text of the rebuttal of the Intelligence Committee report's errors from the men who were on the ground at Benghazi, see Appendix B to this book, the full text of "The CIA Global Response Contractors' Public Response to the November 21, 2014 House Intelligence Committee Report about the September 11 and 12, 2012 Benghazi Attacks: Michael Roger's House Intelligence Report is 'Full of Inaccuracies.'" This document raises other issues—for example, questions about the intimidation of witnesses.

I asked ex-Ranger Kris Paronto what he would most want to communicate to the American public—anything we're not hearing because of all the political smoke. He told me that our political leaders are not listening to the people who were actually in Benghazi at the time of the attacks, but rather are putting a political spin on everything. He was there, and from his perspective it appeared that there was no continuous effort to get to his guys and the ambassador from outside during the attacks. Paronto and the other CIA contractors are by no means peddling conspiracy theories—he has said clearly that he saw no evidence of arms running from Libya to Syria. But there is a lot about Benghazi that still needs to be explained. Paronto believes that the 17 February Brigade (the Libyan militia that, incredibly, we actually trusted to provide security for the American mission compound where our ambassador to Libya was) had already pledged allegiance to Ansar Al Sharia, which attacked our facilities in Benghazi, at the time of those attacks. Benghazi cries out for a thorough investigation by a committee determined to uncover the facts. The hope is that the findings of the U.S. House of Representatives Select Committee on Benghazi, chaired by Representative Gowdy, will be more thorough and accurate than the whitewash from the House Intelligence Committee.

CHAPTER FIVE

Who Lost Iraq?

The surreal thing about war is that for all the bombs, gunfights, death, destruction, and suffering—and the press segments highlighting them—in the vast area of the war zone, life just goes on.

This fact was on my mind one hot evening as I made my way from Baghdad west to Ramadi in a blacked-out helicopter, looking out on a darkened Iraq over the shoulders of the door gunner. Below me were thousands of people just trying to get by. Kids still needed to be educated. Work hours still had to be kept. Tires and diapers still needed to be changed. Faucets still leaked, bills still had to be paid, and traffic still sucked.

This was spring 2005. Tremendous sacrifices had already been made by then, both by coalition forces and by Iraqis, to create a better nation. It would take a lot more sacrifices and a lot more time, but by 2009, American leadership and Iraqi political cooperation finally did create a situation of hope for the majority of Iraqis.

Unfortunately, it would not last long.

When Barack Obama assumed the presidency on January 20, 2009, he had arguably less foreign policy experience than any other new president in American history.

On the campaign trail, Obama had said that his greatest foreign policy experience came from spending four years living in Indonesia as a child.[1] The remark elicited derision from his Democratic primary opponents, including both Joe Biden[2] and Hillary Clinton.[3] Clinton's campaign produced a memorable television ad that asked voters which candidate they wanted answering the 3 a.m. phone call at the White House when the next international crisis struck.[4] The implicit message was that Americans would not be able to sleep soundly at night with the naïve and inexperienced Obama at the helm. Of course later, with Benghazi, Clinton would fail her own test.

Experience or no, one significant thing Obama seemed to lack was an *interest* in foreign affairs. The greatest evidence of this has been his treatment of Iraq during his presidency. Iraq was a problem that he wanted out of sight and out of mind as quickly as possible, from his first days in office. Some of his top advisors have pointed this out.

As we shall see, he did not care. That made it a lot easier to promise to withdraw no matter what, the consequences be damned.

In January 2014, five full years into his presidency, President Obama gave what has since become an infamous interview to the *New Yorker*'s David Remnick. Remnick, the author of a major Obama biography, is also an accomplished journalist who insists on asking critical questions. At one point, Remnick noted that for all of Obama's boasting during the 2012 election about Osama bin Laden's death, "the flag of Al Qaeda is now flying in Falluja, in Iraq, and among various rebel factions in Syria; Al Qaeda has asserted a presence in parts of Africa, too."

Remnick was referring to the Islamic State of Iraq and Syria, or ISIS, which, although no longer part of al Qaeda, was still flying its characteristic black Islamic flag. This is what Obama had to say about ISIS in January 2014, as Remnick reported:

> "The analogy we use around here sometimes, and I think
> is accurate, is if a jayvee team puts on Lakers uniforms that

doesn't make them Kobe Bryant," Obama said, resorting to an uncharacteristically flip analogy. "I think there is a distinction between the capacity and reach of a bin Laden and a network that is actively planning major terrorist plots against the homeland versus jihadists who are engaged in various local power struggles and disputes, often sectarian.

"Let's just keep in mind, Falluja is a profoundly conservative Sunni city in a country that, independent of anything we do, is deeply divided along sectarian lines. And how we think about terrorism has to be defined and specific enough that it doesn't lead us to think that any horrible actions that take place around the world that are motivated in part by an extremist Islamic ideology are a direct threat to us or something that we have to wade into."[5]

Five months later, the jayvee team was dunking on Kobe, and shocking the world. ISIS seized control of Iraq's second-largest city with hardly a fight and continued its bloody advance down the Tigris River. The White House would later claim that Obama was referring to jihadists in general and not specifically to ISIS[6]—but look at the original quote in context, and the president certainly seems to be talking about ISIS. Looking back at the interview, it seems pretty obvious he was blindsided by ISIS's sudden military success, despite their growing competence being in the intelligence briefs. Apparently the president was once again basing his assumptions on theory and abstractions with no connection to the reality of the situation on the ground, the intentions of this particular group, or its demonstrable achievements to that point.

ISIS was a former branch of al Qaeda that had been expelled from that organization for giving Islamic terrorism a bad name. Other terrorists had warned Osama bin Laden about the group's brutality, which had eventually led to its expulsion. Now ISIS was establishing a post-nation state in a transnational territory that would become the new face of world Islamic conquest. ISIS invaded Iraq as it was already in the midst of fighting a two-front war in Syria—against forces loyal to Bashar al-Assad's regime, on the one hand, and against the other groups rebelling against him, such as the secular Free Syrian Army, on the other.

Bashar al-Assad was making cunning calculations, letting his enemies fight amongst themselves, even aiding ISIS against the more moderate opposition to his regime—a smart move. Assad understood that the real crazies would not be acceptable to the West and, ironically, counted on our help to keep his regime in power.

As Remnick mentioned during his interview with Obama, ISIS had established a presence in Fallujah, in the heart of the Anbar province of Iraq, as early as January. But as the quotation from President Obama above suggests, no one took them very seriously. Big mistake.

Obama really should have known better—the facts of ISIS's ascendancy had been included in his presidential daily briefings for a full year by the time the group controlled Mosul, according to reporting by Catherine Herridge of Fox News.[7] Herridge also reported that Obama personally reads those briefings. Perhaps he thought that if he simply minimized the threat he might not have to deal with it on his watch.

Still, the U.S.-allied government of Iraq was on its heels by the end of August, when ISIS had ploughed its way through Iraq's Sunni Arab towns, nearly linking up with its forces in Fallujah and capturing cities all along the fertile crescent almost as far as Baghdad.

In the North, ISIS's rule was brutal. Fighters for the Iraqi army were sometimes lined up, marched out in the desert, and shot execution-style. Shiite mosques were blown up, ancient churches were seized. Under the best circumstances, ISIS gave Iraqi Christians a choice of converting, paying tribute, or fleeing for their lives. In practice, Christians were often simply exterminated. Ancient Christian villages were thus abandoned. Meanwhile, hundreds of thousands of Yazidis—adherents of an older Zoroastrian religion who are accused by fundamentalist Muslims of devil-worship—were forced to flee into the hills. An untold number of the tens of thousands who sought refuge on the barren hillsides of Mount Sinjar would die from the elements and lack of water.

The ones who stayed in their homes found that their Sunni neighbors were turning against them; many Yazidis were rounded up to be killed. Their wives and sisters were captured, raped, and sold by ISIS as spoils of war for as little as twenty-five dollars.

The Islamic State fighters were best known for their cruelty, and apparently that's the way they wanted it. Their approach to public relations contrasted sharply with that of modern armies, states, and even the "more civilized" terrorist groups we are more familiar with. These latter typically conceal or downplay their own atrocities while publicizing the wrongs dealt them by their opponents. This is how modern propaganda works, for good or for ill. Consider, for example, how Hamas publicizes every Israeli strike while hiding its own use of human shields. That's the modern way of waging war as an underdog.

ISIS was doing the opposite. It was publicizing its own atrocities on social media—including the beheadings of non-combatants and the mass execution of captured prisoners—for the purposes of intimidating its enemies and marketing.[8] The modern world has nearly forgotten this way of operating—it's a strategy more like that of Imperial Rome than anything from the last century. While modern combatants seldom put heads on pikes or torture using crude disemboweling devices for shock value, these methods can still be very effective. In a newly connected world, shocking images—whether of a Paris Hilton DUI, a dead bin Laden, or an ISIS beheading—can be either too delicious or too disgusting not to share and comment on.

As ISIS fighters swept across Iraq, they proved how incredibly resourceful a "jayvee" team they could be. They lived off the land, so to speak, in addition to bringing in large outside donations from sympathetic Arab businessmen in oil nations to the south. They collected "alms" taxes ("zakat") from the populations they controlled in Syria and Iraq, and on top of that they extorted businesses. They seized oil facilities and made big money under-selling on the black market. And naturally they seized the weapons of their fleeing and defeated enemies, building up an ever more sophisticated arsenal. By summer's end, they had acquired everything from U.S.-made rifles and tanks to Syrian anti-aircraft systems, and even fighter jets. Hopefully, they never figure out how to fly them, despite reports that they have sought out local pilots as teachers.

The assets ISIS acquired helped make wins on the battlefield progressive as they kept up their momentum. Before the U.S. became involved, even the disciplined Kurdish Peshmerga found themselves outgunned.

ISIS also offered the local population something more than the insurgencies of the past. They weren't just a defensive force, trying to push Americans out of some Arab nation. Rather they styled themselves a caliphate—a successor state to the divinely ordained Islamic kingdom originally founded in Muhammad's time. Muslims eager to help the cause could travel to their country, join them, become citizens, and even carry a black Islamic State passport.

Something else more cutting-edge, if you will, about ISIS was its use of social media. Al Qaeda was so 1990s, with old guys lecturing on grainy videos. ISIS utilized the social media that intended recruits would be using, Twitter and Facebook. ISIS presented an image of youth, action, and generational savvy in an area with tremendously high youth unemployment and not much hope. Wannabe jihadis were inspired by smiling young men posting pictures from faraway battlefields. The stale al Qaeda videos were filled with rhetoric about establishing an Islamic state. But ISIS had actually done it already, on the theory that "if you build it, they will come." Internet echo chambers were filled with their conquests, ideas, and recruitment propaganda from fighters on the ground.

I first realized the power of Twitter during one of my trips to Yemen. It was right in the middle of the Arab Spring, and Ali Abdullah Saleh was still the dictator in charge. The streets were filled with protesters. As I sat at my computer in a desert oilfield near the trouble-spot of Marib, I monitored the escalating situation in the capital, Sana'a. Using Tweetdeck—software that allows you to view several Twitter feeds at once—I had identified credible tweeters who were in the square, a couple of reporters, and a couple of youth protesters. They were posting real-time pictures of the situation. All of the sudden, the computer went crazy with tweets. "Snipers on the roof!" "Shots fired!" "One dead!" "Eight dead!" "Seventeen dead!" Pictures of absolute chaos, blood, and bodies accompanied the very animated tweets.

It was deplorably addicting. It felt as though I was right there in the streets with the protesters, running with the crowd as the snipers opened fire. (I would later meet two of the few Western journalists who were there that day.) My experience suggests how powerful ISIS's social media strategy is; there must be literally thousands of supporters tuned in to its every move while sitting in front of their computers.

ISIS was an offshoot of al Qaeda, and as *National Review*'s Joel Gehrke noted in an insightful piece, it was following the al Qaeda playbook in establishing its caliphate.[9] The U.S. military had obtained and translated an actual al Qaeda manual in 2008. It laid out a three-stage plan for jihadist guerilla war. Phase one involved "spectacular operations," such as 9/11, to improve recruitment and boost morale. In phase two, jihadists were to build a conventional army and seize territory from some government (in the manual, and in theory, it was Saudi Arabia, but in practical terms and on the ground it turned out that Syria worked just as well) to form a base of military operations.

In phase three, the jihadists would use their army to launch invasions as a legitimate state actor. The legitimacy of their state is a very big deal to ISIS. As Gehrke pointed out, the executioner of photojournalist James Foley had uttered a few words about this, and with great pride: "You're no longer fighting an insurgency, we are an Islamic army and a State that has been accepted by a large number of Muslims worldwide, so effectively, any aggression towards the Islamic State is an aggression towards Muslims from all walks of life who have accepted the Islamic Caliphate as their leadership."

Evidently, the ISIS of June 2014 was in an advanced stage of phase three of a plan laid out years earlier. It was our worst nightmare, and a sign that we might be losing the war on terror despite all the years and sacrifices put into it. ISIS had accumulated power and potency and wealth beyond anything Osama bin Laden could have dreamed of establishing.

So the bad guys clearly had a plan. The state of Iraq did not. Did America? Did we have a strategy to counter their marketing and dispel their advertising for a West-versus-Islam holy war in which they could use the power of religion to coalesce disenfranchised youth,

Islamic extremists, and sympathizers to their cause? After more than a year of presidential briefings, three months of Islamic State military victories, the total rout of Iraqi forces within the Sunni Arab areas of Iraq, and the videotaped beheading of an American journalist, President Obama gave a famous press conference in which he reassured Americans that…he was still trying to figure out what to do. "[I] don't want to put the cart before the horse. We don't have a strategy yet. I think what I've seen in some of the news reports suggests that folks are getting a little further ahead of where we're at than we currently are. And I think that's not just my assessment, but the assessment of our military as well. We need to make sure that we've got clear plans, that we're developing them…. But there's no point in me asking for action on the part of Congress before I know exactly what it is that is going to be required for us to get the job done."[10]

Nothing says "I'm in over my head" quite like President Obama in a tan suit, telling it to the world on television in his own words. You almost felt sorry for him. Almost.

U.S. INTEREST IN IRAQ

How did Iraq become such a mess? The short (and obvious) answer: President Obama withdrew U.S. troops prematurely from Iraq based on political considerations ahead of the 2012 election, instead of basing his actions on the facts on the ground and America's long-term interests. The United States failed to follow through on what it had already accomplished in Iraq to keep the country relatively stable and make it a successful new nation.

That's the simple version. In fact, Obama's dereliction of duty is much deeper than even that suggests. In abandoning Iraq to its fate, Obama hasn't just permitted the current bloody mess. He has also forfeited a key element in preserving a long-term U.S. interest. America spent seven decades and invested trillions of dollars and many American lives in order to protect that interest. Obama just ceded a big piece of it voluntarily.

The idealist might say that the American-led invasion of Iraq in 2003 had something to do with ending tyranny and spreading freedom, as President Bush stated in his second inaugural address. The realist might suggest that it has more to do with oil. In fact, it had a little bit to do with both, but more to do with oil. The precise nature of America's interests and historical relationships in the region is worth looking at here briefly.

For most of our country's history, the Arab lands of Mesopotamia were part of a crumbling Ottoman Empire. After World War I, they fell under the domination of the victorious European powers. The U.S. government had little involvement there until about seventy years ago.

American businesses, supported by the American government, got there first with hopes of finding oil, and obviously oil has been the region's main attraction ever since. (It's certainly not the winning personalities of the local political, military, and religious leaders.)

With a bit of help from U.S. diplomats, two American oil companies overcame resistance from France and Britain and obtained stakes in what would become the Iraqi Petroleum Company under the 1928 Red Line Agreement. This let them share in the oil riches of formerly Ottoman-held Arab lands, which England and France had hoped to keep between themselves after World War I.

To the south was Saudi Arabia, which had until recently been a patchwork of Ottoman-controlled cities and independent tribal domains. Even before World War I, King Adulaziz ibn Saud had been gradually consolidating the territory into a unified independent kingdom. Oil was initially discovered on the Arabian Peninsula in the early 1930s. Standard Oil of California obtained rights to explore for oil there and later partnered with Texaco in the venture under the auspices of Aramco. It seemed a risky gamble at that time. By 1938, huge amounts were being discovered in Saudi Arabia. In neighboring Kuwait, a British-American partnership (the Kuwait Oil Company) found oil around the same time.

Thus American oilmen who had cut their teeth in Texas and Oklahoma would be the first to develop the lion's share of Middle Eastern resources. The share of oil in the region controlled by U.S. companies continued to grow through World War II. It became abundantly clear that immense riches were present beneath what had up to then been considered a worthless desert. By 1944, American companies were producing five billion barrels per year in Saudi Arabia alone.

The importance of this discovery is hard to overstate. Eventually, it would turn one of the world's poorest countries into one of its wealthiest. It would also reshape American foreign policy forever.

You have probably heard many people talk about how U.S. policy in the Middle East is all or mostly about oil. And of course this is true, but not necessarily for the reasons you might think. Our interest in the Middle East's oil—and the blood and treasure we have lost over it—is not actually about helping oil companies make money or even about raising our own standard of living. Those are definitely by-products of the policy, but it would be inaccurate to say that business or personal consumption of oil is the driving consideration.

The real reason the United States cares so much about Middle Eastern oil is far more basic than any of that. The architects of our policy there, going back to World War II, were very explicit about this. That oil, to the extent that we control it, will prevent us from being a sitting duck in some future armed conflict.

American leaders learned this lesson in World War II, the most heavily mechanized conflict the world had ever seen. It demonstrated that in modern mobile warfare, powers that lack access to oil will not be powers for long. To the extent that we have ever had a handle on the Middle East, it kept America competitive with the Soviets and made U.S. military superiority possible in the late twentieth century.

You can argue whether this state of affairs has been good or bad for Middle Easterners, but it is the reality. And yes, cheap energy from the Middle East also helped to propel our economy by replacing our own declining production and to rebuild war-torn Europe after World War II.

Before U.S. hegemony in the Middle East, the British were responsible for general security in the region. But they lacked the ability to keep it up. Understanding that with the decline of the British Empire there would be a large security vacuum, the U.S. stepped up to the plate and nudged them out. Our national security and commercial interests were too important to leave in the hands of a declining power.

The immense importance of oil was not lost on the leaders or the generals in World War II itself. German Field Marshall Erwin Rommel noted in his papers that many of his decisions were dictated by fuel shortages rather than tactical considerations—and in fact, this might have been the most important reason for his defeat in North Africa. "The bravest men can do nothing without guns, the guns nothing without ammunition; and neither guns nor ammunition are of much use in mobile warfare unless there are vehicles with sufficient petrol to haul them around," he wrote.[11]

American leaders were alarmed by how much oil was required to wage the war against the Nazis and Japan. This was far more energy-intensive warfare than World War I, in which tanks and planes had played far less important roles. Suddenly, petroleum fuels had become one of the most important ingredients for military victory. And oil was needed for much more than just powering tanks, trucks, and planes—it was also needed to make tires, asphalt (for runways especially), engine lubricants, and other essential war materials. Oil was an even bigger story for the Axis powers. Germany and Japan lost the war in part because they found themselves short of oil and under constant pressure to find more.

In the time since World War II oil has only become more important. In those days, the American armed forces consumed about a gallon of fuel per serviceman per day, which seemed an incredibly large amount at the time. But by the time the United States and its partners invaded Iraq and Afghanistan at the beginning of the twenty-first century, U.S. forces were consuming twenty gallons per soldier per day.[12]

Fortunately, the United States government anticipated this trend. The State Department first established a permanent diplomatic presence in Saudi Arabia in 1942, four decades after the Saudi dynasty had been re-established. Once the war had begun, our government recognized that the American oilmen had found something of great strategic value in the sands.

In 1943, the U.S. started sending foreign aid to the Saudis. That same year, the State Department's Division of Near Eastern Affairs issued a paper that touched on the importance of keeping American companies at the forefront of Middle Eastern oil production, mostly at the expense of British and Soviet interests: "Today, the United States is rapidly approaching a change from an oil exporting nation to an importer, due to the great depletion of American oil reserves as a result of our contribution to the present war. We are consequently much more interested now even than after the last war in maintaining our access to the resources of an area said to contain 40 percent of the remaining proved petroleum reserves of the world."[13]

In 1945, just after his famous Yalta meeting with Joseph Stalin and Winston Churchill, President Franklin Roosevelt himself traveled to the Suez Canal to meet with King Abdulaziz ibn Saud for three days aboard the USS *Quincy*.[14] It was the first such meeting ever, and Roosevelt's efforts paid off. Ibn Saud resisted pressure to submit to British influence, instead keeping his country's oil in U.S. hands, where it would stay for decades. An era of often uneasy Saudi-U.S. cooperation began. In the years that followed, American companies built Saudi Arabia's infrastructure, and ibn Saud agreed to host U.S. airmen and allow TWA planes to land in his country.

ROUGH NEIGHBORHOOD

It all sounds like a picnic. But unfortunately, these world-changing oil discoveries took place in a pretty bad neighborhood.

Many Americans today view the Middle East through the lens of current events. But the region was extremely turbulent in the mid-twentieth century, just as it is now. As the British relinquished control of Palestine in May 1948, forces from Jordan, Egypt, Syria, Lebanon, and Iraq invaded all at once, beginning the first Arab-Israeli War. This conflict, which Israel won, set the stage for several additional Arab-Israeli wars, both large and small. And these in turn helped create the conditions for further conflicts—the Black September War (between

Jordan and Palestinian militias), the rise of the Assad family in Syria, the Lebanese Civil War, and the modern-day Israeli-Palestinian conflict.

Unfortunately, the violence throughout the region became America's problem after World War II. Usually, the United States tried to contain the chaos. At other times, it aided or at least knowingly permitted chaos to advance U.S. interests or prevent something even worse. We didn't always make the best choices. Things got ugly, at times with our involvement. Syria experienced three military coups in 1949 alone, the first of which helped pave the way for construction of the Trans-Arabian pipeline, to bring American-controlled oil from Saudi Arabia to the Mediterranean port of Sidon in Lebanon.

To this day—thirty-five years after the Saudi government bought out Aramco—American involvement in the Middle East continues to revolve around the same strategic interest. The oil must flow, and it must remain available to us. Without it, U.S. conventional military forces would have been at a far greater disadvantage against the Soviets throughout the Cold War era. And yes, the oil was important to our economy as well, as the oil embargoes of 1967 and 1973 demonstrated.

The Cold War is now over, but the possibility of future conflict remains, and the need for oil in war is greater than ever. This is why it has proven so difficult to disengage from the Middle East. Among those helping keep us there are many American liberals who have fought against the exploitation of American natural resources over the last three decades. This may finally be changing today, however, with the advent of fracking and booming U.S. oil production on private lands.

WHAT'S THE MATTER WITH IRAQ?

So where does Iraq fit into this picture? It's probably the roughest spot in this rough neighborhood.

But America's involvement in Iraq doesn't go back very far. Although a few American oil companies were involved there early on, none ever had a controlling stake in Iraqi oil production. And Iraq's oil industry was seized from them and their larger European partners and nationalized in 1961.

Nor did the near-disappearance of Iraq's oil from world markets during the sanctions era of the 1990s cause shortages or price spikes that would have affected the U.S. In February 1999, after several bombings of Iraq by President Clinton and amid a Shiite uprising in southern Iraq, Americans were buying gasoline for just under a dollar a gallon.

Iraq's production, though substantial, is not particularly large relative to its neighbors'. On its best days, it is on par with tiny Kuwait's. If you were an evil overlord and you had to choose which of the two to take over, you'd take Kuwait in a heartbeat. There is a lot of oil in Iraq, but if you want to do anything with it you have to wade through its sharply divisive, violent, sectarian politics.

After World War I, most of Iraq—eventually all of it—fell under the administration of the British. (I had the opportunity to visit their abandoned Royal Air Force base in Habbaniyah as I passed through on my way to Ramadi.)

At first the British found Iraq too hot to handle. After putting down a major rebellion in 1920—a very rare event in which Shiite, Sunni, and Kurd worked together against a common enemy—the British loosened their grip and made Iraq a nominally independent client kingdom under a conveniently available Hashemite monarch who claimed a distant kinship with the Prophet Muhammad.

A 1941 military coup threatened to put the young state in an alliance with Nazi Germany, and so the British re-invaded, restored the monarchy, and occupied Iraq until 1947. They used it as an important source of oil for the war effort.

A 1958 military coup ended the monarchy for good. Two further coups occurred in the 1960s, the last one placing the Ba'ath Party in charge of Iraq. Interspersed with these coups were various internal wars in which Iraq's military suppressed Kurdish attempts at independence or autonomy.

Saddam Hussein became president in 1979. The rest of Iraq's history is probably more familiar. Hussein started the Iran-Iraq War in

1980, and it dragged out to a bloody stalemate. He invaded Kuwait in 1990 and was crushed. America would fight two wars in Iraq—the second leading to Hussein's downfall and the establishment of the current Shiite-dominated government.

Both American wars had motives closely tied to oil production, but neither had that much to do with Iraqi oil *per se*. The underlying reason had more to do with the threat Hussein posed to stability in the region—and thus to the more reliable sources of oil in the region.

Opposition to the Iraq War became very fierce in some quarters of American politics as time went on, and those who opposed it are likely to continue to think they are correct even today. When ISIS began its offensive in Iraq in 2014, some people immediately blamed George W. Bush for invading Iraq in the first place more than a decade earlier—or at least for mishandling the occupation.

That position is not crazy. Having spent many days taking convoys in armored Humvees or in Bradley tanks into the streets of Baghdad and Ramadi—at first worried and then later numb to the potential danger of improvised explosive devices—I can sympathize with doubts about the war, and especially with the idea that the U.S. government didn't properly anticipate the obligations it was taking on with the invasion. As I looked into the faces of Iraqis staring back at us, I could imagine my own city occupied. Historically, occupations don't work out so well.

But whether it was wise or not, at the time the invasion undoubtedly reflected U.S. strategic interests. Even if we could conclude by some objective standard that war wasn't the best option we had, leaders have to make decisions based on the information and context at hand.

To keep Middle Eastern oil flowing, we need to keep the peace. That's no easy task in a region with a history of tension, political violence, and instability. It's even more difficult when someone like Saddam Hussein keeps rocking the boat. He invited his own overthrow by repeatedly causing problems for his neighbors. This is how he ended up becoming part of President Bush's so-called "axis of evil." Furthermore, after he was placed under sanctions and the United Nations established a no-fly zone to contain his ambitions, his regime fired hundreds of times upon coalition pilots. Saddam was the tall grass that got mowed.

The U.S. policy toward Iraq became "regime change" when President Bill Clinton signed the Iraq Liberation Act of 1998. Hussein, with his constant, unsuccessful scheming to establish himself as the preeminent regional military power, had simply proven too belligerent. In 1980, he had invaded Iran, only to find himself in an unexpectedly hard slog. In that war he received extensive U.S. and Saudi help, but only after it looked like the Iranians—who were then far more hostile toward United States interests—might completely overrun him.

A decade later, Hussein invaded and occupied neighboring Kuwait in a dispute over oil production and Kuwait's failure to forgive Iraqi debts. This led to the Gulf War, which expelled him from Kuwait. In revenge, Hussein attempted to assassinate former U.S. President George H. W. Bush when he visited Kuwait in 1993.[15]

By 2003, the Iranians still hated Saddam; the Saudis and Kuwaitis were terrified of him. He had a history of using chemical weapons—not only during the Iran-Iraq War, but also to put down internal rebellions. At the turn of the century, Hussein's hostile and evasive attitude toward United Nations weapons inspections only helped fuel the common Western belief that he was indeed developing weapons of mass destruction. In fact, his own top generals believed almost right up until the U.S. invaded that he had massive chemical and biological weapons stockpiles.[16]

Saddam's evasion of UN inspectors at that point proved to be the last straw. There are only two words of advice you can give any non-nuclear power that causes this much trouble and consistently messes with a vital U.S. strategic interest for as long as he did: "Look out."

■ ■ ■

Of course, there's more than one way to serve a major strategic interest like the one the U.S. had in the Middle East. Was the invasion the best way? Or did it bring on more undesirable chaos than it stopped?

Those are valid questions. They were also academic questions by 2008, because we couldn't undo what we had done.

Barack Obama can rightly say he opposed the Iraq War from its inception. His position has been consistent, at least. He gave a now-famous speech about it in Chicago in 2002 in which he said:

> That's what I'm opposed to. A dumb war. A rash war. A war based not on reason but on passion, not on principle but on politics.... Saddam poses no imminent and direct threat to the United States or to his neighbors...the Iraqi economy is in shambles...the Iraqi military a fraction of its former strength, and...in concert with the international community he can be contained until, in the way of all petty dictators, he falls away into the dustbin of history. I know that even a successful war against Iraq will require a U.S. occupation of undetermined length, at undetermined cost, with undetermined consequences. I know that an invasion of Iraq without a clear rationale and without strong international support will only fan the flames of the Middle East, and encourage the worst, rather than best, impulses of the Arab world, and strengthen the recruitment arm of al-Qaeda. I am not opposed to all wars. I'm opposed to dumb wars.[17]

This was probably the best anti-war argument at the time, and it anticipated many of the problems that plagued our invasion and its aftermath. But at that time, Obama was a state senator with little knowledge or experience in foreign affairs. He had no access to the intelligence that two of his own future secretaries of State—Clinton and Kerry—would use to justify voting in favor of war. He also had very little at stake politically. Obama was somewhat like an NFL fan questioning the judgment of his team's coach during the game. Even if we assume Obama was acting from noble motives—not just to please a crowd of enthusiastic liberals in Chicago who would later fund his U.S. Senate campaign—it was very easy for him to take that stance.

It's also impossible to say for sure how Obama might have voted on the Iraq War in 2002 had he won his 2000 race for the U.S. House. The speech suggests that he probably would have voted against it. But as president, he has moved in quite a different direction from the positions he campaigned on, involving the U.S. in a few wars— not all of them wise or well thought out, without even consulting Congress.

As of late 2014, Obama has authorized strikes in Iraq and has increased troops there into the hundreds if not thousands. The precise number is hard to know, as he uses words such as "advisors" to describe them—so he can make the American people and perhaps himself believe there are not "boots on the ground" or "combat troops." But these "advisors" are disproportionately Special Forces guys.[18] That means they are combat troops.

And of course Obama has appointed two Iraq hawks as his top diplomats since becoming president. Senator Hillary Clinton's floor speech in favor of war supported more or less what President George W. Bush eventually did. She said that Bush should go to the United Nations for a resolution requiring unfettered inspections. And she argued for going to war if Hussein failed to comply, even if a separate UN resolution explicitly authorizing an invasion proved unattainable: "I believe the best course is to go to the UN for a strong resolution that scraps the 1998 restrictions on inspections and calls for complete, unlimited inspections with cooperation expected and demanded from Iraq.... If we get the resolution and Saddam does not comply, then we can attack him with far more support and legitimacy than we would have otherwise."

Kerry took a nearly identical position, even penning a *New York Times* op-ed arguing that the U.S. should invade unilaterally if Saddam Hussein failed to cooperate fully with United Nations weapons inspectors.[19]

But even if we give Obama full credit for opposing the Iraq War in 2002, his position was irrelevant by the time he became president. By then, the wisdom of the war was an academic question—valuable for drawing lessons, perhaps, but irrelevant to the pressing issue of how to preserve the very real gains made by then in Iraq. Obama could not un-invade Iraq, but he could be a good steward of the occupied Iraq he had inherited. He could behave responsibly and make sure he didn't leave complete chaos behind.

That's where he failed. And that is how he lost Iraq.

LOSING IRAQ

Every day when I wake up, I feel Iraq. I feel it in my back; I feel it in my knee; I feel it in my neck. I feel it when I think about my friends I lost there. It is important for veterans who fought to have the belief that they were acting for something greater than themselves, to believe the sacrifice was worth it. Sometimes, our politicians make this difficult.

As part of his 2008 campaign, Obama had promised to withdraw from Iraq by mid-2010. "My first day in office I will bring the Joint Chiefs of Staff in, and I will give them a new mission," he said. "And that is to end this war. Responsibly, deliberately, but decisively. And I have seen no information that contradicts the notion that we can bring our troops out safely at a pace of one to two brigades per month. And again, that pace translates into having our combat troops out in 16 months' time."[20]

Unfortunately the need to fulfill that promise and please his political base in the campaign for the president's 2012 reelection overrode questions of precisely how we were going to leave Iraq.

President Bush had also laid plans to withdraw, but those plans had involved leaving behind a substantial number of troops as a residual force. Beginning in 2008 the U.S. was operating within Iraq under what is known as a "Status of Forces Agreement," which gave legal color to our occupation by making us officially invited guests in Iraq.

Unofficially, we ran Iraq. We cleaned up its messes, fought its terrorists, and eased its internal tensions. We kept the various sects and tribes from killing each other. By 2008, the insurgency had been effectively suppressed. Monthly U.S. combat casualties were down to single digits in six of the seven months before Obama took office.

■ ■ ■

In July 2014, as ISIS swept across northern Iraq and established itself as a new Islamic government, General James Amos, the outgoing commandant of the Marine Corps, made this assessment in an address to the Brookings Institution: "I have a hard time believing that had we been there, and worked with the government, and worked with parliament, and worked with the minister of defense, the minister of interior, I don't think we'd be in the same shape we're in today."[21]

These comments were especially remarkable because they were made to a liberal think tank by a still-serving flag officer under President Obama's command. They represent a complete repudiation of the course Obama took.

A residual U.S. force—even a very modest one—could have prevented the collapse of our hard-won achievements in Iraq. This is not only because U.S. troops would have played a direct military role against the jihadists of the Islamic State when they moved in from Syria. It is also because U.S. forces had served as a politically stabilizing element within the country.

After lots of pain, grief, and death, we finally had something good going in Iraq by 2009. The proper way to leave Iraq was to do so without squandering those gains—without creating a massive power vacuum. It was not an easy proposition, but a necessary one. It would have involved leaving a residual force behind under a new Status of Forces Agreement. This had been Bush's plan. It had been Obama's plan as well. It's just that he lacked the will to see it through. It wasn't important enough for him to raise much of a fuss when his main goal was simply to leave and keep his campaign promise.

That's a serious accusation. It implies extreme cynicism on Obama's part. But it's true. And don't take my word for it. Take that of Leon Panetta, who was Obama's Secretary of Defense at the time. Panetta put it this way in his new book, *Worthy Fights*, in a segment excerpted in *Time* magazine: "We had leverage. We could, for instance, have threatened to withdraw reconstruction aid to Iraq if [Iraqi Prime Minister Nouri] al-Maliki would not support some sort of continued U.S.

military presence.... I privately and publicly advocated for a residual force that could provide training and security for Iraq's military.... But the President's team at the White House pushed back, and the differences occasionally became heated.... [T]he White House was so eager to rid itself of Iraq that it was willing to withdraw rather than lock in arrangements that would preserve our influence and interests."[22]

Panetta recounts that with Obama largely disengaged from the negotiations and more eager to get out than he was to leave responsibly, "al-Maliki was allowed to slip away."[23] Obama's aides in the White House were more interested in minimizing any potential American force in Iraq than they were in guaranteeing that one stayed.

"The president decided he wanted all this behind us," was how Douglas Ollivant, the former Iraq director for the National Security Council, put it in an interview with PBS Frontline. "He didn't want to think about it, he didn't want to talk about it, he didn't want to devote any resources to it. He wanted to 'normalize' Iraq, when it's a country that's not normal. He simply wanted to put it behind us."[24]

Just a few days before Panetta's book was officially released, Julie Pace of the Associated Press gave what was arguably the most concise explanation of what had happened: "It is true that the Iraqis would not give U.S. troops immunity to stay in the country, and that is also something that any U.S. president would require. It is also true, though, that the president of the United States was looking to get out of Iraq, and after it became clear that there was going to be no deal, he went out and sold that as a policy victory, a fulfillment of his political promise. What Panetta and others have said is that it appears as though his desire to get out of Iraq shaped the way he negotiated."[25]

In other words, an initial inability to negotiate a Status of Forces Agreement was not so much the reason we left as it was an excuse for Obama to do more quickly what he already wanted to do.

There is some controversy over just how badly Obama wanted a SOFA—and Obama has helped keep that controversy alive by trying to have it both ways. When the exit from Iraq was still popular and uncontroversial, during the 2012 election season, he owned and even took credit for what he had done. In one of the presidential debates, he castigated his opponent Mitt Romney for suggesting that they had both supported a SOFA that would have left troops on the ground. "What I would not have done," Obama said, "is left 10,000 troops in Iraq, which would have tied us down in the Middle East."

Seventeen months later, in June 2014, with ISIS on the rampage, Obama took the opposite position in a White House press conference: "Keep in mind, that wasn't a decision made by me. That was a decision made by the Iraqi government. We offered a modest residual force to help continue to train and advise Iraqi security forces. We had a core requirement which we require in any situation where we have U.S. troops overseas, and that is that they are provided immunity.... The Iraqi government and Prime Minister Maliki declined to provide us that immunity."[26]

If it seems like President Obama can't keep his story straight, perhaps that's because he is blocking out the memory of what really happened. According to former top officials, Obama went out of his way to put Iraq out of sight and out of mind. "We disengaged not only militarily at the end of 2011, we disengaged politically," former Ambassador Ryan Crocker said of Obama's leadership of the withdrawal. "The war was over. We were out. Let the chips fall where they may. I don't think we thought through exactly how many chips were going to fall, and what the consequences of that were going to be."[27]

In fact, things began falling apart the very minute we left Iraq. The day the last U.S. soldier was gone—literally the first day Iraq was unoccupied, December 19, 2011—Maliki began what would be widely viewed as a Shiite reign of terror when he issued a warrant for the arrest of Iraq's vice president, Tarek al-Hashimi, Maliki's rival and a Sunni Muslim. Al-Hashimi had been tipped off that this was coming and fled to Kurdistan, whence he eventually fled Iraq. Under torture, Hashimi's bodyguards accused him of operating a death squad. He denied the charges, but was tried in absentia and sentenced to death.

Years later, General David Petraeus would tell PBS *Frontline* that this was a major turning point in Iraqi politics. "Tragically, what it did, of course, is it started the process of undoing the process that we'd worked so hard to do during the surge and even in the years after the surge."[28]

Maliki, a deeply corrupt individual who until then had been held in check only by our presence, was just getting started undermining his own country with a reign of sectarian political terror that alienated his countrymen and weakened the fabric of Iraqi society.

He assumed direct control over the security services, in contravention of Iraq's laws and constitution.[29] He forced out officials in charge of fighting corruption.[30] He used security forces to suppress independent journalism. He violently suppressed anti-corruption protestors, suggesting that they were really terrorists.

Maliki essentially tried to establish a system like Saddam Hussein's, except this time he and his fellow Shiites—the majority in Iraq—would call the shots instead of Saddam's fellow Sunnis.

Maliki's closeness to Shiite Iran was also troubling to many Iraqis—not only because of the religious sectarian differences, but also because Iran had been their bitter enemy in the Iran-Iraq War during the 1980s, in which a million people perished.

Maliki used the de-Baathification laws—designed to rid the government of former elements of Saddam's regime—to purge his enemies, mostly Sunnis, from every important institution of government, including the military.

This not only inflamed tensions with Sunnis, but it also weakened his own military (a major problem later on), because he was replacing its competent American-trained Sunni officers with political loyalists. These loyalist generals would later flee in terror when up against ISIS forces that were vastly inferior numerically.

Maliki would cross another Rubicon in August 2013, when he managed to get Iraq's Supreme Court—which has rarely shown much independence—to strike down the law that limited him to two terms as prime minister. Then he promptly announced that he would be running for a third term.

By summer 2014, this had gone so far that much of the regular army didn't consider Iraq to be something worth defending—certainly not against the ruthless jihadists of the Islamic State. Writing for *Foreign Policy*, Zaid al-Ali, a former advisor to the UN in Iraq, noted that "there was very little desire" within the Iraqi military "to take risks on behalf of political elites who were viewed as wildly corrupt."[31]

The U.S.-trained fighters laid down their arms in the face of the oncoming foe, took off their uniforms, and ran for their lives. In the process, they helped equip ISIS, which seized their vehicles and large guns—much of it American equipment.

Meanwhile, many Arab Sunni Muslims in the north, weary of oppression under Maliki, welcomed the jihadists with open arms. These were, after all, their co-religionists. The government of Iraq was run by people they considered heretics.

As Iraqi government soldiers abandoned their posts and lost battle after battle against ISIS, the Kurds tried to fill the vacuum. Thanks to their political autonomy and their relative geographic isolation in northeast Iraq, Kurdistan was already an oasis of stability and prosperity in Iraq, and the last hope for stopping ISIS. The Kurds deployed their large, well-trained army and seized critical oilfields in the Kirkuk region, keeping them out of ISIS hands.

In response, Maliki's government—losing the war everywhere else and fearful of the Kurds gaining more territory and power—actually accused them of aligning with ISIS.[32] This was the last straw for many Kurds. Along with all of Iraq's other problems, this insult helped rekindle a long-held Kurdish desire for independence.

Iraq was falling apart everywhere, and Maliki was hastening the pace of its decline. Before the U.S. intervened with air strikes to stop the Islamic State's genocide campaign in the north, Maliki found himself with no useful allies left. He was finally removed as prime minister by his own political party.

No one was more directly responsible for Iraq's disintegration than Maliki, but consider the circumstances in which it happened. At least in part, Maliki was reacting to Obama's total disengagement from the situation. Once he had announced the coming timeline for the U.S. withdrawal, Obama rarely engaged or even spoke to Maliki, something President Bush had done frequently.[33] Without American backing,

Maliki sought to consolidate his power by other means. The means he chose were a stronger alliance with Iran and repression of his political opponents.

As a consequence of Obama's disengagement, Maliki (quite willingly) fell entirely within Iran's sphere of influence. He began to do things that were consistent with his new America-free environment. For example, he permitted Iran to use Iraqi airspace to provide aid to Syria's Bashar al-Assad in 2012, at a time when the secular Free Syrian Army was still a viable force and the dictator's main military opponent.[34]

LEADERS TAKE RESPONSIBILITY

Obama's withdrawal from Iraq is arguably the most consequential example of how he has subordinated national and strategic interests to politics. With Iraq's parliament seemingly unwilling to cooperate, Obama took the path of least resistance. He cut corners before bailing out of Iraq completely.

And, of course, once ISIS was on the move, he and his top aides would blame everyone but themselves. They cited Bush's framework for withdrawal, omitting that it had included a status of forces agreement. They blamed the Iraqis for not wanting to grant immunity to U.S. troops serving there, even though we had overwhelming leverage to demand it.

And in terms of accepting responsibility, it only got worse from there. In September 2014, as the U.S. began its intervention against ISIS in Iraq and Syria, Obama would try to shift the blame for failing to detect ISIS's ascendancy onto America's intelligence services. In an interview with *60 Minutes* he argued, "Our head of the intelligence community, Jim Clapper, has acknowledged that, I think, they underestimated what had been taking place in Syria."

But in fact Obama had actually been warned repeatedly about ISIS, even at the time he was still describing them as "jayvee." The Daily Beast's Eli Lake followed up by contacting a source who was quite unrestrained in offering his response: "Reached by The Daily

Beast after Obama's interview aired, one former senior Pentagon official who worked closely on the threat posed by Sunni jihadists in Syria and Iraq was flabbergasted. 'Either the president doesn't read the intelligence he's getting or he's bullshitting,' the former official said."[35]

Both Clapper and the head of the Defense Intelligence Agency, Lieutenant General Michael Flynn, had testified before the Senate Armed Services Committee in February 2014. Their testimony, both written and spoken, has been available on the internet ever since, and there's no doubt President Obama had access not only to the testimony but also to the intelligence that backed it up well before it was delivered.

These two officials told Congress that ISIS was likely to "take territory in Iraq and Syria to exhibit its strength in 2014." Flynn's written testimony was especially explicit: "While most Sunnis probably remain opposed to [the Islamic State's] ideology and presence in Iraq and Syria, some Sunni tribes and insurgent groups appear willing to work tactically with [them] as they share common anti-government goals. Baghdad's refusal to address long-standing Sunni grievances, and continued heavy-handed approach to counter-terror operations have led some Sunni tribes in Anbar to be more permissive of [the Islamic State's] presence. Since the departure of U.S. forces at the end of 2011, [the Islamic State] has exploited the permissive security environment to increase its operations."[36]

Given these details, it's pretty hard for Obama to maintain that he was blindsided by what came next.

SO, WHO LOST IRAQ?

The rise of ISIS has made Obama's declarations of success from the withdrawal era ring very hollow today.

"With our diplomats and civilian advisors in the lead, we will help Iraqis strengthen institutions that are just, representative, and accountable," Obama said. "We'll build new ties of trade and of commerce, culture, and education that unleash the potential of the Iraqi people."

Had no one explained to him that, the moment we left, Iraq's leaders would ignore our advice, subordinate the nation's institutions to their personal ambitions and sectarian loyalties, fall under Iran's influence, and create new demand among disenfranchised Sunnis for something like ISIS?

Obama talked of our withdrawal from Iraq as if it were ushering in a new age of world peace. "I would note that the end of war in Iraq reflects a larger transition," Obama said. "The tide of war is receding." This is perhaps the most ignorant statement of his presidency. In the end, Obama's decision to withdraw irresponsibly mattered a lot, as subsequent events demonstrated.

The fact that the U.S. failed to obtain a new Status of Forces Agreement that would have allowed us to leave a small stabilizing force behind was also one of the greatest failures of Hillary Clinton's State Department. Obama clearly didn't care, and she was one of the few people (along with Panetta) who had his ear and might have been able to convince him that he was making a big mistake. Obama's administration understood that Maliki was untrustworthy.

As even Panetta has pointed out, a U.S. presence during the last three years could have prevented a lot of horrors from happening—including the genocide campaigns in northern Iraq against the Shia, Christian, and Zoroastrian religious minorities. It would have helped keep Maliki in check. He would have thought twice about purging the government and military of his sectarian opponents.

But Obama and Secretary of State Clinton let themselves be convinced by their own attorneys that this would have required a politically impossible vote in Iraq's parliament. These legal niceties helped usher in genocide, and the U.S. had to send forces back into Iraq anyway.

This failure was one of historic proportions. Far from ending U.S. involvement in the Iraq War "responsibly," Obama got out to help his own reelection prospects. He got out irresponsibly—dishonorably, even. It was a case of political propaganda taking priority over the national security, foreign policy, and responsibilities of the United States—all of which are much more important than one man's reelection efforts. Social media lit up with veterans of the Iraq War who felt betrayed by the president and Clinton. Imagine, if you were running through the streets of Fallujah, clearing house by house under fire, watching the last dying gasp of your platoon mate, and nursing your own shrapnel wounds—and a couple years later you see this BS in the news.

The rise of ISIS will also have further consequences outside of Iraq, especially if the caliphate continues to exist as a state. It's going to mean more atrocities, greater risks to the strategic oil in the region, and more terrorism—perhaps eventually even in our homeland. If the situation in Iraq and Syria is allowed to fester, we will likely see more post–nation-state disruption by other transnational groups that will try to rape, pillage, and plunder their way to statehood.

There is one other grave consequence. It is a sad sentence to write, but the rise of ISIS means that everything we did in Afghanistan to destroy al Qaeda's safe haven there was wasted. That was, after all, the reason we went in—to overthrow a government that was harboring the terrorists responsible for 9/11. Now, a group so brutal that al Qaeda actually expelled them has established its very own government—and done so by defeating armies we trained, using our stolen weapons, in a country we had largely pacified six years earlier.

Many Iraq War veterans continue to feel deflated. Their sacrifices have been squandered, as have those of the Iraqis who fought alongside them. Our weak leadership has abandoned the Iraqis and our gains. They can see for themselves that the reality falls far short of President Obama's premature rhetoric about a new partnership with a pacified Iraq.

Veterans, including myself, have watched with disgust and disappointment as cities we fought in fell like so many dominoes despite their defenders' superior numbers. Our soldiers did their part and held up their end of the bargain. Then they watched the failures and unabashed self-centeredness of leaders who placed their own political gain over the nation's best interest as they frittered their victory away. The loss of what we won in Iraq has widened the trust deficit between America's veterans and the current civilian leadership in power. It is in itself a form of post-traumatic stress.

CHAPTER SIX

"Chickensh*t Diplomacy"

When Israel invaded Gaza in early 2009, I was in Sana'a, the capital of Yemen, as part of my job working security management for an oil company. It was amazing to watch Yemen's government and its state-run media exploit that crisis to improve its own image. Makeshift tents were set up in the middle of the city, where hundreds of chronically unemployed men (there is no shortage of them in Yemen) could sign up to fight against Israel; hundreds of them did.

The media were ablaze with angry denunciations of the Jews and their American allies. Of course, this is always convenient, because it helps distract from the dire poverty and acute mismanagement that plagues Yemen.

That's the main purpose of all this propaganda, but it also has the effect you would expect. This was driven home for me in a jarring conversation I had with one of the nicest Yemeni ladies I had ever met.

"I hate Jews," she proclaimed. I asked her why. "Because they kill Muslims."

"Have you ever met one? Have you ever met a Palestinian?" I asked. "No," she answered.

This exchange illustrates why I think we are at least a generation away from peace between Israel and Palestine, and perhaps a lot further than that. All around the Arab world in places like Yemen, the stirring up of hatred against unknown outsiders is the best defense for ineffective, corrupt, and widely despised governments. Hatred of Jews—or whomever else, but it's usually Jews—deflects the people's hostility from the government.

This gives the state media and politicians a constant incentive to focus on the Palestinian conflict, no matter how distant it is from the life of their own nation or the good of their own people. It has thus become a much higher priority for some of these governments than actually improving the lives of their citizens.

And then there is a feedback effect, because all of the propaganda helps to undermine the peace process in Palestine as well. No settlement will ever be reached that puts an end to continuing violence or injustice if years of propaganda have hardened most of the Arab world against accepting anything short of Israel's annihilation.

THE ARAB WORLD'S RESPECT FOR POWER

An understanding of the conflicts in the Middle East—of which the Israeli-Palestinian is the most intractable—requires a cultural sensitivity that Americans often lack. Too often, we project our Western values and ways of thinking onto peoples whose mentality, experiences, and assumptions are vastly different from ours. As a result, the conflicts we see in those parts of the world remain incomprehensible to us. "Why do they do that?" we ask ourselves when encountering behavior that seems alien to our own cultural mentality. We fail to grasp that what seems alien to us can often be second nature in other parts of the world—and vice-versa, from the perspective of other peoples.

In May 2008, while running for president, Obama was facing criticism from all sides about his lack of foreign policy experience. He made one of his more creative attempts to assuage people's concerns in an interview with the *Atlantic*'s Jeffrey Goldberg: "It's conceivable that there are those in the Arab world who say to themselves, 'This is a guy who spent some time in the Muslim world, has a middle name of Hussein and appears more worldly and has called for talks with people, and so he's not going to be engaging in the same sort of cowboy diplomacy as George Bush,' and that's something they're hopeful about."[1]

The most obvious problem with these comments is the self-centered belief that one man's personal qualities would somehow open the door to solutions no one had previously considered to major world problems that lots of smart people had previously tried and failed to fix. But they also reveal a lack of cultural understanding.

One could even accuse Obama here of unintentional cultural chauvinism. "Engagement," as a good in and of itself, is a thoroughly Western concept. The one thing that surely earns respect in the Arab world is not "engagement," but power.

This was the most important lesson I learned from my time in Yemen. I deployed there nine or ten times over three or four years, all the while studying International Relations at Harvard University through its extension school. As long as the tribes in the desert were not cutting my power lines, or the power was not going off in the capital city, I was getting a world-class education, taking courses in Islam and Arabian anthropology, all the while experiencing it firsthand.

Yemen is a different world, far removed from the American mindset. It is constantly experiencing critical shortages of food, water, and drugs. It is a horribly poverty-plagued part of Arabia. Education is scarce. Women's rights are almost non-existent in parts of the country and everywhere fall far short of what we view as basic.

While in the capital, I networked with many embassy and security officials. I met with other private companies' security officials as well. This was all in an attempt to understand the potential threats to our people and our facilities. My time in South America had taught me to find the influencers—the few people in town who could get something accomplished. It might be the British or the Russians who let you know about an al Qaeda–related threat to your compound. If you have a problem in the desert—where I spent much of my time—you need to know which tribesmen are the key figures, the guys who can make things happen. This is not the sort of thing one can grasp intuitively from the comfort of an air-conditioned office in the American capitol or a university classroom.

I managed a security apparatus for a facility in the desert. The Yemeni government supplied about 150 troops as part of its contract with the company I worked for, and fifty or so local tribal guards also worked there. We placed the troops on the outside perimeter, and the guards would ride with me as I went out to meet and negotiate with tribe members. The tribal custom was that if a tribal member accompanied me, no one else could harm me, or else the tribe was shamed. Of course, not everyone always adhered to this custom, but it was by far the best guarantee available.

Many of my days were spent talking armed men out of hijacking trucks, shooting at us, or stopping the flow of work. It was an interesting cross-cultural problem-solving task. We made big efforts to get to know who was who in the tribe—the influencers. Many times, work stoppages would affect other, more powerful tribal members, and so I could play them against each other.

My education from Harvard helped put my experiences in context. I had read quite a bit about tribal law and custom. Here I had the chance to put it all to practical use, and to learn a lot more than you can learn from books. Text is helpful, but it is only with context that deep understanding is achieved.

The most important lesson, by far, was that this is a culture that respects power and ruthlessly exploits weakness. This is a lesson our political leaders don't seem to understand, and I believe the failure to grasp it is part of the reason America's role in the Israeli-Palestinian conflict has become such a train wreck.

One day in the Arabian desert, we had three or four oil service contractors working for us in the field—this might cost us tens of thousands of dollars a day. I got a call saying that all work had stopped. Word had gone out: a threat had been issued by someone that anyone caught working would be shot.

This sort of threat was fairly routine, so I wasn't immediately worried. But this time was different. None of my private security guards would go outside the wire with me. They were armed, but they were not hard men—not hard like the guys I had served with.

I went to their barracks to see what the hell was going on. One of them tried to explain: "No, we can't go. It's *Nagi* out there, and he has hired guns. One of the guys with Nagi *shot his own brother* in the head!"

So much for guard protection, I thought to myself.

I sent our army detachment to see if they could handle the people causing the stoppage. I could always tell how powerful a tribal sheik was based upon the military's reaction to him, or lack thereof.

Time passed and nothing happened. Finally, my interpreter radioed in, saying that the army was up on the dune with the group and that there seemed to be a stalemate of sorts. I grabbed an AK-47 and convinced a *sheba*—or old Bedouin—to go out with me, along with an interpreter. We made our way up the sand dune.

The scene was pretty amazing. There were approximately fifteen Bedouins on one side of the dirt road, all armed, some carrying fully automatic machine guns, as opposed to just AK-47s. On the other side of the road were our army soldiers and a gun truck. Both groups were in firing positions. There were a few people, including this Nagi character, in the middle of the road between the two potential firing lines.

As we pulled up and got out, I remember very distinctly smelling the air and saying to myself, "I wonder who the hell else in the world is doing anything like this right now." Probably no one.

It could have turned into a really ugly scene. All it would have taken was one nervous tribesman or soldier making a wrong move—or worse, discharging his weapon. You can't call 911 in the middle of the desert— that reality is partly responsible for making the local culture what it is.

I sat down in the middle of the group, feeling surprisingly calm. I knew I would have to take a hard stance. Nagi, who was high on Qat—a narcotic leaf that many Yemenis chew—was extremely nervous, and I didn't like that. He got up and walked away. The Bedouin who had supposedly shot his own brother in the head served as the nego-tiator. His outfit was different from the rest, mostly black. He seemed like a hard man, the type I had served with. I have no idea whether he actually shot his own brother, but I can say that he was the most ratio-nal person on the scene.

He handed me over his AK-47, a cultural gesture suggesting that he meant no harm. He outlined their demands through my interpreter. Nagi wanted a contract from us to deliver fuel between the facilities. Unfor-tunately, we had already given out that contract. However, we had given it to one of his fellow tribesman, and so probably something could be worked out between them that wouldn't harm us financially or contrac-tually.

I looked right in the Bedouin's eyes very confidently: "This is the deal, I don't care if you and your people stay here for three weeks in this desert. I will not help you. In fact [and I was totally bluffing here], I will make sure that you never receive any work in this field again.

"But if you agree to allow work to continue, send your gunman away, and come see me in my office two days from now, with no guns or Qat, then I will help you. I will work with our contracting office to help you get some of the contract."

He was surprised, paused, and looked at me, "We respect you for coming out here to meet us like this. We did not expect it. Nagi will come to the office in three days, as you said."

"No!" I interrupted. "He needs to be there in two days." I wanted to make it clear that I was the one setting the conditions. The Bedouin agreed, and they withdrew their men. Two days later, Nagi came to the office as agreed. He ended up with half of his tribesman's con-tract—and his peer never complained at all.

I share this experience to make a simple point. In Arabia, power is the one thing that brings true respect. It got Nagi what he wanted. It helped me avoid what I wanted to avoid. Your own strength is the one thing that makes "engagement" worthwhile—otherwise, any engagement is probably going to be counterproductive.

In the tribal world, it is practically suicidal to make unilateral concessions, to appear weak, or to weaken the position of one's allies. The only way to keep or establish peace or command any respect or retain any influence is to demonstrate one's strength. The application of this concept to our current foreign policy situation in that part of the world is probably rather obvious.

A COLLEGE THESIS IN ACTION

In October 2014, U.S.-Israeli relations hit their all-time low-point. That was when an anonymous White House aide referred to Israeli Prime Minister Benjamin Netanyahu as "a chickensh*t," which was clearly intended to send a message.

And it wasn't just about Netanyahu personally. In the same story reporting the slur, journalist Jeffrey Goldberg wrote, "By next year, the Obama administration may actually withdraw diplomatic cover for Israel at the United Nations."[2]

It was a long road that led to this dark moment. Incredibly, one can pick up this thread as early as 1979.

When Barack Obama was a freshman at Occidental College that year, he enrolled in Political Science 94, an introductory American foreign policy course in which students were required to write and present papers examining various foreign policy questions.

According to a classmate, Obama was usually "relatively quiet" in class.[3] But he became "very vocal" when he was assigned to a group exploring the Middle East peace talks. The Camp David Accords had concluded a year earlier producing the historic Egypt-Israel Peace Treaty—which, among other things, made Egypt the first Arab state to officially recognize Israel. The Accords also provided a framework for peace in the Middle East.

Obama's main contribution, according to David Maraniss's biography *Barack Obama: The Story*, was a critique of the Camp David Accords. Specifically, Obama's group's paper rejected the idea that

"Egypt and Israel can solve the delicate problem of Palestinians, with the U.S. overseeing and insuring the whole process." The critique continued, "This takes a naïve faith in American ability to control the world according to its whims. In actuality, this has not been the case for some time—the U.S. today has limited influence in the Middle East, and must be viewed as a participant, rather than a controller, of the world system."

Obama's group concluded that "only by transcending [the Camp David Accords] and allowing the Palestinians and Arab nations to participate in the settlement can the problem be solved."[4]

Few of us would want to be judged as middle-aged adults on arguments we made as teenagers. Nevertheless, it is striking how much President Obama's actions in the Middle East today echo the conclusions he and his group reached in that college class thirty-five years ago.

Those conclusions—on the limits of the United States' ability to influence world affairs, and in particular the impotence of the U.S. and Egypt to bring about a sustainable peace between the Israelis and Palestinians—seem to be guiding his Middle East policy as president.

Israel is an ally of the United States. The relationship hasn't always been perfect, and Obama is not the first president to have strained relations with Israel. But it is by far the closest and most important relationship we have in the region.

Yet throughout his presidency, Obama has worked very hard to undermine Israel's position vis-à-vis the Palestinians. He has acceded to and even helped expand the demands of the latter, while making unprecedented and unreasonable demands of the former.

This is not an accident—it has been part of his stated strategy. The strange result has been to bring Egypt and Israel together for a common purpose, while marginalizing the U.S.

OBAMA AND ISRAEL: IT'S COMPLICATED

As a candidate for president, Barack Obama cast himself as a backer of Israel, as all serious U.S. presidential candidates are expected to do. But his candidacy raised serious questions among Israelis and other supporters of Israel.

The infamous BUD/S Bell—to quit, simply ring it three times, place your helmet under it, and you're out of SEAL training

Serving with the SEALs in Trinidad

Ship boarding/takedown training off the coast of Puerto Rico

In the "kill house"—
training for close-
quarters and urban
combat

In Panama with a platoon mate in the SEALs

In La Paz, Bolivia

Sniper shot in La Paz

Training host country forces in Bolivia

Teaching Peruvians—including one who later came to the U.S., joined the Army, and died in Iraq

On a ship off the coast of Panama, conducting interoperability operations with other nations' militaries

In Ramadi, Iraq, 2005

In Yemen,
working as
a security
consultant, with
Taleb, from a
Marib tribe

In the Yemeni desert, watching a suspicious vehicle with a Bedouin guard

Mentoring our security force of Yemeni soldiers

On the trip to Egypt with the Westminster Institute delegation

With General Abdel
Fattah al-Sisi, now
the president of Egypt

There was the Reverend Jeremiah Wright, Obama's former pastor and mentor, who had made numerous anti-Semitic statements from his pulpit. His church—where Obama was baptized into the Christian faith, and where he sat through Sunday sermons for years—published a bulletin containing an "open letter" that bizarrely charged Israel with building an "ethnic bomb" that would only kill blacks and Arabs while leaving others unharmed.[5]

On the campaign trail, Obama caused more alarm by pledging to meet, without preconditions, with the president of Iran. The Islamic Republic is a longtime sponsor and major funder of Hamas, a terrorist group that controls Gaza in Israel's southwest corner and is devoted to Israel's destruction. It was the founding principal and continues to be the main funder of Hezbollah, the Shiite militia in Lebanon that has repeatedly harassed Israel from the north. Adding insult to injury, Iran's president at that time, Mahmoud Ahmadinejad, was a radical among Iranian radicals. His threats to "wipe Israel off the map" were among his more inflammatory public comments.[6]

At a campaign rally in Cleveland in February 2008, Obama said, "There is a strain within the pro-Israel community that says unless you adopt an unwavering pro-Likud [Israel's center-right party] approach to Israel that you're anti-Israel."[7]

It was a provocative comment, given that Israel was in the midst of its own campaign season. Benjamin Netanyahu, the head of Likud, Israel's main conservative political party, looked like an easy bet for prime minister. In his book *Leading from Behind,* journalist Richard Miniter quotes an aide to Netanyahu: "Imagine Netanyahu saying that just because you don't take a pro-Democratic [Party] position does not mean that you are anti-American." This is "just not done."[8]

Throughout the 2008 campaign, Obama's opponents raised questions about his commitment to Israel. John McCain used comments supportive of Obama's candidacy by an advisor to Hamas to suggest that the terrorist group wanted Obama to win the election.[9]

All of this was enough to make many Israelis and other supporters of Israel nervous about the prospect of an Obama presidency. In fact, in the weeks leading up to the election, polls showed that the citizens of nearly every foreign country wanted Obama to win the presidency, the Israelis being the notable exception. A poll of five hundred voting-age Israelis commissioned by the Rabin Center for Israel Studies had McCain ahead of Obama by a twelve-point margin.[10]

That skepticism was reinforced by some of Obama's initial actions as president. He gave his first television interview as president to the Saudi-owned television network Al-Arabiya. During his first presidential trip to the Middle East, in early April 2009, Obama visited two majority-Muslim countries, Turkey and Iraq, but bypassed Israel. Obama wouldn't set foot in Israel for another four years.

Administration officials later acknowledged the error of snubbing Israel. "We made a mistake," a senior administration foreign policy advisor later told *New York* magazine about not visiting Israel during Obama's June 2009 trip to Cairo. "Nobody thought of it as a big deal at the time, but, I mean, you're in the neighborhood, you're right down the street, and you don't stop by for coffee?"[11]

If this was an oversight, it demonstrates a glaring lack of diplomatic competence. It would be more understandable as an intentional snub.

Obama later told a group of Jewish leaders that during George W. Bush's presidency "there was no daylight" between the U.S. and Israel, "and no progress [on resolving the Israeli-Palestinian conflict]."[12]

At a minimum, Obama was suggesting that America's credibility with Arab states suffered when American and Israeli policies are too close together.[13] But he was also implying that he intended to put some "daylight" between his country and its only reliable Middle East ally. His strategy would generate no more "progress" than Bush's had, but it would create a whole host of other problems.

OBAMA'S SETTLEMENTS OBSESSION

Early in his administration, Obama placed an emphasis on pursuing an agreement to end the Israeli-Palestinian conflict. On his third day in office, he named former Senate majority leader George Mitchell as special envoy for Middle East peace.

But Obama also took another action that would undermine all of Mitchell's efforts: he made halting the construction of Israeli settlements in the West Bank a precondition for the resumption of peace talks. The settlements in question are civilian homes built in areas claimed by both Israel and the Palestinians—in East Jerusalem in particular. Jerusalem is Israel's capital, but the U.S. and other countries still don't recognize Israel's annexation of the eastern part of the city. As a result, many consider new construction there to be illegitimate.

Obama raised the settlements issue with Benjamin Netanyahu in the newly elected Israeli prime minister's first visit to the White House in May 2009. Two days earlier, Secretary of State Hillary Clinton had put the administration's position in very explicit terms. The administration wanted "to see a stop to settlements—not some settlements, not outposts, not natural-growth exceptions," Clinton said at a joint press conference with Egypt's foreign minister. "And we intend to press that point."[14]

Israel responded by stating that it would not construct new settlements, but would continue to build homes as needed in existing settlements.

Obama was unmoved. In sharp contrast with past American presidents, he was adamant that nothing new be built—not even a new school or synagogue or a new apartment to meet natural population growth among the Jewish population in the existing settlements — never mind the fact that many Palestinians had sold that land or their homes to Israelis.

It was an untenable position—not just politically, since Netanyahu's conservative coalition draws much of its support from the settlement community, but also in practical terms. The settlement population at that point was more than three hundred thousand. To demand that Israel promise not to build a single new house was unrealistic. This was a domestic Israeli political issue that Clinton and Obama just did not seem to grasp. And they were making this a precondition for peace talks when the Palestinians themselves had made no such demands.

This is why Obama's preoccupation with the expansion of Israeli settlements was so surprising—even the Palestinians had not taken such a hard line. There were already enough grievances and bad blood between the two sides, and Obama's first act was to create an additional sticking point. As Robert Malley, a former special assistant for Arab-Israeli affairs to President Clinton, put it in an interview with the *Guardian*: "The surprise in this is not the Israeli position [on settlements]. The surprise is the forcefulness of the American one. Rarely have we seen it at this pace and with this intensity and unambiguity. The U.S. has taken a position that doesn't give much wriggle room at all to the Israeli government."[15] Obama made settlements a focal point of his "A New Beginning" speech in Egypt the following month. "The United States does not accept the legitimacy of continued Israeli settlements," he told the audience at Cairo University. "This construction violates previous agreements and undermines efforts to achieve peace. It is time for these settlements to stop."[16]

Two weeks later, Netanyahu made his own demands in a speech at Bar-Ilan University in Tel Aviv: that the Palestinians renounce terrorism and formally acknowledge Israel's right to exist as a Jewish state. The construction of homes for Israelis was not the main obstacle to peace in the Middle East, Netanyahu argued; rather, it was a side issue that would be worked out once these fundamental issues were addressed.[17]

It's worth recalling here how other governments in Arab and Islamic countries use the Palestinian-Israeli conflict to mollify their own populations. I ran into quite a few people who openly despised Israel and Jews in Yemen, but I never—not once—heard anyone discuss settlements as a key component blocking the peace process. The settlement issue plays some small role in stoking anger against Israel, to be sure—there have been *fatwas* issued to ban its practice, and it is viewed as one form of oppression of the Palestinians—but it is not in itself the fundamental roadblock to peace. Obama was raising issues to complicate the negotiating process for the side that is presumably our ally. He was operating based on his preconceived assumptions about what the Palestinians should achieve in the process, rather than what was feasible in talks, and he was undermining any real chance at progress toward peace.

Obama and Netanyahu's dueling speeches highlighted how frayed their relationship had become only a couple of months into their respective terms, five full years before the "chickensh*t" incident. From the very beginning, Obama's "daylight" strategy was working to weaken Israel's hand.

Later in 2009, Israel agreed to temporarily halt residential construction. But it exempted schools, hospitals, and buildings already in the process of being constructed, including three thousand houses and apartments in the West Bank.[18] This ten-month moratorium was a sign of Israel's good faith in the peace process.

It is perhaps no surprise, given the history of the conflict, that this small gesture was not reciprocated by the Palestinians, but the nature of their response was especially interesting. Palestinian Authority head Mahmoud Abbas specifically cited Obama's position in refusing to enter into direct talks with Netanyahu without a complete settlement freeze.

This demonstrates that Obama was the main problem preventing any new talks. As a result, the temporary halt in construction ended in September 2010 without any progress in getting the two sides to the negotiating table. Less than two years into his first term, Obama had become an obstacle to negotiations in the peace process—perhaps the principal obstacle.

As foreign policy scholars Michael O'Hanlon, Martin S. Indyk, and Kenneth Lieberthal wrote in their 2012 book *Bending History: Barack Obama's Foreign Policy*, "Seven months of U.S. diplomatic effort had been wasted and Obama's credibility damaged for no good purpose."[19]

In a moment of candor, Obama later acknowledged that he hadn't proceeded in the right way. He told *Time* magazine's Joe Klein that his administration had "overestimated our ability to persuade [the Israelis and Palestinians] to [engage in a meaningful conversation] when their politics ran contrary to that.... If we had anticipated some of these political problems on both sides earlier, we might not have raised expectations as high."[20]

In March 2010, Vice President Biden traveled to Jerusalem on a fence-mending trip. During his visit, Israel's interior ministry announced its approval of 1,600 new housing units in a suburb of East Jerusalem. The announcement made Obama livid, because Netanyahu had agreed that his government would not authorize any new housing. That the announcement coincided with Biden's visit made matters even worse.

Biden denounced the move as "precisely the kind of step that undermines the trust we need right now."[21] He said that the announcement "runs counter to the constructive discussions that I've had here in Israel." Hillary Clinton bragged to Obama that she had upbraided Netanyahu for more than forty minutes by phone and publicly rebuked him.[22] Obama senior advisor David Axelrod appeared on ABC's *This Week* and said that the administration felt insulted by the timing of the settlement announcement, which, he said, "seemed calculated to undermine" peace talks.[23]

Netanyahu claimed that he had been caught off guard by the announcement. Perhaps that was even true. But of course, this sort of thing—whether it was a misunderstanding or a passive-aggressive reaction by Israeli officialdom—tends to happen when you antagonize your allies in the first place. When you fail to establish a friendly relationship with your next-door neighbor, something as simple as a misplaced garbage can or a badly behaving dog can become a new cause for hostility.

And that's the way Obama's relations with Israel proceeded. When Netanyahu visited the White House two weeks later, Obama extended none of the respect that usually greets foreign heads of state. Obama arrived late to a meeting with Netanyahu and handed him a list of thirteen demands Obama felt were necessary to bring the Palestinians to the negotiating table, including a halt to new settlements in East Jerusalem. Then Obama abruptly left the room to go have dinner with his wife and children.[24]

"There is no humiliation exercise that the Americans did not try on the prime minister and his entourage," *Maariv*, an Israeli newspaper, opined. "Bibi received in the White House the treatment reserved for the president of Equatorial Guinea."[25] Actually this may have been an understatement. When the president of Equatorial Guinea, whose government has been tied to serious human rights abuses, visited Washington in 2009, he got what one human rights activist called "the red-carpet treatment."[26]

BIBI AND BARACK

The relationship between Israel and the U.S. has long been very close. What's amazing is how Obama allowed his own ideological preconceptions, held as early as his college years, to damage it so severely in just a matter of months. During Obama's first term, the growing rift between the United States and Israel centered on a personal animosity between Obama and Netanyahu. The contentious nature of their relationship was captured in a short conversation that took place at the G-20 summit in Cannes, France in 2011.

In what they no doubt thought was a private conversation, President Obama and Former French President Nicolas Sarkozy exchanged thoughts on the Israeli prime minister. "I cannot bear Netanyahu; he's a liar," Sarkozy told Obama in range of a microphone. Instead of challenging Sarkozy's characterization, Obama replied, "You are fed up with him, but I have to deal with him even more often than you."[27]

Sarkozy and Obama's hot-mic moment over Israel caused a lot of embarrassment for all three countries. But it was a moment of clarity about the relationship between the U.S. and Israel. It was common knowledge by then that Obama and Netanyahu did not get along, but this was perhaps the best proof yet. Despite assurances to the contrary, after more than half a century of unshakeable support for the Jewish State, the United States no longer had Israel's back—at least not as long as Obama and Netanyahu were both in office. This was not the first time two heads of state had not gotten along, with serious effects on both countries' foreign policy. But the relationship between Israel and the U.S. is much more important than either man.

The consensus was that the Obama administration had poisoned the atmosphere by demanding a full settlements freeze as a precondition to peace talks. "I think we raised the bar too high on Netanyahu," a senior Obama national security aide told journalist Richard Wolffe, one of Obama's most sympathetic biographers. "We asked [Netanyahu] to do things he couldn't possibly do, and ironically the Palestinians weren't even asking for a total settlement freeze. We created the dynamic where we raised the bar so high, the Palestinians couldn't lower it: 'The U.S. has demanded it; how can we expect anything less?' In retrospect, that wasn't the best way to proceed."[28] Wolffe's administration source was right: Mahmoud Abbas confirmed to *Newsweek* that it was not the Palestinians but "Obama who suggested a full settlement freeze." And the Palestinian president said he later felt betrayed by Obama on the issue. "I said OK, I accept. We both went up the tree. After that, he came down with a ladder and he removed the ladder and said to me, jump."[29]

When you think about it, it's pretty hard to blame Abbas for the mess Obama got him into by raising the expectations of his constituency.

Hillary Clinton also later acknowledged that the Obama administration had erred in taking such a hard line on settlements. In *Hard Choices*, Clinton writes,

> In retrospect, our early hard line on settlements didn't work. Israel initially refused our request, and our disagreement played out in public, becoming a highly personal standoff between President Obama and Netanyahu, with the credibility of both leaders on the line. That made it very hard for either one to climb down or compromise. The Arab states were happy to sit on the sidelines and use the dustup as an excuse for their own inaction.[30]

It is not surprising that Clinton now wants to distance herself from Obama on this question ahead of an expected run for the presidency. But what is fantastical about this statement and others from Hillary Clinton in her launching-pad book is that she was the top diplomat implementing this feckless foreign policy. This happened on her watch.

In the military, we don't get to blame our commanding officers for our failures in the field—that's something only their superiors can do.

That Hillary would throw her boss under the proverbial bus for her own personal and political gain seems to indicate a character issue. And here Clinton resembles Obama. Abdication of responsibility for failures and spiking the football on successes are standard operating practice for both Clinton and Obama.

The settlements issue would continue to bedevil the peace process in Obama's second term.

When Netanyahu visited the White House in October 2014, he seemed prepared to restart peace talks. Netanyahu said that the rise of ISIS was pushing former foes such as Saudi Arabia to closer relationships with Israel and that those relationships could be the basis for a renewal of Palestinian peace talks. He probably had a point.

But Obama was too busy obsessing over settlements to use the situation on the ground to advance the peace process. Another 2,600 new homes had just been approved in East Jerusalem. The lead paragraph of a *New York Times* piece in October 2014 captured the dynamic: "Prime Minister Benjamin Netanyahu of Israel on Wednesday raised the tantalizing prospect that a new Arab alliance could resuscitate Israel's moribund peace talks with the Palestinians, but President Obama responded with a familiar complaint—that Jewish settlements are the real problem."[31] White House spokesman Josh Earnest said that the new housing "will only draw condemnation from the international community, distance Israel from even its closest allies, poison the atmosphere, not only with the Palestinians but also with the very Arab governments with which Prime Minister Netanyahu said he wanted to build relations."[32]

But again, even the Palestinians hadn't made housing construction into as much of an issue as Obama was making it now. He was undoing any chance for peace and continuing to create new obstacles to it.

SWAPS

On March 19, 2011, Obama gave a speech on the Middle East at the U.S. State Department. Referring to the peace process, Obama suggested that an agreement should be based on borders that existed before the 1967 Six Day War. He said, "We believe the borders of Israel and Palestine should be based on the 1967 lines with mutually agreed swaps, so that secure and recognized borders are established for both states."[33] Obama was demanding that peace talks begin with Israel forfeiting territory (the West Bank including East Jerusalem) won in the 1967 war, in which it had been attacked. As many observers noted, this was a striking break from what American presidents had supported for decades.

Lyndon Johnson, the American president in 1967, said that for Israel to withdraw to those lines "is not a prescription for peace but for renewed hostilities."[34] In 1969, Israeli Foreign Minister Abba Eban referred to the 1967 lines as the "Auschwitz borders" because they left Israel vulnerable to attacks by neighbors who had by then shown a propensity to launch such attacks routinely.[35]

Obama's remarks provoked an immediate backlash. The Israeli government had been given less than twenty-four hours' advance notice of the content of the speech. When Netanyahu's advisors reviewed it, as is common practice, they suggested changes. But the Obama administration had intentionally sent the speech too late for any changes to be considered, and so none were made.

Netanyahu visited Obama two days later for a very tense meeting. Netanyahu lectured Obama for nearly ten minutes in front of reporters on Israeli history and the struggles of the Jewish people. He also warned, "A peace based on illusions will crash against the rocks of Middle Eastern reality." As one Israeli advisor put it to Richard Miniter, watching Obama during this meeting "was like watching the [space shuttle] Challenger explode."[36]

At the annual conference of the American Israel Public Affairs Committee (AIPAC) a couple of days later, Obama tried to clarify what he meant by "the 1967 lines with mutually agreed swaps." "By definition," he said, "it means that the parties themselves—Israelis and Palestinians—will negotiate a border that is different than the one that existed on June 4, 1967.... It allows the parties themselves to account for the changes that have taken place over the last forty-four years, including the new demographic realities on the ground and the needs of both sides."[37]

This put the U.S. position more in line with the policy elaborated in a letter President Bush had written to Prime Minister Ariel Sharon in 2004. Bush's letter stated that when the borders are agreed upon Jewish settlements should be incorporated into Israel.

Perhaps this really was all that Obama intended in the first place, when he made his original comments. But what's telling is that by that point, he had done so much to poison the relationship that the Israelis were no longer giving him the benefit of the doubt. For all intents and purposes, Israel's government no longer considered the U.S. under Obama to be a reliable ally.

As Obama was putting daylight between himself and Israel, the opposite was happening on the Palestinian side. Abbas's more moderate political party, Fatah, reconciled with the terrorists of Hamas that same summer of 2011. Obama had helped eliminate the "daylight" between the more moderate and the more radical Palestinian factions. Obama's special envoy for Middle East peace, George Mitchell, resigned in frustration.

In this failure, Obama also set up for failure all of his second-term efforts at getting Israel and the Palestinians to the negotiating table. Israel's U.S. ambassador, Ron Dermer, said he was "deeply disappointed" that the U.S. would work with Hamas, but in reality there was no danger that anything would come of it.[38] And he was right—all attempts to work with a "unity" Palestinian government backed by Hamas would prove futile.

KERRY FAILS TO WIN THE PEACE PRIZE

At the beginning of his second term, President Obama encouraged John Kerry, his new Secretary of State, to enter into the Israeli-Palestinian peace process and re-start negotiations. As they say on the internet, you won't believe what happened next.

Over the next year and a half, Kerry would visit the Middle East at least a dozen times in a vain (in every sense of the word) attempt to get both sides to the negotiating table. The Palestinians refused to talk until Israel ceased settlement construction—as we have seen, a position basically created and hardened due to Obama's rhetoric—and Israel was unwilling to talk until the Palestinians recognized Israel's right to exist. Meanwhile, Israel released hundreds of Palestinian prisoners just to try to induce the Palestinians to the negotiating table.

Kerry's frantic efforts succeeded only in driving the Israelis away. In early 2014, Israeli Defense Minister Moshe Ya'alon called Kerry "obsessive" and "messianic" for his efforts to broker Middle East peace.[39] "The only thing that can 'save us' is for John Kerry to win a Nobel Prize and leave us in peace," he said. Kerry took the insult in stride, but it was clear that the two sides would not be entering serious talks any time soon. Obama's behavior during his first term had nearly guaranteed it.

Kerry didn't help his own cause with inflammatory remarks that alienated Israel. In February 2014, Kerry was criticized for suggesting that Israel would face new economic boycotts if it did not make compromises for peace. Many saw his remarks as legitimizing boycotts that had hurt Israel's economy already. The same month, Kerry told a group of world leaders that if a two-state solution to the conflict wasn't agreed to soon, Israel would be in danger of becoming "an Apartheid state."[40]

Apartheid is a crime involving systematic oppression by a minority racial group against a majority population of a different ethnicity. Kerry's use of that extremely loaded term evoked images of pre-Mandela South Africa. In his burning desire to do something relevant, Kerry had joined Obama and others in the administration in a pattern of running off at the mouth irresponsibly in a way that made peace less likely, not more.

President Obama's approval among Israelis hit rock bottom in early 2014. In February, the Israeli weekly *Sov Hashavua* published a poll in which 70 percent of Jewish Israelis said they did not trust Obama to safeguard their nation's vital interest in talks with the Palestinians.[41] The *Times of Israel* published a poll in which a mere 20 percent of Israelis said they trusted Obama to prevent Iran from obtaining a nuclear weapon.[42] Another poll, published in the *Jerusalem Post*, found that only 21 percent of Israelis trusted Obama to manage U.S. policy in the Middle East. Just 25 percent felt Obama was a "true friend of Israel."[43]

OPERATION PROTECTIVE EDGE

In June of 2014, Hamas began firing rockets and mortar shells into Israel from Gaza, breaking a cease-fire the two governments had signed in 2012. A violent offshoot of the Muslim Brotherhood that also receives funding from Iran, Hamas is a terrorist group whose charter states that "Islam will obliterate" Israel.[44]

By early July, Hamas was sending scores of rockets into Israel every day. On July 8, Israel launched airstrikes on Gaza in what it called Operation Protective Edge. On July 17, Israel expanded its assault to include a ground invasion to destroy the sophisticated tunnel system Hamas had constructed to smuggle arms and carry out attacks and kidnappings of Israeli citizens. After a couple of cease-fires, all of which Hamas violated, the fifty-day war ended with at least 2,100 Palestinians and 71 Israelis dead.[45]

Two previous wars between Israel and Hamas had ended the same way this one did—with overwhelming military victories for Israel but public relations victories for Hamas. As always, Israel was broadly condemned for inflicting heavy casualties on the people of Gaza. The United Nations even investigated Israel's conduct for possible war crimes.[46]

But in fact Hamas, not Israel, deserved most of the blame for the high civilian death toll. Hamas had deliberately placed much of its arsenal in densely populated civilian areas—near and inside homes, schools, hospitals, and other places where women, children, and other noncombatants were located. Using civilian buildings to store munitions violates the Geneva Conventions. Hamas also fired weapons from those areas, inviting return fire that was sure to cause unnecessary civilian casualties.

If any other country had to endure thousands of rockets being fired at it for over a decade, as Israel had, it would have responded strongly to destroy the enemy. And it would have been justified in doing so. The Israeli government has an obligation to protect its citizens. Can you imagine if Mexico started to fire hundreds of rockets into the U.S.? It took a lot less than that for us to invade Mexico and seize its capital in the 1840s. As Israeli Prime Minister Benjamin Netanyahu told *NBC Nightly News*'s Brian Williams, "What would you do if American cities, where you're sitting now...would be rocketed, would absorb hundreds of rockets?...You'd say to your leader, 'A man's got to do what a man's got to do.' And a country's got to do what a country's got to do. We have to defend ourselves. We try to do it with a minimum amount of force or with targeting military targets as best as we can. But we'll act to defend ourselves. No country can live like this."[47]

The Israeli military sent text messages to Gazans, dropped leaflets, even employed what it calls "roof knocking"—sending non-explosive devices onto buildings to warn the inhabitants of a building before it is bombed to give them time to flee the attack.

But many citizens didn't flee, because Hamas encouraged them to stay in their homes. Hamas had learned from previous wars that images of Palestinians, particularly dead children and grieving parents, elicited sympathy for its cause.

So Hamas was creating an environment in which civilians would be killed. How do we know Hamas likes civilian casualties? Because as the *New Republic*'s Leon Wieseltier has pointed out, "A combat manual of the Shejaiya Brigade of Hamas advises its fighters to deploy in densely populated areas because 'the [Israeli] soldiers and commanders must limit their use of weapons and tactics that lead to the harm and unnecessary loss of people and civilian facilities,' and adds that 'the destruction of civilian homes' is a boon to the cause, because it 'increases the hatred of the citizens toward the attackers and increases their gathering around the city defenders.'"[48]

Throughout the war, Hamas claimed that it wasn't using human shields, but rather that many Palestinians had nowhere to flee. There is ample evidence that this wasn't true. Mudar Zahran of the Gatestone Institute, a think tank led by former U.S. ambassador to the United Nations John Bolton, asked dozens of Gazans about Hamas. Here is a sample of their responses to Hamas's conduct during the war:

"If Hamas does not like you for any reason all they have to do now is say you are a Mossad agent and kill you." —A., a Fatah member in Gaza.

"Hamas wanted us butchered so it could win the media war against Israel showing our dead children on TV and then get money from Qatar." —T., former Hamas Ministry officer.

"They would fire rockets and then run away quickly, leaving us to face Israeli bombs for what they did." —D., Gazan journalist.

"Hamas imposed a curfew: anyone walking out in the street was shot. That way people *had* to stay in their homes, even if they were about to get bombed. Hamas held the whole Gazan population as a human shield." —K., graduate student.

"The Israeli army allows supplies to come in and Hamas steals them. It seems even the Israelis care for us more than Hamas." —E., first-aid volunteer.

"We are under Hamas occupation, and if you ask most of us, we would rather be under Israeli occupation.... We miss the days when we were able to work inside Israel and make good money. We miss the security and calm Israel provided when it was here." —S., graduate of an American university, former Hamas sympathizer.[49]

As Netanyahu said, "Here's the difference between [Israel and Hamas]. We're using missile defense to protect our civilians, and they're using their civilians to protect their missiles."[50]

Look at the people Obama had lined himself up with. Over the side-issue of filling in well-established and long-existing Israeli settlements that aren't going anywhere no matter what anyone thinks, Obama gave extra ammunition to a gang of war criminals to win the public relations war against one of our closest allies.

With friends like Obama, Israel hardly needs enemies.

OBAMA PUNISHES ISRAEL

As the fighting in Gaza escalated, American officials constantly complained that Israel wasn't showing enough restraint in firing on civilian areas. Obama issued numerous statements urging Israel to agree to "immediate and unconditional" cease-fires. While acknowledging that it was "unacceptable" for Hamas to fire rockets at Israeli civilians, White House spokesman Josh Earnest told reporters that "Israel must take greater steps to meet its own standards for protecting civilians from being killed, and we'll continue to . . . send that message directly to the Israelis."[51]

The White House often plants stories in the media that Obama is seething about one thing or another, and this was one of those occasions. He was described as having become "enraged" at the Israeli government for its actions and treatment of Kerry. And Obama would take out his rage on Israel. In mid-August, it became public that the White House was now subjecting Israeli requests for ammunition shipments to more scrutiny than it had previously.[52] Weapons transfers had always been conducted through the respective governments' militaries. But Obama began making each shipment subject to review by the White House itself. This, according to the *Wall Street Journal*, had the effect of "slowing the approval process and signaling to Israel that military assistance once taken for granted is now under closer scrutiny."[53]

Weeks into the fighting, the U.S. Department of Transportation issued a warning to U.S. air passengers urging them to "consider the deferral of non-essential travel to Israel." The putative excuse was the barrage of Hamas rockets. One rocket had landed within a mile of Ben Gurion International Airport in Tel Aviv. But as Noah Pollak pointed out in the *Weekly Standard*, this was very interesting timing.

By the time the warning was issued, the greatest threat from the rockets had already passed. Pollak suggested, with some justification, that this was an attempt to pressure the Israeli government into signing on to a cease-fire:

> Israel earned over $10 billion last year from 3.5 million visitors, the plurality of whom were Americans. Coming at the height of summer tourism season, State's warning could cost Israel many millions of dollars in lost revenue....
>
> [The travel warning] could be a shot across the bow—a deniable but very real signal to Prime Minister Netanyahu that the Obama administration's support for Israel's operation in Gaza has come to an end, and that there will be consequences for its continuation. And at the same time the State Department was delivering a blow to the Israeli tourism industry, Kerry was showing solidarity with Gaza by announcing a $47 million aid package ... [54]

Meanwhile, most other countries' airlines continued their flights into Israel's airports. One Israeli business newspaper estimated the damage to Israel's economy from the U.S. travel warning at $200 million.[55] If it was even half that, it was significant. Again, with friends like these...

And just think—Obama, whose number one priority is to protect American citizens, would not institute a travel ban from West African countries affected by the deadly Ebola epidemic in 2014, but he banned flights to Israel based on one rocket that landed over a mile away from the tarmac.

KERRY'S SPACY CEASE-FIRE PROPOSAL

On July 15, just a few days into the fifty-day war, Hamas had rejected an Egyptian-Israeli cease-fire plan that would have ended the war early on and allowed Israel to destroy the tunnels Hamas had been using to attack civilians within Israel. Hamas refused the cease-fire—a break in hostilities to begin talks about demands—unless its full laundry-list of demands was met in advance. The terrorist group was most incensed that the temporary cease-fire agreement remained silent on the crucial issue of Israel's blockade of Gaza.

Obama dispatched Kerry to build on the Egyptian plan, but Kerry's initial proposals were rejected by both sides; in fact, neither Egypt nor Israel wanted Kerry to be involved in the process at all. As we will see in the next chapter, Obama and Clinton had already alienated our Egyptian allies as well. Kerry then began working on a cease-fire proposal with Hamas and two of its biggest state supporters, Turkey and Qatar, without consulting Israel, Egypt, or the Palestinian Authority.

On July 25, Kerry's office sent Netanyahu a confidential draft of his cease-fire proposal called "Framework for Humanitarian Cease-Fire in Gaza."[56] The draft wasn't meant to be presented to the Israeli cabinet, but Netanyahu's office leaked it to the press and presented it for a vote anyway. It was rejected unanimously.[57] Kerry was supposed to be brokering a peace involving a U.S. ally, and that ally rejected his draft proposal *unanimously*, across all Israeli political parties. Think about that for a moment. What would we say about a treaty that received zero votes in the U.S. Senate—not a single one from either party?

Michael Oren, former Israeli ambassador to the U.S., told the *Wall Street Journal* that Kerry's draft reflected an approach "completely out of sync with Israel, not just on a governmental level but on a societal level."[58] Oren continued, "The best thing that Kerry can do is stay out.... We need time to do the job, we need to inflict a painful and unequivocal blow on Hamas. Anything less would be a Hamas victory."[59] Anonymous Israeli government officials derisively referred to Kerry's negotiating initiative as a "strategic terrorist attack." He was described as having "dug a tunnel under the Egyptian ceasefire proposal."[60] One left-wing Israeli journalist said the proposal "raises serious questions over his judgment." Barak Ravid, a correspondent for *Haaretz*, a major left-wing Israeli publication, wrote, "It's as if he isn't the foreign minister of the world's most powerful nation but an alien who just disembarked his spaceship in the Middle East."[61] If nothing else, the reaction from Israelis demonstrates that Kerry was faithful to Obama's strategy of putting "daylight" between the U.S. and Israel. Deputy Likud leader Tzipi Hotovely said that with Kerry's cease-fire proposal, "Incredibly, America now seems to be serving only the interests of Hamas."[62]

And the Palestinian Authority was just as upset. A PA official told the newspaper *Asharq Al-Awsat* that "Kerry tried to sabotage the PA by ignoring the Egyptian cease fire plan that we [Palestinian Authority, but not Hamas] and Israel had already both accepted."[63] Kerry's plan, the PA official said, "repeatedly demonstrates a complete and fundamental misunderstanding of the Middle East.... [It was designed to] appease Hamas and its allies, Qatar and Turkey."[64]

Kerry's mishandling of the cease-fire negotiations marginalized America once and for all. He was a hamster running up a wheel trying to achieve some sort of accomplishment for his tenure. Israel, observing that it could no longer trust the Obama administration for anything, turned to Egypt, which, by that point was led by recently elected president Abdel Fattah al-Sisi, a former army general. As the *Wall Street Journal* put it, "[A]s Egyptian officials shuttle between representatives of Israel and Hamas seeking a long-term deal to end the fighting, U.S. officials are bystanders instead of in their historic role as mediators. The White House finds itself largely on the outside looking in."[65] In fact, when a final breakthrough was achieved on August 26, Kerry and the Americans were so marginalized that many American officials first heard about the cease-fire via social media rather than from the Israeli or Egyptian governments.[66]

Think of this new Egyptian-Israeli alliance, which leaves us out in the cold, as the one salutary outcome of Obama's total mishandling of the Middle East. Naturally, it was something that President Obama neither intended nor expected. But it is probably one of the only positive outcomes his administration has produced.

Perhaps Obama's insight from his college days—that America cannot control events in the Middle East—had become a self-fulfilling prophecy.

THE IRAN IMPASSE

During his first term, when Obama was still obsessing over Israeli housing construction, he seemed far less concerned with a much more serious threat to peace in the Middle East: Iran's nuclear program.

In fact, this would ultimately be the subject of the infamous conversation referred to above, in which a top Obama administration official called Netanyahu "a chickensh*t" and "a coward" in October 2014. As another anonymous administration official explained in the same *Atlantic* piece, the advantage of Netanyahu's cowardice was that it had enabled Obama to string Netanyahu along, persuading him not to take any military action against Iran's nuclear program until it was too late: "It's too late for him to do anything. Two, three years ago, this was a possibility. But ultimately he couldn't bring himself to pull the trigger. It was a combination of our pressure and his own unwillingness to do anything dramatic. Now it's too late."[67]

Obama had long been seeking a way to mend relations with what he calls the "Muslim world." He felt that a less combative relationship would benefit both the U.S. and Israel, and he had a point, at least in principle. As he told an Israeli television audience in 2010, "[T]he truth of the matter is, is that my outreach to the Muslim community is designed precisely to reduce the antagonism and the dangers posed by a hostile Muslim world to Israel and to the West."[68]

On March 20, 2009, Obama delivered a four-minute speech to the Iranian people and its government through Voice of America, the official external broadcast organ of the U.S. government. Calling for "engagement that is honest and grounded in mutual respect," Obama told Iranians that his administration was "committed to diplomacy that addresses the full range of issues before us" and that the process "will not be advanced by threats."[69] Obama also sent a private letter to Iran's Supreme Leader, Ali Khamenei, asking that the two countries restart a dialogue.

Apparently Obama believed that he would not be able to marshal international support for continuing economic sanctions against the Islamic Republic if he did not at least try diplomacy. Or as Hillary

Clinton put it to reporter David Sanger, the administration reached out "[n]ot because we thought it would necessarily work...but because we knew that without trying, we'd never get the allies to sign on to a much, much tougher approach."[70] That sounds like a reasonable policy in theory. But appeasing Iran's *mullahs* had some nasty side effects in practice. When millions of Iranian citizens began publicly protesting the reelection of President Mahmoud Ahmadinejad in June 2009, Obama was virtually silent. As the Iranian government brutally suppressed the protests, Obama ignored pleas for help from opposition groups. Obama's subdued response was noticed by the protestors, some of whom took to the streets of Tehran, chanting, in Persian, "Obama, Obama, you're either with them, or you're with us!"[71] Evidently, from the comfort of the White House, Obama saw the world in a much more nuanced light than those experiencing the evil within Iran did.

Later, Israel would watch with concern as Obama worked to conciliate Iran and restrain Israel from taking military action against its nuclear facilities. Relations between Israel and the U.S. became especially tense in July 2009, when Hillary Clinton said that the United States would consider extending a "defensive umbrella" over the Middle East if Iran developed a nuclear weapon.[72] Dan Meridor, Israel's minister of intelligence and atomic energy, told Sanger that the remark made it seem "as if [the Americans] have already come to terms with a nuclear Iran. I think that's a mistake."[73]

These comments by Hillary Clinton marked a huge shift in American national security and defensive posture—with potentially grave consequences should she be elected president. Her suggestion that somehow a defensive umbrella against a nuclear Iran would yield the same results as deterrence against the Soviet Union or North Korea shows an ignorance of the Middle Eastern mind. Further, allowing an Iranian bomb would escalate a nuclear arms race in the most volatile region of the world, with the Saudis, Turks, and potentially others creating their own nuclear arsenals.

The prospect of Iran building or obtaining the bomb worried Obama—after all, he had campaigned against nuclear proliferation in

2008. But Iran's nuclear program wasn't the same kind of existential threat to the U.S. as it was for the Israelis—or for the other regional players. I remember sitting with a very high-ranking general of the Supreme Council of the Armed Forces of Egypt in Cairo in 2013. I asked him if he thought the Iranian program was peaceful. He simply smiled at me and said, "Of course not, they are trying to get a bomb. We do not want a nuclear-armed Middle East."

Netanyahu could no longer be certain that Obama was serious about his stated intention to keep "all options on the table"—including a military strike—if Iran didn't stop trying to get the bomb. And so the stringing-along of Israel began. In 2013, Iran's new president Hassan Rouhani and Obama became the first Iranian and American presidents to speak by phone since 1979. In November 2013, the United States and five other world powers came to a temporary agreement with Iran over its nuclear program. Iran agreed to freeze its program for six months in exchange for an easing of economic sanctions, which had crippled the Iranian economy. Netanyahu called the interim deal "a historic mistake" because it didn't require Iran to dismantle its centrifuges.[74] These types of weak negotiations do damage to our status in the world—and are a dream come true for those who seek more opportunities to expand their power at our expense.

The interim agreement was supposed to provide time to reach a comprehensive agreement, but the deadline came and went without one. In July 2014, with Iranian negotiators giving little ground and Obama giving much more, the U.S. extended the deadline through late November 2014. In late November 2014, the U.S. extended the deadline another seven months.

When Hassan Rohani addressed the UN General Assembly in October 2014, he gave a positive assessment of the nuclear talks and said that he had "no doubt that the situation between the U.S. and Iran will be completely different" and that there were "many potential areas of cooperation in the future" if a deal could be struck.[75] But back in the real world, Iran was already cheating on its agreements—blocking American weapons inspectors from the International

Atomic Energy Agency and infusing uranium gas into state-of-the-art IR-5 centrifuges.[76]

And there are other signs that the U.S. may opt for a policy of containing a nuclear Iran rather than preventing it. In the fall of 2014, Colin Kahl was appointed as Vice President Joe Biden's national security advisor and to head up Iran policy. Before holding that position, Kahl had co-authored a report called, "If All Else Fails: The Challenges of Containing a Nuclear-Armed Iran." According to the *Weekly Standard*'s Lee Smith, this report was "widely regarded as a trial balloon to gauge public response to a policy, containment, that the administration claimed to oppose."[77]

As of the last extension—which the Iranians likely view as a nice way of getting seven additional months of loosened economic sanctions—the Iranian regime seems to be getting the better of Obama in nuclear negotiations. As former George W. Bush speechwriter David Frum wrote in October 2014, "On the present trajectory, any final agreement will leave Iran paused on the verge of nuclear-weapons capability—and this time, with the U.S. having signed away any non-military means of preventing Iran's final drive to complete a bomb."[78]

Why has Obama given so much ground on nuclear negotiations? Obama sees conciliation with Iran as key to a more balanced, and thus more peaceful, Middle East. He told the *New Yorker*'s David Remnick in early 2014—in the same interview in which he called ISIS the "jayvee" team, "Although it would not solve the entire problem, if we were able to get Iran to operate in a responsible fashion—not funding terrorist organizations, not trying to stir up sectarian discontent in other countries, and not developing a nuclear weapon—you could see an equilibrium developing between Sunni, or predominantly Sunni, Gulf states and Iran in which there's competition, perhaps suspicion, but not an active or proxy warfare."[79]

There is no question that the United States, from the time it assumed responsibility for general security in the Middle East up until the Iranian revolution, pursued a policy of balancing between the two regional powers, Saudi Arabia and Iran. But to accept a nuclear-armed

Iran would not only upset that balance—it would explode it. And to lift crippling sanctions and extend that abatement without getting fundamental concessions on the nuclear program is an amazing mistake.

Iran is currently flexing its muscles in other ways as well, taking advantage of American mistakes as it goes. In 2014, the Iranian-backed Houthi Rebels overthrew the government of Yemen, in Saudi Arabia's backyard. And despite Obama publicly stating that Bashar al-Assad of Syria must go some time ago, our president's policies have helped to ensure that the Iranian-backed Assad will stay in power long after Obama is gone.

Thanks to the work of Obama and Hillary Clinton, and Obama's politically minded, hasty withdrawal from Iraq, Iran now exerts more influence over Baghdad than the United States does—which is a damned shame, considering the blood and treasure lost there.

A surrender to the inevitability of a nuclear-armed Iran would solidify that theocratic regime as the regional hegemon in the Middle East.

Obama is in the process of trading away the allies we have—Israel and the friendlier Sunni nations such as Saudi Arabia—in exchange for unclear and probably illusory improvements in our relationship with a sworn enemy, Iran. If we didn't have an election in 2016 and an opportunity to reverse course completely, we would probably end up with no friends in the region at all.

CHAPTER SEVEN

Who Lost Egypt?

E gypt is the largest Arab nation. A quarter of all Arabic speakers live there. When people talk about opinion on the "Arab Street," they're probably talking about Egyptians.

And for decades Egypt has held a special place in American interests in the Middle East. The Egyptians help us with strategic negotiations. They give us over-flight of their airspace. They secure the Suez Canal and allow us head-of-the-line privileges there. They also recognize and keep peace with Israel.

That fact made Egypt's Arab Spring Revolution of 2011, as inspiring as it was, a very perilous moment for America—and a very important one for the region's future.

Egypt under Hosni Mubarak, who was deposed at the end of those protests, was no Jeffersonian democracy, to be sure. In fact it wasn't a real democracy at all. It was a brutal, repressive, and corrupt autocracy with only the thinnest veneer of elections and popular legitimacy.

But Mubarak was also a strategic ally and vital partner in America's fight against al Qaeda. As Mubarak frequently reminded visiting American diplomats, he was a lot easier to deal with than the alternative—Islamists who would turn the Arab world's most populous country into a breeding ground for terrorists. If he had to be replaced, America had to hope it would not be by someone significantly worse.

By the end of President Obama's sixth year in office, Mubarak was gone. And Egypt's relationship with the United States was badly damaged—perhaps irrevocably. Egypt was snubbing American diplomats and ignoring American foreign policy advice. The reason for the dramatic deterioration in our relations with Egypt? As street protests in 2011 threatened to topple Mubarak, the Obama administration's incoherent response alienated both the regime and its opponents.

The administration's subsequent support for the Muslim Brotherhood backfired when a second popular uprising ended its corrupt, incompetent, and mercifully brief reign—a fact that became profoundly clear to me when I was there in 2013 with the delegation of the Westminster Institute. I attended a meeting that included multiple senior Egyptian officials, culminating in a meeting with General Sisi himself.

With popular anti-American sentiment reaching an all-time high in Egypt, the United States has seen its influence dwindle as the new military-led government has forged closer relationships with other countries, including Russia and Israel. The Obama White House and the Clinton State Department risked reversing perhaps the most significant diplomatic coup in world history (the Camp David Accords) by flipping Egypt from our side to Russia's.

CONFUSION ON THE CRESCENT

Almost nobody anticipated the uprisings that swept through North Africa and the Middle East starting in December 2010. Sparked by a revolution in Tunisia that brought down the government of Zine El Abidine Ben Ali, what came to be known as the "Arab Spring" quickly spread to other countries, including Egypt in the following month.

When demonstrators in major cities across Egypt clashed violently with state police, the Obama administration initially stood by Mubarak, America's long-time ally. Secretary of State Hillary Clinton said, "Our assessment is that the Egyptian government is stable and is looking for ways to respond to the legitimate needs and interests of the Egyptian people."[1] When Press Secretary Robert Gibbs was asked whether the administration still backed Mubarak, he replied, "Egypt is a strong ally."[2]

But as the violence escalated, the Obama administration began sending mixed signals. When a reporter asked Gibbs whether Obama still supported Mubarak, Gibbs said, "This isn't a choice between the government and the people of Egypt."[3] Actually, it was—the Obama administration just didn't know it yet.

Gibbs also said that the administration was not "taking sides" in the uprising, although Obama did begin calling on the regime to make democratic reforms.[4]

Adding to the confusion, Vice President Joe Biden said that he "would not refer to [Mubarak] as a dictator."[5] Hillary Clinton also seemed to side with Mubarak. In 2009, she had told an Arab television audience that she considered him a "friend of my family."[6] After Mubarak announced that he would implement some democratic reforms, Clinton angered demonstrators by saying that the U.S. backed "the transition process announced by the Egyptian government."[7]

When Mubarak deployed troops to quell the protests, and protestors began to be killed, Gibbs suggested that the U.S. might reconsider the $1.5 billion in annual aid it sent Egypt if protestors were fired upon and if reforms were not implemented.[8] This contradicted what Hillary Clinton had said just two days earlier: "There is no discussion as of this time about cutting off any aid."[9]

One American official told the *New York Times* that the administration's haphazard response to the crisis was a result of its being completely caught off-guard by the uprising. "This is what happens when you get caught by surprise," he said. "We've had endless strategy sessions for the past two years on Mideast peace, on containing Iran.

And how many of them factored in the possibility that Egypt moves from stability to turmoil? None."[10]

Nearly two weeks into the increasingly violent protests, the administration was still sending mixed signals. On Clinton's advice, Obama deployed veteran diplomat Frank Wisner to Egypt to tell Mubarak that neither he nor his son should stand for the presidential election in September. Wisner delivered that message, but soon after leaving Egypt he told a security conference that Mubarak "remains utterly critical in the days ahead as we sort our way toward the future."[11] Wisner was fired and the State Department quickly disavowed his comment.

As Mubarak continued to dig in, Obama called on him to hand power to his vice president, Omar Suleiman. When Mubarak wouldn't commit to doing so, Obama delivered a live televised speech from the White House saying that an "orderly transition must be meaningful, it must be peaceful, and it must begin now."[12]

By this point, the administration's response had already upset nearly everyone involved. The Mubarak regime and its allies, including Israel, were upset that Obama was trying to push a long-time ally out the door—Mubarak had consistently supported the Egypt-Israel peace treaty and a two-state solution for the Israelis and Palestinians. The demonstrators were angry because Obama had stopped short of demanding that Mubarak resign. They felt that Obama had abandoned them. Protestors carried signs that said, "Shame on you Obama!"[13] The sentiments of ordinary Egyptians were summed up by Amin Iskander, an official of the opposition El Karama party, who told the *Los Angeles Times,* "[The Americans] are just waiting to see which side wins and then they will claim to have backed them all along."[14]

Mohamed ElBaradei, former head of the International Atomic Energy Agency and an Egyptian opposition leader, offered this message to Obama in an interview on CBS News, "You are losing credibility by the day. On one hand, you're talking about democracy, rule of law and human rights, and on the other hand, you're still lending your support to a dictator that continues to oppress his people."[15] (ElBaradei's comments would find a new application two years later—they were also a perfect description of Obama and Clinton's support of the Muslim Brotherhood before it was driven from power by another popular uprising.)

As Mubarak ratcheted up the violence against the protestors in the original 2011 Egyptian revolution, the White House was divided about how to proceed. The more idealistic advisors who had come up through the campaign, such as deputy national security advisor Ben Rhodes, wanted Obama to back the protestors. On the other side, Secretary of Defense Robert Gates and Secretary of State Clinton wanted Obama to continue to urge an "orderly transition" that involved Mubarak stepping down at election time in September. They feared that a hasty exit by Mubarak would leave a vacuum that would be filled by Islamists. (Though of course, when that happened later, Clinton's State Department would give its full support to the Islamists.)

According to Rhodes, Obama was "consistently the most forward leaning" in advocating for Mubarak's removal.[16] If this were actually true, it is puzzling why he was not so forward-leaning when similar protests broke out in Iran—where siding with the protestors would have aligned much better with American interests.

On February 11, 2011, after eighteen days of protests, Mubarak stepped down, handing authority to a council of military leaders. Most Egyptians were jubilant, but few gave any credit to Obama. As David F. Sanger recounted, "Obama's careful approach pleased no one. To Egyptians in Tahrir Square, it was wishy-washy. One activist I spoke with later balked at the notion that the US government had been supportive, and asserted, 'We got no solidarity with Obama.' To other leaders in the region, however, Obama's decision to pressure Mubarak at all was a sign of weakness, and perhaps a troubling indication that the president would willingly abandon a longtime ally."[17] The protestors felt Obama had played both sides for too long. As Lisa Anderson, president of the American University in Cairo, put it to Sanger, "Obama came too late here. He didn't get any points for dismissing Mubarak."[18]

At one point during the protests, an aide asked Obama what he thought would happen in Egypt. "What do I want to happen, or what do I think?" Obama replied, according to Sanger. "What I want is for the kids in the square to win and that Google guy to be president. What I think is we're going to be in for a long, protracted transition."[19]

But "that Google guy" (Wael Ghonim, the Google marketing executive who helped launch the protests) and the "kids in the square" didn't represent the only alternative to Mubarak. In fact, they weren't even the most likely alternative. After decades of dictatorship, Egypt didn't have a party system or strong institutions. The strongest group was the long-persecuted Muslim Brotherhood. They were already preparing to fill the post-Mubarak vacuum. Obama's statement showed a striking lack of understanding of the political and social situation in Egypt.

As Vali Nasr, former senior advisor to Ambassador Richard Holbrooke, explains in his book *The Dispensable Nation: American Foreign Policy in Retreat*, "America would have liked to see Egypt's Facebook generation—young, technologically savvy, and relatively liberal—inherit Egypt, but they had no organization to sustain their political drive or charismatic leader to guide them. In time, the Muslim Brotherhood (and the bevy of more radical voices to its right), with its much sharper and more numerous cadres, would make mincemeat of them. The administration could only hope that the Brotherhood would stay the course with democracy—that our enthusiasm for Mubarak to go would not come back to bite us."[20]

But come back to bite us it did.

THE BROTHERHOOD FILLS THE VOID

Eighteen days after the protests started, Hosni Mubarak's twenty-nine years in power ended. Egypt was ruled by the Supreme Council of the Armed Forces (SCAF) from February 2011 until late June 2012, when presidential elections took place.

The transition was chaotic not only for Egypt but also for its neighbors, particularly Israel. Egypt lost control of parts of its border with Israel, allowing Palestinian terrorists from Gaza to launch attacks on Israeli civilians via the Sinai Peninsula.

As Egypt prepared for parliamentary elections in the fall of 2011, the Obama administration made it clear that it expected the Islamist parties—not only the Muslim Brotherhood but also the more extreme Salafis—to be included. Obama said that elections should be held in a "just and inclusive manner."[21]

This had a very specific meaning; it was an implicit threat to the military. The administration called on the military to begin a "full transfer of power" to a civilian government. Martin S. Indyk, a former United States ambassador to Israel, told the *New York Times*, "What we're now doing is saying to the military that if you think you're going to maintain military power, we're not going to support that. We want you to play the role of midwife to democracy, not the role of military junta."[22] That might have been reasonable—if the viable alterative to the military hadn't been radical Muslims deeply hostile to the United States. The administration's antagonism toward the military would hurt American interests in Egypt.

Indyk seemed almost to admit that the administration was in danger of undermining American interests when he conceded that that strategy was "a high-risk one, because the ones who benefit most from it are the people who don't necessarily have our best interests in mind— the Islamists—who might not be as wedded to the peace treaty as the military. We are essentially coming down on the side of democracy."

This assumed that the Islamists would respect Egyptian democracy.

The administration was trying to have it both ways. As the *New York Times* reported, "The Obama administration appears now to be openly hedging its bets, trying to position the United States in such a way that regardless of who comes out on top—the army or the protesters—it will still maintain some credibility, and ability, to influence the government and ensure a level of stability in Egypt, and to continue to uphold the Egyptian-Israeli peace deal, which the United States views as central to stability in the region as a whole."[23]

But the policy backfired. The administration achieved the exact opposite of what it had intended to achieve by hedging its bets. It lost all credibility and influence with Egyptians. In parliamentary elections held from November 2011 to January 2012, the Muslim Brotherhood's

Freedom and Justice Party won a near-majority in the new lower house of the Egyptian legislature. The more puritanical Salafist Al Nour Party took another 25 percent of the vote.[24]

In the run-up to the elections, the Muslim Brotherhood had suggested that it might abandon the Egypt-Israel Peace Treaty.[25] Once in power, the new Islamist-dominated parliament issued a statement urging the government to cut diplomatic ties with Israel over its ongoing conflict with Hamas.

"Revolutionary Egypt will never be a friend or ally of the Zionist regime, which we consider the primary enemy of Egypt and its Arab people," the statement read. "[Egypt] will treat this entity as an enemy. The government is urged to reexamine its relations and agreements with this enemy."[26] It also encouraged the government to extend aid to the Palestinians and adopt "all forms of resistance" against Israel.[27] From the American point of view, this was backward progress.

Then came the real kicker. Three days before the presidential election in late June, Hillary Clinton signaled what many in Egypt saw as support for the Muslim Brotherhood's candidate, Mohamed Morsi. In a speech at the State Department, she said it was "imperative that the military fulfill its promise to the Egyptian people to turn power over to the legitimate winner." She also said that if a candidate from the military were to win, it would constitute "backtracking."[28] Clinton's apparently innocuous remarks were loaded with hidden meaning that any Egyptian could understand. As Army veteran and Egypt expert Spencer Case wrote, "The rub is that Morsi's competitor, Ahmed Shafiq, was a military man denounced by critics as a throwback to the Mubarak regime. Clinton's uttering of these words in the eleventh hour of the campaign—without any warning about the dangers of Islamist government—could only have undermined him."[29]

And not only did the U.S. Secretary of State publicly offer her support, but the U.S. Ambassador to Egypt, Anne Patterson, appeared in public with Morsi prior to the elections as well. This would become a sore point for Egyptians with a wide variety of political affiliations.

America was giving Morsi our blessing—and it's very puzzling that we did so.

THE BROTHERHOOD'S MISRULE

On June 24, 2012, Morsi became Egypt's new Islamist president. In his victory speech, Morsi promised several times to be "a president for all Egyptians."[30] The Obama administration hoped that the Muslim Brotherhood would govern not as Islamists intent on instituting Sharia law, but as pragmatists focused on fixing Egypt's ailing economy. This view, this hope, was both irresponsible and profoundly naïve. Where the original confusion can be excused because Mubarak's ouster was undoubtedly a difficult situation to handle, U.S. support for a Muslim Brotherhood candidate aligned with Salafists was an unforced error.

The administration engaged in significant outreach to the Brotherhood. It hosted a delegation of Brotherhood members at the White House to discuss political and economic issues. And Hillary Clinton was dispatched in July 2012 to try to convince skeptical Egyptians to accept the Brotherhood's rule. Several groups, including Coptic Christian activists, refused to meet with her.[31] Their apprehensions would later be vindicated.

The administration seemed to think that the Muslim Brotherhood was legitimate because it had been democratically elected. Obama didn't understand that the Brotherhood's totalitarian nature is incompatible with democracy. Once in power, it quickly moved to consolidate power, punish dissent, and establish a constitutional order that would make its removal nearly impossible. Clinton, who has traveled the world speaking out on women's rights, was in essence supporting a government that was certain to make them recede.

Morsi was elected democratically, winning approximately thirteen million votes and scoring just under 52 percent in his runoff. But as many have pointed out, elections alone do not necessarily guarantee democracy or a liberal society. There must also be checks and balances on power. By the time of his ouster, Morsi was ruling the country more like a dictator. He wasn't replacing Mubarak's regime—he was simply replacing Mubarak.

During his time in office, Morsi worked to intimidate the few independent media outlets that covered his country. He took important steps to undermine the independence of the judiciary (one plan involved lowering judges' retirement age so that they could all be replaced by his own hand-picked appointees) and consolidate power in his own office. In November 2012, he granted himself the power to "issue any decision or measure to protect the revolution," with the added note that "constitutional declarations, decisions and laws issued by the president are final and not subject to [judicial] appeal."[32] In order to further delegitimize the judiciary, he used rhetoric tying its members to the Mubarak regime.

The internationally respected Mohamed ElBaradei, former director general of the International Atomic Energy Agency, responded on Twitter by commenting that Morsi had "appointed himself Egypt's new pharaoh."

Morsi worked to cripple foreign non-governmental organizations, perceiving a threat in groups that tried to work for democracy and human rights.[33] He funneled money to Hamas, allowing it to re-arm with more sophisticated rockets with which to target Israeli citizens. In a low-turnout referendum boycotted by several important parties, he installed an Islamist constitution whose provisions were so repugnant to Egypt's ancient Christian community that its representatives had walked out during the drafting.

Under the Brotherhood's rule, Sinai—the huge area of desert land in Egypt's northeast that borders with Israel—was allowed to become even more lawless than usual. At the meeting I attended in Egypt in 2013 with the Westminster Institute, I heard then-General (now President) Sisi speak about weapons being smuggled from a destabilized Libya into Sinai as well. Sisi made it clear that Morsi and allies allowed or aided this activity and that it threatened Egyptian stability.

The result was numerous assaults on Israel and a constant flow of weapons and people to and from Gaza. The weapons used in the short 2014 war between Israel and Hamas are believed to have been transferred during this time.

Not only was the Muslim Brotherhood corrupt, it was also incompetent—and this was its real downfall. Egyptians are accustomed to corruption and dictatorship, but they expect results, and nothing had prepared them for rule by people so incapable. Morsi did almost nothing to address the economy, energy shortages, or soaring crime rates. According to one poll, after one year in office, only 13 percent of Egyptians said Morsi had improved living conditions in the country. Seventy-three percent believed he had not made a single good decision during his first year in office.[34]

By spring 2013, millions of Egyptians were ready for change—again. In April, disaffected Egyptians launched Tamarod, "a mirror for the street," a grassroots movement to collect signatures to call for an early election. By late June, twenty-two million signatures had been collected. In a meeting I had with the leaders of Tamarod on my trip to Egypt a few months later, they expressed their grievances with Obama and Clinton. They didn't understand how the U.S. could have backed the Brotherhood regime, both before and after the elections. The policies being forced on them, they protested, were the antithesis of American values. Tamarod spokesperson Mohamed Nabawy stated that Clinton's State Department was supporting the Brotherhood, Obama was generating Egyptian hate, and Egyptians viewed the administration as weak.

On June 30, the first anniversary of the start of Morsi's term, fourteen to thirty million protesters demonstrated across Egypt against the Muslim Brotherhood's rule. It was an immense demonstration, possibly the largest in world history and certainly much larger than the one that had predated Mubarak's ouster. The following day, one million demonstrators appeared in Cairo's Tahrir Square demanding early elections.

The Egyptian military quickly sided with the protestors. On July 3, despite vague warnings and threats from the Obama administration, a coalition led by Egyptian army chief General Abdel Fattah al-Sisi suspended the constitution and arrested Morsi, later placing him under house arrest.

Adly Mansour, head of the Supreme Constitutional Court, became acting president. As I sat with Sisi and others on the Westminster Institute delegation in September 2013, he explained the "coup" or "non-coup" that he had just helped happen. "In Egypt, the military is the protector of the state and has been for a very long time," he said:

Morsi's decree placing him above the constitution and judges started a second revolution. The Muslim Brotherhood militias were becoming violent with the protestors. I wanted Morsi to be successful. He appointed me to Minister of Defense. I personally called him during this time and asked him to let opposition re-enter into government or hold early elections. The military would not allow Egypt to descend into civil war. He refused.

I then went on state media and told the Egyptian people if they wanted the army to step in they would have to come to the streets in a sign to do so. This is when there were approximately thirty million Egyptians across the country that did so.

Sisi offered his definition of a "coup": "A coup is if we came in the middle of the night, killed or jailed a leader, then took power. That is not what happened. We stopped a civil war and we handed over power to civilians."

A practicing Muslim himself, Sisi echoed every other group we had met with: "we must not allow political Islam." He went on to explain the timeline of events that would follow—a new constitution, elections for parliament, then a presidential election. The constitutional committee would be inclusive, even having Salafists on it. There would be protections for minority religious groups and for women. Egypt would move towards democracy. Then Sisi said something that I will never forget: "If you look at Egypt from the lens of American democracy, you are not being fair. We are two hundred years behind you."

OBAMA AND CLINTON SIDE WITH THE BROTHERHOOD

During the street protests against Morsi, the Obama administration had made its position worse by subtly signaling its support for the deeply unpopular president and his Islamist party.

U.S. ambassador to Egypt Anne Patterson delivered a speech urging against "street action" and tried to discourage Egyptian groups from participating in the protests.[35] As Marc Thiessen observed in the *Washington Post*, this was the second time the administration had opposed the popular will of the Egyptian people: "Once again, Tahrir Square was awash in anti-U.S. signs: 'Obama and Patterson support terrorism' read one. Another said: 'Wake Up America, Obama Backs Up a Fascist Regime in Egypt.' Another showed Patterson shaking hands with the leader of the Muslim Brotherhood with the caption: 'We know what you did last summer.' In other words, Obama had blown it a second time."[36]

The Obama administration was still at least coy enough not to label Morsi's ouster a "coup," which would have required a cutoff of U.S. foreign aid. Obama was trying to perform a delicate balancing act once again. Once again, it wouldn't work.

The new interim government banned the Muslim Brotherhood and arrested thousands of its members, many of whom were given death sentences. More than one thousand people were killed during the crackdown on the Islamists—more than eight hundred in one incident.[37] For their part, supporters of Morsi began attacking and terrorizing Coptic Christian communities all over Egypt.[38]

I remember the expression on Egypt's Coptic Christian pope's face very vividly, as we sat in a fourth century monastary in the middle of the desert during my visit to Egypt with the Westminster Delegation. "If we Christians have to sacrifice for the good of Egypt we will," the Coptic pope declared. I could almost feel his pain; chills ran down my spine. He continued, "Attacks are the price of freedom in Egypt, the price of love." He said he had noticed a change in the administration, that he saw the U.S. as a Christian nation, and questioned why the administration supported the Muslim Brotherhood, only three quarters of one percent of the population; they had left the Egyptian people behind. His words were powerful.

Obama, on the other hand, was powerless to influence the unfolding violence because he had burned all his bridges at this point. His administration urged Sisi to reconcile with the Brotherhood. Sisi ignored him. Obama demanded that the new government not arrest Morsi; and after Morsi's arrest, that it release him. The military didn't listen. The administration encouraged the new government to be inclusive of Islamist parties and members. Aside from allowing Salafists to be included in the forming of the new constitution, it outlawed Islamist parties and arrested or killed thousands of their members.

The military also installed a curfew in Cairo, which my delegation was under whilst there. What was incredible was that most people simply accepted the curfew. The economy in Egypt had been devastated, and people just wanted order and security back. It was another example of how different cultural values can be—Americans would never tolerate such a situation.

As an article in the *New York Times* explained, the administration's efforts were fruitless: "All of the efforts of the United States government, all the cajoling, the veiled threats, the high-level envoys from Washington and the 17 personal phone calls by Defense Secretary Chuck Hagel, failed to forestall the worst political bloodletting in modern Egyptian history."[39]

By seeming to side with the Muslim Brotherhood, the United States had lost most of its influence with the new regime and a majority of the Egyptian public. "America is losing Egypt," Dr. Mohamed Abou El-Ghar, leader of the Egyptian Social Democratic Party, said in a meeting with western journalists in August 2013. "There is a very strong perception that they are supporting the Muslim Brotherhood and they are against other parties."[40]

The administration denied the allegation. Secretary of State John Kerry said, "We firmly reject the unfounded and false claims by some in Egypt that the United States supports the Egyptian Muslim Brotherhood or any specific Egyptian political party or movement."[41]

But it was hard for Egyptians to reach any other conclusion given the administration's actions toward the new government and its public appearances of support for the Brotherhood prior to the elections. Kerry's words fell short, mainly because of the actions of his predecessor, Hillary Clinton, and, of course, of Ambassador Patterson.

In October 2013, Obama cut hundreds of thousands of dollars in military aid to Cairo, a symbolic gesture that many Egyptians considered retaliation for the military's crackdown on the Muslim Brotherhood.[42] Washington blocked a scheduled delivery of four F-16 Block 52 fighters, cut off sales of some military equipment, and cancelled a joint military operation with Egypt. In March 2014, the Obama administration rejected an appeal by Egypt for helicopters it needed for counterterrorism operations in Sinai. U.S. officials said this was in response to the military's ousting of Morsi.[43]

All of this convinced the new government and many Egyptian citizens that Obama was intent on subverting their second revolution. "You left the Egyptians, you turned your back on the Egyptians and they won't forget that," Sisi said about the United States. "Now you want to continue turning your backs on Egyptians?"[44]

It is hard to overstate the depth and breadth of anti-American sentiment that Obama's actions have engendered in Egypt today. In a complaint submitted to the International Criminal Court by a group of Egyptian lawyers, Obama was even accused of crimes against humanity for his perceived support of the Muslim Brotherhood.[45]

Egyptian conspiracy theorists make New World Order believers seem quite harmless. For example, one common belief among the population is that U.S Ambassador to Egypt Anne Patterson directed snipers affiliated with the Muslim Brotherhood to murder Egyptian soldiers.[46] The pro-regime media have smeared Obama as mentally unfit, labeled his late mother a prostitute, and called his administration the "Adolf Obama Reich." An article in an Egyptian newspaper even included a prayer that Obama die in agony.[47] Clearly, this is not something I'm cool with. He is my president. But this is where America's leadership stands in the popular Egyptian mind. It's Obama's fault that it's come out this way, and that result is undermining American interests.

As Marc Lynch wrote in *Foreign Policy* magazine in July 2013, "Even longtime observers of Egyptian rhetoric have been taken aback by the vitriol and sheer lunacy of the current wave of anti-American rhetoric. The streets have been filled with fliers, banners, posters, and graffiti denouncing President Barack Obama for supporting terrorism and featuring Photo-shopped images of Obama with a Muslim-y beard or bearing Muslim Brotherhood colors."[48]

Why would the Sisi regime risk losing American support (financial and otherwise) by brazenly defying the Obama's administration's wishes in their banning of the Muslim Brotherhood as a political party?

Put simply, Egypt no longer needs the U.S. as much as the U.S. needs Egypt. That's a possibility that Obama apparently never considered. When the United States refused to label the removal of Morsi a "coup," which would have forced it to cancel aid to Egypt, the new regime realized that it could defy the U.S. with impunity. "That taught the Egyptian military that we need them more than they need us and that we will not even enforce our own law," said Elliott Abrams, a deputy national security advisor under President George W. Bush.[49]

Stephen McInerney, executive director of the Project on Middle East Democracy, told the Daily Beast's Josh Rogin in August 2013 that the administration was "too deferential to the Morsi government and also to the Egyptian military and failed to build constructive relationships with all sorts of other actors inside Egypt. And now they are desperately clinging to their relationship with the military, which is hanging by a thread, because they don't have any other allies."[50]

BYE, BYE, AMERICA

With its relationship with the United States in tatters, Egypt began bolstering ties with its oil-rich allies. Saudi Arabia, the United Arab Emirates, and Kuwait together provided the military regime some $13 billion in the first two months after its takeover.[51]

Russia has also stepped up. In late 2013, Egypt agreed to buy $2 billion worth of military equipment from Russia.[52] They used to buy this stuff from us.

More deals may be in the works. Speaking in Washington, D.C., in August 2014, Egyptian Foreign Minister Nabil Fahmy said that while his country values its relationship with the U.S., it also has "an emerging relationship with Russia [that] we will seek to nurture and leverage."[53] He was quite open in stating that confidence in the Obama administration among Egyptians had "eroded" after aid was cut.[54]

"This news doesn't really come as a surprise," Anna Borshchevskaya, a fellow at the European Foundation for Democracy, told the *Washington Free Beacon* about Egypt's turn towards Russia. "When we cut off aid to Egypt, we lost leverage over Egyptian military, and others were more than happy to fill the void."[55] Although I want to see foreign aid revamped, as I'll discuss later, U.S. aid to Egypt has a strategic purpose. Its value far exceeds the cost of the investment.

Residents of Alexandria, Egypt's second-largest city, are well aware of how the balance of influence has changed. Billboards have been erected across the city showing an image of Russian President Vladimir Putin with the caption, "Bye Bye America."[56]

EGYPT AND ISRAEL

Anti-Israel sentiment runs high in Egypt, and when Egypt had helped broker Israeli-Palestinian peace agreements in the past, it had usually been seen as working on behalf of the Palestinians. Sisi himself expressed the need to resolve inadequate living conditions of Palestinians in our meeting.

But by instituting a variety of security measures—from cracking down on the Islamists and outlawing Hamas to destroying hundreds of Hamas's tunnels running from Sinai to Gaza—Sisi gradually convinced the Israelis that he was someone they could work with. The days of Morsi helping arm the terrorists who threaten Israel had ended. The Egyptian military also largely shut down the Rafah crossing, the only border crossing in and out of Gaza that Israel does not control. The Egyptian and Israeli governments began strengthening their ties, and the two countries soon began to increase their security cooperation.[57]

During our meeting with Sisi, I was surprised and happy to hear of Egypt's cooperation with Israel. Sisi explained that the weapons coming in from Libya, the Hamas tunnels, and the rise in militants posed a threat to both Israel and Egypt. Egypt would go to the Israelis to ask for cooperation, he said, and the Israelis would offer coordination, intelligence, money, or arms. The Egyptians, careful of public perception, nonetheless negotiated and received the blessing of Israel to put their troops in the Sinai (despite a treaty between the two countries keeping it military-free) to root out the tunnels and stop the arms smuggling. Representatives of the two countries met on intelligence matters weekly.

This coordination and friendship is exactly what we as Americans want to transpire. It is exactly the opposite of what was transpiring under the leadership of Morsi. And it's somewhat ironic that this cooperation is happening now, only in our absence, and that it has happened in part because the leaders of both countries are so fed up with Obama's meddling in their affairs.

By the time of Israel's war with Hamas in the summer of 2014, relations between Egypt and the United States were so strained that when U.S. Secretary of State John Kerry visited Cairo to discuss a cease-fire, Sisi forced him to walk through a metal detector—an indignity that was well-calculated. The *International Business Times* noted that foreign governments "normally trust U.S. officials enough not to check them with such stringent security measures" and that when the courtesy is not extended, it could be "viewed [as] a sign of distrust."[58]

With Kerry almost a *persona non grata* in Israel, Sisi and Egypt were more than happy to reinforce Egypt's alliance with Israel and shut us out of regional affairs. Actually, several Arab governments secretly sided with Israel during that war—including Saudi Arabia, Jordan, and the United Arab Emirates. They all want to destroy Hamas. But Egypt was by far the most important and the most vocal ally of Israel in the conflict.

Egyptian and Israeli intelligence and security officials spoke at least daily during the war. Israel wanted to make sure that Sisi was comfortable with how it was conducting the operation.[59] "We knew we could not do something that went beyond what they could digest," a senior Israeli official told the *Wall Street Journal* about the Egyptians. Israeli officials said Egypt's perspective mattered more to them than America's, which says a lot.[60]

Egypt also stepped up to play a crucial role in mediating the cease-fire. Meanwhile, the United States's role in negotiations was proving so toxic that Egypt and Israel rejected America's requests even to be involved.[61] In fact, both Israeli and Egyptian diplomats argued that Egypt's initial attempt to produce a cease-fire had collapsed mostly because Kerry's involvement had motivated Hamas to hold out for something better.[62]

When a cease-fire finally did take hold, it was Egypt, not the United States, that engineered it. "A previously closed door had been strategically opened," Israeli deputy minister of defense Danny Danon wrote after the war about Egypt's welcome help in leading cease-fire proposals. "The fact that Egypt was willing to play such a constructive role is an exceptionally encouraging sign for Israel."[63]

Foreign policy scholar Aaron David Miller gave Egypt high marks for brokering the cease-fire. From an American standpoint, it was an extremely encouraging development, despite our current administration's views. "Egypt's new government under President Abdel Fattah al-Sisi actually comes out of this round faring better than anyone else," Miller wrote in August 2014.[64] Egypt's main goal was to damage Hamas and, despite Kerry's efforts, keep Turkey and Qatar on the sidelines. And it did just that. Kerry had been desperately trying to keep Turkey (whose current regime is very sympathetic toward the Muslim Brotherhood) and Qatar involved.

What's more, Egypt solidified an alliance with Israel that continues to flourish. In August 2014, the two countries negotiated deals that will send $60 billion worth of Israeli natural gas to Egypt.[65] Now, you might consider this a happy ending, depending on your view of the region. Two nations that were at war with one another last century now seem closer to one another than either one is to us.

But it isn't a happy ending for America when a U.S. president steps in and destroys American prestige with two key allies in the world's most volatile region. This is precisely what Obama did. He placed ideological considerations from his college days ahead of smart dealings with Israel. Clinton's State Department publicly supported a group who would seek to reduce women's rights and religious minority rights and manipulate democracy in order to take it away. The President bungled his way through our diplomacy with Egypt, clumsily attempting to hedge his bets and siding with an Islamist government that had no common cause with American interests. As a result, where the U.S. government was unwilling to stand up for or promote U.S. interests in the region, two other countries excluded us and advanced and promoted (as it happens) our interests themselves.

This is a devastating commentary on Obama's tenure. America has an enormous national interest in keeping stability in the Middle East. This is why the United States has always been viewed as a key player in bringing about peace there. It is why American negotiators have been involved in so many peace deals.

But the U.S. can have no role in brokering an Israeli-Palestinian peace process if both Israel and Egypt view us as part of the problem. Unfortunately, thanks to Obama's passive-aggressive behavior toward Israel and his incompetent, at times desperate handling of Egypt, that's where we are now.

American leaders who look out for American interests are much easier for friendly governments to deal with, because they're predictable. Obama is not, and it will probably take a new U.S. president to begin to restore ties with both Egypt and Israel.

CHAPTER EIGHT

The Current Mess— and Solutions Moving Forward

I n this book we have examined how the Obama White House has leaked sensitive information and implemented questionable national security and foreign policies. At some critical moments—as with Benghazi and the withdrawal from Iraq—national interests were irresponsibly and dangerously sacrificed to serve short-term political goals, perhaps more so than at any other time in our nation's history. At others—such as with our original "light footprint" intervention in Libya, our failure to help Iran's resistance, and the mixed messages we have sent to the Egyptians—those interests were apparently sacrificed for other reasons: to fit the ideologies of academic theorists, out of President Obama's general aversion to foreign affairs, or—as with our rapidly deteriorating relationship with Israel—based on Obama's personal feelings dating back to his college days.

We have also looked at several immediate or potential hazards that Obama's fecklessness has helped create or aggravate—including the ascendancy of ISIS, the aggression of Vladimir Putin, the collapse of the Libyan state, and the deterioration of America's relationship with traditional allies such as Egypt and Israel.

No one can say for sure how long this damage and these threats will persist in their current forms. Perhaps Libya will mend—although more likely it will be taken over by a new Islamist government. Perhaps ISIS's small empire will self-destruct—or perhaps it will fall prey to Iran's ambitions, or, on its current trajectory, survive our bombardment and end up with its own seat at the United Nations.

These threats are quite unpredictable. What we can predict is that America's most important geopolitical foes of this decade—Russia, always powerful and ambitious, and Iran, an aspiring nuclear power and regional hegemon—will be around and threatening us for many, many years to come, no matter what else happens. And, unfortunately, Obama's foreign policy blunders and Hillary Clinton's mismanagement of our diplomatic apparatus have ensured that we'll start from a position of weakness in addressing those threats. In the game of world politics and diplomacy this is a dangerous position to be in—our weakness and lack of leadership could eventually affect the American way of life. It is imperative that our next leader not only understands the way the world really works but also is committed to putting us back on the right course. He or she must be able to look world leaders in the eyes with the confidence and belief that our way of life, ideals, and country are exceptional.

Hillary Clinton's comments that we should "empathize" with our enemies suggest someone not really up to the job of the presidency. The apology tour around the world for the last six years has clearly failed. Respect is earned. Any "empathizing" the U.S. does should be about understanding the true intentions of our "enemies," not making excuses for them—and certainly not accommodating them in their desire to impose their values on us, as when the Obama administration and the Clinton State Department "empathized" with Muslims' anger at "blasphemy" against Mohammed instead of standing up for the First Amendment. The next president must be someone who has the rock-solid conviction that America, despite its flaws, is great.

PUTIN'S SYRIAN SWINDLE

The story of Obama's relationship with Russia is still unfolding as I write these words. The terrible, tragic ending that many people fear could still come about. The funny part is, Obama had ample warning of Russia's bad intentions from its behavior late in the Bush years. Critics have said that Bush misjudged Vladimir Putin, and they're right. But Putin's intentions were much clearer by 2009 than they were in 2001 or 2006, and now we've misjudged him again, without learning from what happened before.

Ignoring all the obvious warning signs, Obama bent over backwards to accommodate the Russians throughout his first term—and is now being rewarded with a kick straight in his backside from the shirtless Russian bear.

Many people like to begin the story of Russo-American relations in the Obama era with a famous gaffe that occurred near the beginning of Obama's presidency. It's not the most important incident, but it deserves a brief mention. Secretary of State Hillary Clinton met with her Russian counterpart, Foreign Minister Sergey Lavrov, in March 2009 and presented him with a big red "reset" button that had been plundered from a hot tub.[1] It sounds amusing now, but the idea at the time was that she and Obama would "reset" America's relationship with Russia, which President Bush had supposedly allowed to deteriorate.

As a telling aside, the State Department staff who set the gimmick up apparently were not proficient in Russian—the word on the button, "*peregruzka*," translated not to "reset" but to "overcharge" or "overload"—a concept that some might say has proven a more fitting characterization of our relations with the Russians during Obama's presidency.

America's relationship with Russia has been frosty for decades. The only time we've seen it melt a little was when we had a powerful leader in the White House containing Russian ambitions. Otherwise, a Russian nationalist like Putin will push as far as he can go. A President Obama and an aspiring president Hillary Clinton as head diplomat was the realist Putin's dream combo.

This became most evident in Syria, which is a far more illustrative example than the "reset" incident in explaining U.S.-Russian relations in the Obama era. It might sound unrelated at first, but bear with me for a few paragraphs.

Syria's civil war has caused untold human misery. It has given birth to ISIS. Western Syria is now a major source of revenue for the new caliphate, and a base of operations for the Islamic State's attempt to force the collapse of Iraq.

In late summer 2012, when ISIS was still just another warring militia and American intervention in Syria's civil war might have accomplished something, President Obama was not interested in getting involved. In his defense, neither were most Americans.

Even so, he drew a "red line," as he put it—or a "line in the sand," as those familiar with Syria's history might.[2] He said that he was not considering military intervention or large-scale military aid to the opposition at that point, but that that could change: "We have been very clear to the Assad regime, but also to other players on the ground, that a red line for us is we start seeing a whole bunch of chemical weapons moving around or being utilized. That would change my calculus. That would change my equation."[3]

As it turned out, Obama's staff was floored by his comment. Apparently, this "red line" talk was genuinely off-the-cuff—something they had not planned on at all, and not a part of Obama administration policy up to that date.[4] It was a pure, unscripted Obama gut reaction. And as such, it would prove to be an idle threat that would undermine American credibility vis-à-vis Syrian dictator Bashar al-Assad.

On August 21, 2013—almost exactly a year after Obama's "red line" comments—Assad crossed Obama's red line. Assad's army used chemical weapons against rebels and civilians in Ghouta, a suburb of Damascus.

According to the United Nations report on the matter, there was "clear and convincing evidence that surface-to-surface rockets containing the nerve agent sarin were used in Ein Tarma, Moadmiyah, and Zamalka in the Ghouta area of Damascus."[5] Horrific images and videos of victims desperately gasping for breath as they struggled to survive the nerve agent made their way onto the internet.

But of course Obama did not act on his "red line" threat. Whatever you feel about America playing any role in the civil war in Syria, most Americans would agree that if our president, ostensibly the most powerful man in the world, draws a line in the sand, he should back it up—or that he should not draw such lines in the first place. By late summer 2013, when the chemical weapons were used in Ghouta, the radical Islamic fighters in Syria—those affiliated with ISIS and al Qaeda—were clearly the most powerful force among the anti-Assad rebels. Many Americans were justifiably concerned that any intervention against Assad would only make matters worse, helping jihadists who might be at least as dangerous to American national interests as Assad himself. (Their concerns would be vindicated when ISIS marched into Iraq months later.)

No one was terribly impressed by the arguments set forth by Obama and Secretary of State John Kerry in favor of "unbelievably small" (Kerry's infelicitous description) air strikes against Assad.[6] Probably the least impressed of all was Assad himself.

The planned intervention was unpopular enough in the U.S. that President Obama abandoned it, but only after the Arab League and the Parliament of the United Kingdom had rejected it as well.

Empty threats are no way to conduct foreign policy. Obama was flailing as he continued to threaten some kind of attack. In diplomacy, when someone is cornered this way, the easy way out is for someone smarter and more levelheaded to give him a way to save face. Lo and behold, Russian President Vladimir Putin found a way to ride to Obama's rescue—and to Assad's. The incident was a great example of how wily Putin really is, and how weak Obama is.

Putin brilliantly exploited the incompetence of the Obama administration, saved the Syrian dictator from any consequences for his actions, and let Obama come away claiming a foreign policy victory. Putin's intervention allowed the Russian president to play the role of global statesman, even as he hatched plans for aggression against Eastern Europe.

The episode began with another careless remark from the Obama administration—this one from Secretary of State Kerry. Asked whether there was anything Assad could do to avoid war, he told reporters:

"Sure, he could turn over every single bit of his chemical weapons to the international community in the next week—turn it over, all of it without delay and allow the full and total accounting (of it), but he isn't about to do it and it can't be done."[7]

Almost immediately, Sergey Lavrov, the Russian foreign minister, offered to broker just such a deal. And Assad announced that he would agree to it in principle. In less than a week it was done—Kerry had blundered his way into peace while trying to start an "unbelievably small" war. After his comments, and with the Russian government and Assad offering to cooperate, what choice did he have but to accept the deal? (If Assad is still alive and in power by the time you read this, he owes John Kerry a case of beer.)

We know that Kerry did not mean to do what he did because the State Department at first tried to walk back his comments, issuing a statement claiming it was merely a "rhetorical argument about the impossibility and unlikelihood of Assad turning over chemical weapons he has denied he used.... [Secretary of State Kerry's] point was that this brutal dictator with a history of playing fast and loose with the facts cannot be trusted to turn over chemical weapons, otherwise he would have done so long ago. That's why the world faces this moment."[8]

This clarification only made Kerry look even more foolish a few days later when he accepted the framework for a deal with Assad. Kerry was trusting Assad to deliver on precisely what he had said "can't be done"; he was "trusting" this "brutal dictator" who "cannot be trusted to turn over chemical weapons."

This deal unquestionably damaged the United States' interests, undoubtedly to Putin's great delight. The U.S. had been hostile toward Assad (when President Obama drew his "red line" against the use of chemical weapons), then effectively neutral (with Obama's failure to follow through after Assad was caught using them). Now we were actively legitimizing Assad's government and trusting him to dispose of chemical weapons—right after pointing out the obvious fact that he couldn't be trusted. And we were allowing Russia's Putin to play the role of peace-making deal-broker.

Obama, and thus the United States, looked ridiculous. Within a space of days he had gone from wanting to bomb Assad to forming a tacit alliance with him.

But at least the chemical weapons were destroyed, right? Wrong. In a turn of events that should have surprised absolutely no one, Assad didn't honor the deal. In summer 2014, the UN and the Organization for the Prohibition of Chemical Weapons reported that Assad's army was still using chlorine gas "systematically and repeatedly." A full year after the deal, as our Russian "partner" in negotiating it was busy stomping his boots on Ukrainian soil, it was discovered that Assad had also failed to disclose four chemical weapons sites—and who could say for sure there weren't more?[9]

By then, there was no reasonable way to hold Assad accountable. No, we had basically ensured his legitimacy, much to the chagrin of our NATO ally Turkey, which wants Assad gone. Assad had had time to decimate the Free Syrian Army (the main non-jihadist opposition to his government), a relatively palatable option for Syria from an American point of view. The Obama administration was now at war with ISIS (the main jihadist opposition to Assad)—not to mention watching Libya collapse in Africa and trying to fight off a Russian invasion of Ukraine with Twitter hashtags (#UnitedForUkraine!) and toothless economic sanctions that applied only to Putin's inner circle.

Putin's smooth swindle in Syria illustrates much of what is wrong with Obama's foreign policy. Lacking clear goals and leadership, but overflowing with noble-sounding sentiments and idle threats, Kerry and Obama walked right into the trap set by a smarter leader. Putin understands that reality reigns over rhetoric in international relations. I hope the next American president understands that too.

GEOPOLITICAL FOE

At one point during the 2012 election, Republican nominee Mitt Romney called Russia America's "number one geopolitical foe."[10]

Obama mocked him for this in a debate, delivering this zinger: "The 1980s are now calling to ask for their foreign policy back."

Perhaps Obama didn't realize that the 1980s culture is still popular in parts of Russia. In case you wonder what denial looks like, Obama still would not admit two years later that Romney had been right—not even as Putin was annexing Crimea and seizing control of other large parts of eastern Ukraine.[11]

And it's not just that Romney has been proven right in that single statement. It's equally important to go back and look at the full context of Romney's remarks, because he said much more. It was March 2012, and President Obama had just been caught on a live mic reassuring then–Russian President Dmitry Medvedev (widely perceived as Putin's puppet), apparently in the course of promising some kind of nuclear arms concession to the Russians. "After my election," he said, "I have more flexibility."

Romney's reaction to this would be prophetic as far as Syria goes. But people only started to realize it when Putin invaded Ukraine. Romney began his remarks on Russia, in a March 26, 2012 interview, by cataloging every Obama sell-out to the Russians up to that date, pointing out that at nearly every step since the "reset" Obama had been placing dangerous and unwise levels of trust in Putin.

Romney noted that "Russia continues to support Syria. It supports Iran, has fought us [over] the crippling sanctions we wanted to have the world put in place against Iran." Romney also brought up a few important and well-known concessions Obama had made to Russia during his first term.

Chief among them was the New START (Strategic Arms Reduction Treaty) Treaty. Its predecessor, called START I, had been signed by President George H. W. Bush and Russian President Mikhail Gorbachev in 1991. It limited the number of nuclear warheads and other missiles the signatories could deploy. START I expired in December 2009, which is when Obama picked up the ball. After much negotiation, in April 2010, Obama and Medvedev signed the New START Treaty, which cut their countries' respective strategic nuclear missile launchers by half and established a new inspection and verification regime.

After signing the treaty, Obama delivered some remarks that seemed over the top then and are downright embarrassing now. Declaring that the agreement marked a "milestone for U.S.-Russia relations," Obama said, "Together, we have stopped the drift [between the two countries], and proven the benefits of cooperation. . . . This day demonstrates the determination of the United States and Russia—the two nations that hold over 90 percent of the world's nuclear weapons—to pursue responsible global leadership."

Actually, that day demonstrated how impatient Obama was to strike a deal—so desperate that in his impatience some experts felt he was bamboozled. This, clearly, has become a dangerous pattern of putting a political win over what is best for the country. Former CIA chief and START I advisor James Woolsey wrote that in his eagerness to sign a deal Obama "agreed to a treaty that limits our nonnuclear long-range weapons and runs the risk of constraining our missile defenses."[12] Hillary Clinton's reset button and Obama's inked nuclear deal are both symbolic of the desire of two individuals to get a short-term win and appear as if they were doing something good for the American people, all the while undermining our standing in the world and our national security.

Russia only agreed to New START on the condition that Obama nix plans for missile defense installations in Eastern Europe. Obama had complied with this in September 2009—another item Romney brought up.[13] The missile defense system was not designed to prevent Russian attacks on the U.S. (which would go over the North Pole instead) but potential Iranian missile attacks on Europe.

Obama backed down, faced with Russian objections to our encroachment on what Putin and Medvedev still consider their sphere of influence—or even part of their territory. Our president's willingness to accommodate a calculating Putin this way probably played a part in what followed five years later, in the Ukraine crisis.

Giving up proposed missile defense sites harmed U.S. relations with very staunch American allies Poland and the Czech Republic—

two nations that still remember what it's like to be under Russia's thumb.

And as the crisis in the Ukraine unfolded in summer 2014, Polish Foreign Minister Radosław Sikorski called the U.S.-Poland relationship "worthless" because Obama was conceding too much to Russia. He expressed fear that Poles had acquired a false sense of security against Russian threats because of their ties to an America that probably wouldn't deliver when the chips were down.[14]

Romney's March 2012 remarks included this broader characterization of Russia: "Russia is not a friendly character on the world stage. And for this president to be looking for greater flexibility, where he doesn't have to answer to the American people in his relations with Russia, is very, very troubling.... They fight every cause for the world's worst actors.... in terms of a geopolitical foe, a nation that's on the [United Nations] Security Council, that has the heft of the Security Council and is, of course, a massive nuclear power, Russia is the geopolitical foe and the idea that our president is planning on doing something with them that he's not willing to tell the American people before the election is something I find very, very alarming."

Eighteen months after Romney made his comments—including the line about Russia's continued support for Syria—Putin would outwit Obama over Syria. Six months after that, he would invade and annex Crimea and infiltrate Ukraine with militias that seized control of several major cities. Putin's men—pro-Russian Ukrainian militia soldiers loyal to him and serving under Russian officers—shot down a civilian airliner heading toward Malaysia over the war-torn area. Unashamed by his indirect involvement in this atrocity, Putin then threatened to cut off or sharply reduce Europe's supply of natural gas during the winter of 2014.

Putin has played Obama like a fiddle. He's figured out that there will never be any serious consequences for his actions, beyond Obama and Kerry disparaging him for behaving "in 19th century fashion."[15] That joke might play well to an affluent audience who believe themselves more enlightened than the rest of the world, but Putin doesn't mind these worthless slights; he operates in the real world. It is important that someone who does the same lead America next.

At a 2014 fundraiser, Obama was caught telling donors why he had no interest in seriously challenging Russia's actions in Ukraine. "We do very little trade with Ukraine and, geopolitically... what happens in Ukraine doesn't pose a direct threat to us," he explained.[16] But the U.S. signed an agreement to protect Ukraine in 1994, in exchange for the newly independent nation giving up its nuclear arsenal—the world's third-largest at the time.[17] Given his incompetent handling of Russia throughout his presidency, it is apparently too much to ask that Obama should be aware of this when raising money for his political party. When Obama extended the hand of friendship and the "reset" button in 2009, he was in part making a political point that he had repeated throughout the 2008 election campaign. Where the Bush administration had grown wary of Putin and relations had grown frosty, he would come in as Mister Nice Guy. Obama either failed to realize—or failed to care—that this meant letting his guard down and thus betraying vital U.S. interests.

Obama was effectively rewarding the bad Russian behavior that had inspired Bush's distrust—the August 2008 invasion of Georgia, its neighbor to the south. Instead of learning from his predecessor that Putin could not be trusted, Obama assumed that he could do better. After all, Obama had such a winning personality.

The next U.S. president can't operate this way toward Russia. He (or she) can't construct a foreign policy on the idea that he is the nicer, smarter guy who can do things better and make everybody happy without reference to what went before.

There is a lot at stake in America's relationship with Russia. The last thing the world needs is a war between nuclear powers; the second-to-last thing it needs is for the Russians to take advantage of our aversion to such a conflict in order to work their will unchecked. America can and should take a firm stand towards Russia. Putin and our allies should know that the leader of the free world will not tolerate Russia's geopolitical threats and will take measured and decisive actions in countering them.

YIELDING TO THE MULLAHS

Aside from Russia, America's biggest problem at the moment is Iran, whose nuclear program—and Obama's half-hearted efforts to derail it—are certain to create headaches for the next U.S. president.

Obama desperately wants a permanent nuclear agreement with Iran as the defining feature of his foreign policy legacy, and in late 2014 he seemed to be on the edge of obtaining one. But while Obama seems convinced that he can make a deal, he does not seem very concerned about whether that deal serves America's best interests.

A deal that would actually uphold American interests is highly unlikely. Iran managed to gain an additional seven months' time—its second extension—by hardening its demands. And why wouldn't it? It stands as a pseudo–regional hegemon, controlling Yemen (via the Houthi rebels), Iraq (through the Shiite government), Syria (through Assad), and Lebanon (through Hezbollah).

Obama sees Hassan Rouhani, who became Iran's president in August 2013, as someone he can work with. Unfortunately for Obama, Rouhani and his lieutenants see him as someone they can walk all over.

That's not just my opinion. In October 2014, Ali Younesi, a senior advisor to Rouhani, told an Iranian publication that Obama was "the weakest of U.S. presidents" and that Obama's presidency has been "humiliating." According to Younesi, "Americans witnessed their greatest defeats in Obama's era: Terrorism expanded, [the] U.S. had huge defeats under Obama [and] that is why they want to compromise with Iran."[18]

Iran should have been the one eager to compromise with the United States. Its economy has been in the tank for years, in large part because of American and European sanctions placed on the regime's banks and oil exports. But the Iranian economy rebounded after Iran signed a preliminary nuclear deal with Obama in July 2013, which eased some of those sanctions. And since then, it is the United States that has been acting like the weaker side—the one that's desperate for an agreement. Obama, the president of the world's most powerful country, has maneuvered himself into a position of negotiating from desperation.

The media often label Rouhani a moderate. And he is a moderate compared to his predecessor, Mahmoud Ahmadinejad, an Islamist with what can best be described as apocalyptic nuclear ambitions. But Rouhani's moderate rhetoric should not be mistaken for truly moderate policy, especially when it comes to Iran's nuclear program. When Rouhani addressed the United Nations General Assembly in late September 2014, he gave a positive assessment of the nuclear talks, saying that he had "no doubt that the situation between the U.S. and Iran will be completely different" and that there were "many potential areas of cooperation in the future" if a deal could be struck.[19]

But he also made it clear that Iran now had the leverage in the talks. As the *Wall Street Journal* editorialized about the speech, "The fabled Iranian moderate's unsubtle message: You'll play by our rules now."[20] As talks over a permanent deal proceeded in the summer and fall of 2014, Iran turned down several unprecedented offers. One would have required Iran to disconnect all of its centrifuges from one another—but not destroy them.[21] This would mean that Iran could have simply plugged the machines back in if it wanted to start enriching uranium again. Probably sensing it could get an even sweeter deal, Iran declined this offer.

At one point, Iran became so emboldened that it offered the United States assistance in fighting the Islamic State in exchange for more sanctions relief. "Iran is a very influential country in the region and can help in the fight against the ISIL terrorists," a senior Iranian official told Reuters. "But it is a two-way street. You give something, you take something."[22]

It took a lot of chutzpah for Iran to offer to help the U.S. against ISIS, given that Iran played a role in its creation and growth. It was the Iran-backed Maliki government in Iraq whose incompetence and corruption made ISIS's rise possible. And Iran's support for Assad in Syria against the Free Syrian Army and other pro-Western forces also helped ISIS gain control of large swaths of Syria.

Meanwhile, as its leaders called the shots in negotiations with the U.S., Iran wasn't even abiding by the conditions of the interim deal it had signed. In September 2014, the International Atomic Energy Agency published a report detailing how Iran continued to stonewall the inspectors' efforts to explore the "possible military dimensions" of its nuclear program.[23] Its scientists also began putting uranium gas through its modern IR-5 centrifuges—a fact that Iranian state news organs have been boasting about.[24]

In an interesting piece in the *Atlantic*, former George W. Bush speechwriter David Frum detailed how the Iranian regime had gotten the better of the United States in the talks:

> This most recent proposal [the one allowing Iran to "disconnect" its centrifuges] marks the latest in a series of American climb-downs. Iranian negotiators have sniffed at each round of American concessions and insisted on more. As best as outsiders to the talks can tell, they have obtained them. On the present trajectory, any final agreement will leave Iran paused on the verge of nuclear-weapons capability—and this time, with the U.S. having signed away any non-military means of preventing Iran's final drive to complete a bomb....
>
> The talks began because the United States possessed powerful means of compulsion against Iran: from sanctions, to sabotage, to military force. But the rulers of Iran...recognized that their counterparts were nearly as averse to using those means of compulsion as were the Iranians themselves. A stick that your adversary dreads using is no stick at all.
>
> The United States also had carrots to offer, above all the relaxation of sanctions and a more normal U.S.-Iran relationship. Yet even before ISIS advanced in northern Iraq, the Obama administration had made up its mind that this carrot was something that the United States needed even more than Iran did. Just as a stick that you dread using is no stick at all, so a carrot that you yourself crave ceases to be much of a carrot.
>
> The unsurprising result: The United States—which began the nuclear talks from a position of strength—has acted throughout the negotiations like the weaker party.[25]

Frum was right. But the Obama administration wasn't done scaling back its own demands or accommodating those of the Iranians. It later made an offer that would have allowed Iran to operate 4,000 centrifuges, instead of the previous limit of 1,300.[26]

There were also other signs that the White House had already resigned itself to a nuclear Iran and was looking for a way to introduce a policy of containment. In September 2014, Colin Kahl was appointed Biden's national security advisor to head up Iran policy. Kahl's earlier report, called "If All Else Fails: The Challenges of Containing a Nuclear-Armed Iran," was seen as "a trial balloon to gauge public response" to containment, according to the *Weekly Standard*'s Lee Smith.[27]

Iran's nuclear ambitions threaten us and our allies—not just Israel, but also the Sunni nations of the Arab Peninsula, and Saudi Arabia most of all. Even worse, if Iran gets the bomb, many other nations will claim a right to follow suit, creating a far more dangerous situation for the entire region.

A nuclear Iran would bring about the real possibility of a Sunni-versus-Shia war in a part of the world where we've invested much blood and treasure to maintain stability. Such a war has long been on the agenda of radicals on both sides of the religious divide. It would be a tragic outcome, and an ironic one for President Obama, who, as we've seen, told David Remnick of the *New Yorker* in early 2014 that he saw conciliating Iran as key to a more balanced and peaceful Middle East. The remarks bear repeating, especially in light of the intervening events that have highlighted the degree of wishful thinking in the president's analysis: "Although it would not solve the entire problem, if we were able to get Iran to operate in a responsible fashion—not funding terrorist organizations, not trying to stir up sectarian discontent in other countries, and not developing a nuclear weapon—you could see an equilibrium developing between Sunni, or predominantly Sunni, Gulf states and Iran in which there's competition, perhaps suspicion, but not an active or proxy warfare."[28]

The United States has long desired a balance between Iran and Saudi Arabia in the region, but this administration's policies are leading to a very imbalanced Middle East, one that is certainly not in America's or the world's interest.

As this book was being prepared to go to press, the November 24 deadline for a comprehensive agreement passed without an agreement. Talks were extended another seven months. Although an extension is better than a bad deal, a bad deal after an extension is probably worse than either. Iran has now bought itself seven more months of sanctions relief—and perhaps more time to covertly enrich uranium.[29] Congress might have to step in and save Obama from himself—a veto-proof majority exists that could impose new sanctions and end this charade.

Of course, that's why Obama is openly trying to bypass Congress with whatever deal he ends up signing. In April 2014, Secretary of State Kerry told the Senate Foreign Relations Committee that the administration "would absolutely" obtain congressional approval for any deal it struck with Iran. "We'd be obligated under the law," he said.[30] But the White House subsequently went back on this, announcing the administration's intention to suspend sanctions on a temporary basis through executive action once a deal was reached.[31] It's kind of funny—during the election season, Obama took credit for the sanctions, which Congress had passed almost unanimously over his opposition. Now he maintains a right to suspend these sanctions indefinitely without another vote of Congress.

There is a reason Congress is usually involved in these decisions— a reason the Founding Fathers gave the Senate a role in ratifying treaties, and Congress a role in declaring war. Decisions made by one man are far more likely to be bad ones. Decisions on Iran made by Obama seem almost certain to be bad ones.

REALISM AND THE DELICATE BALANCE

One day at the oil facility in Yemen where I was a security consultant I got a call from my interpreter, Mohammed, telling me there was a Bedouin blocking our food truck at the gate. Our facilities had no guns inside, in a land where everyone over eleven years of age has an AK-47. But I could not take any chances, and I didn't want this guy to set a precedent by causing problems inside the wire, which would put my people in danger. So I sent in several army soldiers to disperse him.

But the army and the tribes have a tense relationship. Three armed soldiers approached the man and within thirty seconds there were about twenty tribesmen who joined the incident, picking up pipes and sticks.

I grabbed my interpreter and we quickly drove down to the spot to prevent any further escalation.

In Arabia, there is no give—men consistently show foolish pride, and this simple incident threatened to end with someone dead. We had 150 Yemeni soldiers and they easily outnumbered the tribesmen. But if there were a killing, we might end up with a thousand tribesmen coming over the sand dunes to take revenge.

Mohammed and I tried to break up the confrontation, without much success at first. My own Arabic was limited, and Mohammed's language skills were of little use in the middle of twenty men yelling at each other at the top of their lungs. It was at that moment that I remembered that I was wearing my New York Giants ball cap. With a little bit of information gleaned about tribal law from my studies in the Harvard program, I got an idea.

Because personal pride is so important to tribal life, the tribes have developed a mechanism in their customs to counter it—to require a retreat from conflict. To signal to an adversary that you want a peaceful resolution, you simply remove your headdress and place it on his head. If he does not respond in kind he is shamed amongst his tribe.

Stepping forward, I removed my ball cap and placed it on the head of the Bedouin who was blocking the food gate. Instantly, the yelling stopped. Two dozen Bedouins looked at me and clapped. The gate opened, and the man followed me to my office to negotiate a solution.

I share this story because it demonstrates how sometimes we need leaders who think outside the foreign policy box and understand the thought process of those they are confronting. That Obama has shown no aptitude for this is evident. But Obama won't be president much longer. The next president has to be someone ready to transcend his own preconceived ideas and embrace what works.

get picked on and perhaps accidentally cause a huge brawl is to walk in and act like you're everyone's best friend, loudly talk as though you are better than everybody else there, and make threats you are not prepared to back up.

Beyond questions about the use of military force, the maintenance of world power requires smart diplomacy in peacetime. Sometimes foreign policy is about war, yes, but usually it's about avoiding wars. It's about not diminishing America's credibility with unrealistic and idle threats. It's about giving adversaries the opportunity to do what we want them to do and to save face at the same time.

How should a president confront nuclear Russia, given that a war is completely unpalatable? One lever Obama has that he has failed to pull—again, because of political considerations and a desire to please his base—is energy. Energy is a universal world need, and one of the few levers that the world's less savory characters—from our uneasy friends in Saudi Arabia to Venezuela's leftist dictator to Putin himself—still use against their neighbors. But despite the Obama administration's war on coal, the U.S. is on the verge of becoming the largest producer of oil and natural gas—which means we have the opportunity to level the playing field for the kids on the playground who are being bullied.

Energy is an ideal tool for America to use for soft power around the world in advancing our interests.

Given what is happening now in Russia, there is no good reason the Obama administration is not conducting a full-court press to remove all restrictions on the strategic export of U.S. fossil fuels. The economic reasons alone justify it—exporting the fuels might even let us start running trade surpluses—but such a move would be incredibly beneficial for foreign policy as well.

There is no reason for President Obama's delay of the privately funded construction of the Keystone XL Pipeline. Well, okay, there is a reason—just not a good one. Tom Steyer, a hedge fund billionaire who hates fossil fuels, promised to spend $50 million for Democrats in the 2014 midterm elections on the condition that they prevent the pipeline from being built. But just because Obama subordinates national interests to politics doesn't mean the next president has to be so foolish. Here is a chance to do a favor for our northern neighbor, helping Canada's oil go to market, at the expense of bad actors such as Venezuela, Russia, and the Middle East. There is no downside.

The pipeline is more than just a business or a political matter. It is potentially one piece in a much larger puzzle of how energy can help us conduct foreign affairs. More than half of the Russian government's revenue comes from oil and gas. To the extent that the United States can displace Russian market share or drive down world prices, it can hold Putin's ambitions in check.

In emergencies like the one Europe experienced in 2014, when Putin threatened its supply of natural gas in the wake of the Ukraine crisis, an America with the proper infrastructure—most of which would cost the government nothing—would be able to move oil and gas quickly to anyone threatened by Putin or any other bad actor. This is why pipelines and terminals must be built immediately. While we should use our boom in natural gas to propel our domestic economy forward, much as we did with oil in the twentieth century, some permits for natural gas export terminals should be fast tracked as a national security priority. When crises like the one with Putin emerge, American companies should be encouraged to sign gas contracts with European countries.

It might take a few years for the U.S. to supply a significant percentage of Europe's energy needs, but a move in this direction would have immediate market impact and let our allies know that they can depend on us—and that they can simply outlast the likes of Putin rather than acceding to his threats. As I write this, oil prices are going down. This is a blow to Putin and the Russian economy financed by oil and gas. Supplying our allies in Europe will both support their national security and keep Putin in check.

Energy could also play a key role in the long term—not only in defusing the threat of a nuclear Iran but also in offering a real chance for a better relationship with its leaders—one that doesn't involve letting them obtain a nuclear bomb and then having to contain a nuclear-armed Islamic Republic.

U.S. scientists are currently revisiting the idea of using thorium—a nuclear fuel far less dangerous than uranium and not so easily weaponized—in the next generation of nuclear reactors. There is virtually zero chance for a meltdown with thorium reactors, as there is with uranium reactors. This is a proven technology, but one into which the government discontinued research during the Cold War in favor of uranium reactors. Thorium is a more abundant and more efficient fuel—our interest in uranium derived from its role in producing nuclear weapons, which at the time was something we wanted to do.

But as thorium technology is revived and developed on a suitable scale, it should be used as a foreign policy tool as well. Imagine if the world community agreed to build peaceful thorium nuclear energy plants for Iran in exchange for its enriched uranium. At the very least, it would remove any excuse for bad behavior. At best, it could fulfill Iranians' energy needs, allow their government to continue proudly touting the scientific advancements of the Islamic Republic (this is an example of face-saving), and obviate any need for uranium enrichment.

Imagine the markets the U.S. would open up and the soft diplomacy it could wield in helping to build, supply, and underwrite peaceful energy to other countries.

Energy is one piece of the puzzle—but it isn't the only one. It's just an example of the sort of practical thinking that is missing from our foreign policy today. When there's a problem in the world, we should be looking for what weapons—hopefully not military weapons—we have in our arsenal to make things better. Energy is one such weapon.

"DON'T DO STUPID SH*T"

The Obama White House's stated rule of operation—"Don't do stupid sh*t"—is actually not bad as part of a policy.[34] But it hasn't been working because Obama's White House isn't adhering to it. And in any case, it's not a complete foreign policy.

In addition to changing our diplomatic approach to include more pragmatic and sensible thinking, we will always need intelligence work, the occasional covert mission, and, on very rare occasions, larger military actions. These all help obviate the need for endless wars to maintain stability. After all, endless war is no stability at all.

To keep this balance requires an extremely skilled and competent team dedicated to American goals that are clear to friends and foes alike.

On all of these counts—the goals, the competency, the clarity—President Obama has been a failure, as I have discussed at length in these pages. This is true even at the most basic level, simple competence.

A 2014 report from the Inspector General for the State Department suggests that during Hillary Clinton's tenure as Secretary of State, far more energy was spent retaliating against whistleblowers and covering up for whore-mongering ambassadors than responding attentively to Chris Stevens' urgent requests for extra diplomatic security in Libya.[35]

But on a more fundamental level, the grand strategy is simply absent. The vision for American leadership just isn't there.

Obama and Clinton employed military force where no American interest was apparent, with disastrous results for Libya.

By embracing Egypt's Muslim Brotherhood, Obama and Clinton managed to help Hamas arm for its 2014 conflict with Israel. They infuriated Egyptian citizens, who watched the resulting Brotherhood government dismantle their new post-Mubarak constitution—and then Obama also alienated the leaders of the Egyptian government that followed.

In attempting to put "daylight" between the U.S. and the Israeli government over the Palestinian question, Obama has not made America a more credible broker in the peace process, nor has he made an inch of progress toward an acceptable settlement. But he has lost the good will of the Israelis, helped plunge them into their biggest shooting war with Hamas in decades, and made Egypt (at least for now) the ally Israel turns to before it looks to us.

Obama pulled out of Iraq prematurely in order to fulfill his campaign promise. It was a popular decision at the time, but now even his former top officials admit it was an error. The results were not only predictable, but in fact predicted by his predecessor. As President Bush had warned while still in office, an overly hasty and irresponsible pullout from Iraq created a need for Americans to return there yet again with guns blazing—this time against a stronger terrorist enemy than America ever faced in al Qaeda.

Finally, Obama's "can't-we-all-just-get-along" attitude toward both Russia and Iran has allowed two key foes to take advantage of his naiveté—with huge ramifications for Eastern Europe, Syria, Iraq, the nuclear future of the Middle East, and America's strategic interests.

In short, Obama has managed to wound or alienate most of our allies, embolden our enemies, and undermine all of the progress of the previous decade in combating Islamic terrorism. Meanwhile, he thinks he's making progress by not using phrases like "Islamic terrorism."

As for the leaks—the original reason that I and all the military and intelligence personnel who are members of OPSEC got involved in the political debate—they are simply inexcusable.

If the leaks were just mistakes and not politically motivated acts, they would be bad enough for threatening all of the worthy goals that America has in the world today. The political motive makes them even more despicable. And OPSEC will be around to challenge any politician of any party who tries the same thing in the future.

This stuff matters—a lot. It may determine what kind of world our children live in. Given how badly our world standing has deteriorated under Obama, it's going to be that much more important that our next president takes these things seriously. Hillary Clinton has already been tested on the most important job of an American president—protecting Americans—and she has failed. She was unsupportive prior to, unresponsive during, and unaccountable after her 3:00 a.m. phone call test in Benghazi.

MOVING FORWARD

As Americans, we need a strong leader to lead not only us, but the world as well. He or she must understand the world as it is, with a view based in reality. This view must remain consistent and change only with circumstances. It should not change to suit different audiences or domestic political situations. For example, an American leader should never claim more flexibility in foreign policy after an election is over. No occupant of the White House should ever utter such a sentence again.

Our goal is a more peaceful world for our descendants and ourselves. We can use both soft and hard power to achieve this, in a push-pull balancing act orchestrated by robust leadership.

Our foreign aid should form part of our soft power—and I'm sad to say that right now, we are not taking advantage of what we already give. For example, the United States is the second-largest donor of aid to Yemen, but you really wouldn't know it if you lived there. As a result, anti-American attitudes are probably more common there than they should be.

I find this fact amazing. The U.S. is home to the best marketers on the planet—people wear Michael Jordan T-shirts in the Congo and drink Pepsi in Paraguay—yet none of these professionals' efforts seem to be employed (or at least successfully employed) in demonstrating to people abroad how we are helping them. It seems absurd that we give foreign aid packages to so many—without making sure they know whom to thank.

Let's use the talents of what is arguably the most American industry ever to let the world know where the help is coming from. That's probably a better strategy for winning hearts and minds than broadcasting to them, through self-aggrandizing leaks to the *New York Times*, that our president is personally approving every single drone strike in their country.

When it comes to hard power, we should immediately rescind sequestration—the draconian and untargeted cuts made to our military in 2013 because Congress failed to reach an agreement on cutting the budget in any more rational way.

Any runner knows it is much easier to keep up than catch up. We can definitely find savings in the Pentagon budget, but the sequestration cuts are indiscriminate. Leaders need to roll up their sleeves and find the savings, not take the easy way out and place the burden on the backs of our brave men and women.

Our men and women serving are the best in the world, and they represent the one percent of us who voluntarily go forward on our behalf. We should never take them for granted. Our way of life and our reluctant role in the world ultimately rest upon them. That is the reality.

International terrorism—including by transnational actors—has become increasingly common. American leadership is needed to convince our allies to help us, because it tells them we will have their backs when they need us. We need a leader whose policies aim at the root cause, rather than addressing the symptoms. An ever expanding kill list and unaccountable drone strikes may kill a few terrorists here and there, but they also serve as better recruitment for terrorist groups than Guantanamo Bay ever did. The next president should be able to assure the American people without hesitation that there will never be drone strikes on our own soil and—given easy proliferation—should forge international law on armed drone usage. This is our responsibility.

The various groups we face in asymmetrical warfare—ISIS, al Qaeda, and so forth—will adapt and take on new strategies over time. If we make the decision to engage them, we must do so wholeheartedly—and wipe them out. "Unbelievably small" is not a word that any American leader should use to describe one of our military operations. That's a sign that we're not serious.

And American leaders must not be afraid to call Islamic terrorism what it is. Leadership matters. We must be clear, principled, and consistent; this will embolden our allies to do the same. This includes our Islamic allies, who as Muslims can in some respects play a much more robust role in discouraging Islamic terrorism through persuasion than we can by simply striking back. But of course, this would require being a true ally to our traditional Muslim allies—not selling them out for an uncertain relationship with Iran, whose regime is fomenting unrest in their countries and funding terrorism to this day.

Being on a team means you are interdependent—not independent, trying to go it alone. We can change our policies only if we elect someone who truly believes in our team, its greatness, and what we can achieve together. We haven't had that kind of leader in the last six to seven years, and that fact has helped remind Americans, war-weary as they may be, that these issues do matter. We cannot afford another president—whatever his or her party, and whatever his or her view of world affairs—who plays politics with our national security and foreign policy for personal gain the way Obama and Clinton have, subordinating what matters to what does not.

But we can always start again. We fall down, but we can rise again, dust our knees off, and press ahead. This is who we are. This is how we started, and it will be how we move forward. We must elect someone who, no matter what the challenge, will stand shoulder to shoulder with us as Americans, seeking our interests first, proving to our allies that they have no greater friend than us, and convincing all others that they can make no worse enemy.

APPENDIX A

FRANK R. WOLF
10TH DISTRICT, VIRGINIA

COMMITTEE ON APPROPRIATIONS

SUBCOMMITTEES:

CHAIRMAN—COMMERCE-JUSTICE-SCIENCE

TRANSPORTATION-HUD

STATE AND FOREIGN OPERATIONS

CO-CHAIR—TOM LANTOS
HUMAN RIGHTS COMMISSION

Congress of the United States
House of Representatives
July 16, 2014

241 CANNON HOUSE OFFICE BUILDING
WASHINGTON, DC 20515-4610
(202) 225-5136

13873 PARK CENTER ROAD
SUITE 130
HERNDON, VA 20171
(703) 709-5800
(800) 945-9663 (IN STATE)

110 NORTH CAMERON STREET
WINCHESTER, VA 22601
(540) 667-0990
(800) 850-3463 (IN STATE)

wolf.house.gov

Mr. Scott Taylor
Special Operations Education Fund
POB 1096
Alexandria VA 22313

Dear Mr. Taylor:

I just wanted to write to thank you and OPSEC for all your efforts to help establish House Select Committee on Benghazi. The time, energy and effort OPSEC put into helping get the committee created did not go unnoticed. OPSEC's ability to harness the grassroots power of veterans across the country was impressive and made a difference on Capitol Hill. The fact that OPSEC, in a very short period of time, helped to generate more than 14,000 contacts to Members of Congress made an impact, as we quickly added co-sponsors to H. Res 36 in response to the letters, calls and emails generated by OPSEC contacts in the intelligence, special operations and veterans' communities. From a personal standpoint, I can't tell you the number of times my staff reached out to OPSEC's leadership for advice, support and critically important information during the 18 months it took to get the select committee established.

I am deeply grateful for your support and appreciate all that you and OPSEC have done, and continue to do, to find out what happened in Benghazi. Our veterans – and those who will serve in the future – deserve nothing less than the truth.

Best wishes.

Sincerely,

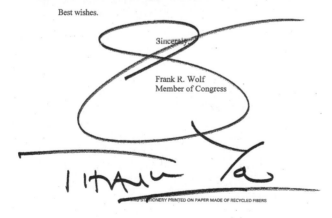

Frank R. Wolf
Member of Congress

THIS STATIONERY PRINTED ON PAPER MADE OF RECYCLED FIBERS

The CIA Global Response Contractors' Public Response to the November 21, 2014 House Intelligence Committee Report about the September 11 and 12, 2012 Benghazi Attacks

Michael Roger's House Intelligence Report is 'Full Of Inaccuracies'

BY JOHN 'TIG' TIEGAN and KRIS 'TANTO' PARONTO, CIA Contractors on the Ground in Benghazi, Libya on September 11, 2012

Since the release of the November 21, 2014 U.S. House Intelligence Committee's report, many uninformed people in the political world including several national media outlets want to believe that this reports "debunks" what really happened in Benghazi. The report, however, is full of inaccuracies—and the authors of the report printed them anyway despite testimony and other truthful information that proved those statements wrong.

Testimony was provided by the Global Response Staff, security contractors on the ground working for the CIA in Benghazi on, September 11, 2012 to September 12, 2012. These CIA contractors debunked these conclusions. The team of CIA security contractors consisted of Kris "Tanto" Paronto, John "Tig" Tiegen, Mark "Oz" Geist, Ty "Rone" Woods (now deceased), Jack Silva and DB Benton –all sources of the book, 13 Hours, which is a first-hand account of what happened at both Benghazi locations during the attacks on September 11, 2012.

We provided the same unchanging and accurate information of what took place in Benghazi on September 11, 2012 through September

12, 2012 to our immediate chain of command in the CIA's office of security, during several FBI interviews, and to Congressman Rogers and his committee. So it comes as a very big disappointment to us as those on the front lines that this report is full of inaccuracies and bias.

We can only assume that this is the case because Rogers and others are attempting to protect their reputations, and protect, or further the careers of others, but that should be left for another time. The purpose of this article that we are writing as former CIA Global Response Staff security contractors, who fought and bled together that night in Benghazi, Libya, is to point out the major inaccuracies in this faux "investigative" report.

We are standing up and speaking out to set the record straight yet once again because some in Congress and in the mainstream media refuse to accept the facts about what happened to us as witnesses, combatants, and survivors of the Benghazi attacks on September 11, 2012 and September 12, 2012.

If one wants to separate facts from biased political beliefs then one needs to get their facts correct. The report Congressman Rogers and his Democratic committee's ranking member Congressman Dutch Ruppersberger completed got several facts wrong about the basic timeline of events that took place on the ground in Benghazi. So, if this "official" report cannot get its facts correct, it cannot be deemed the "final" investigative report by the mainstream media. We, as the men who protected other Americans on the ground in Benghazi, as best we could, are here to point out specifically what this HIPSC report and Mike Rogers got wrong. What follows is a detailed breakdown of some of the inaccuracies in Rogers' report.

FALSE FINDING #1:
POLITICIANS IN WASHINGTON, D.C. CLAIM:

Page 8, paragraph 2 of the US House of Representative Intelligence Report states:

"Security Officers from the CIA's Benghazi Annex recalled hearing explosions from an unknown location around 9:40 p.m."

FROM THE CIA CONTRACTORS ON THE GROUND:

This is incorrect. As we and others stated during our testimony before the House of Representatives' Committee (date), we were first contacted at 9:32 p.m. and the explosions and gunfire were known to be at what was known to us as the U.S. consulate, which per security requirements after the attack, was changed to the U.S. Special Mission and was then called the "Temporary Mission Facility" by U.S. Department of State, and later in this report. Note that the location of all gunfire and explosions were known to those of us at the U.S. Annex. At no time did we state to the committee that we did not know the location of the gunfire or explosions. We had visited what we knew to be the U.S. Consulate on a weekly basis.

FALSE FINDING #2:
POLITICIANS IN WASHINGTON, D.C. CLAIM:

Page 8, paragraph 1 of the U.S. House of Representative Intelligence Report states:

"Due to the thick smoke, the DS agent lost contact with Ambassador Stevens and Mr. Smith along the escape route. After crawling out the window and realizing the Ambassador and Mr. Smith were not with him, the DS Agent under gunfire, repeatedly re-entered the burning building to search for them, but was unsuccessful."

FROM THE CIA CONTRACTORS ON THE GROUND:

This is extremely unlikely. Ansar Al Sharia and Al-Qaeda in the Islamic Maghreb (AQIM) terrorists had taken complete control of the U.S. compound in Benghazi, and had one of the villas there completely surrounded and were within only feet of each window and door opening. If the Diplomatic Security (DS) agent repeatedly went in and out of the window under gunfire how was he not hit? The terrorists would have been no more than 10 feet from him shooting into an area that was 4 feet wide by 8 feet long with no cover. The DS agent may have been able to complete this move once, but doing so repeatedly would have been impossible without injury or death. Also, Rogers' report makes no reference that the DS agents individually testified to Mike Rogers and the committee. We, CIA Contractors on the ground, have remained close friends with one of the DS agents, and he stated to us that he was never asked to testify before Mike Rogers's House Intelligence Committee. How can the report be deemed a complete investigation when the members don't speak to all who were on the ground and in combat?

Former Deputy CIA Director Mike Morrell, Mike Rogers and James Clapper were not in Libya during the attack, nor were any member of House Intelligence Committee. CIA Chief of Station and CIA Chief of Base "Bob" did not assist us (the GRS Security Team- the CIA Contractors) at the Temporary Mission Facility. The CIA Team Leader also waited at the vehicles 400 meters from the Temporary Mission Facility allowing all 6 GRS CIA Security Contractors to clear and secure it before driving our SUV onto the Temporary Mission Facility. What we're getting at here is this statement in the report is taken from those who did not physically see or experience what took place during the initial attack and subsequent GRS response early on at the Temporary Mission Facility.

FALSE FINDING #3:
POLITICIANS IN WASHINGTON, D.C. CLAIM:

Page 9, Paragraph 4/Page 10, Paragraph 1 states: "Within approximately one hour, at about 12:30 AM, the attackers began one of several attempts to assault the Annex. Some of this attack was captured on video. CIA personnel recounted that the attacks included RPG's, satchel charges, gelatin explosives, and small arms fire, with around five to ten people amassing in the adjacent field. These security personnel were able to repel the attackers. Around 2:00 to 2:30 AM, there was a second attempt on the compound that lasted 5 to 10 minutes that was also repelled."

FROM THE CIA CONTRACTORS ON THE GROUND:

This portion of the report significantly downplays the ferocity of the multiple attacks on the Annex. The second attack involved closer to 20 or more terrorists and was much longer and more aggressive than the first. We have stated this on many occasions to all that have interviewed us including Mike Rogers and his committee. **It should also be noted emphatically that the GRS security contractors—the Kris "Tanto" Paronto, John "Tig" Tiegen, Mark "Oz" Geist, Jack Silva, and DB Benton—were the only CIA personnel who saw the attackers from start to finish, and we were the only CIA personnel who were involved in both firefights.**

Both the Benghazi Chief of Base and CIA GRS Team Leader hid in Building C during both attacks and the following mortar attack. Neither the Chief of Base "Bob" or the GRS Team Leader came up to the Annex Roofs or fighting positions to see what was going on outside the Annex walls. Any testimony outside that coming from the GRS Security Contractors holds limited value since no one except the GRS Security Contractors saw or was involved with both attacks in their entirety.

FALSE FINDING #4:
POLITICIANS IN WASHINGTON, D.C. CLAIM:

—Page 11, Paragraph 4 reads: "Meanwhile, the other Tripoli Teams officers spread out to assess the situation, locate all personnel and fill any security gaps."

FROM THE CIA CONTRACTORS ON THE GROUND:

This is entirely incorrect. Once the Tripoli element—GRS and Delta Force arrived, all of them entered and stayed in Building C until approximately 5 minutes after the end of the mortar attacks that killed Glen Doherty and Tyrone Woods. Those attacks also severely injured Mark "Oz" Geist and Dave Ubben. The only member of the Tripoli element that joined the Benghazi GRS security team upon arrival was Doherty. He climbed to the roof of Building C. Mike Rogers and his committee were told this in testimony from us. Further, Paronto stated he called on the radio to the Tripoli element asking for relief in order to use the bathroom immediately after they arrived. The request was never answered by any CIA personnel in Building C or by the Tripoli element.

FALSE FINDING #5:
POLITICIANS IN WASHINGTON, D.C. CLAIM:

Page 12, Paragraph 1 reads: "Following the mortar fire, the remaining members of the security team rescued and began treating the wounded officers while repelling attackers who continued to fire on the Annex for a short time."

FROM THE CIA CONTRACTORS ON THE GROUND:

This is also incorrect. Once the final mortar fell, the Libyan Militia, who brought the Tripoli team from Benina Airfield, went in the direction of the mortar fire as ordered by their commander who was trapped in Building C. Tiegen was the only one who went to Building C immediately to assist the wounded. Paronto, Jack Silva, and DB Benton were the only GRS security contractors who remained outside to defend the Annex. Tiegen was never under fire when he went up the ladder, or the whole time he was on the roof treating the four down Americans. It took the Tripoli Team and Delta Force several minutes before coming out of Building C to assist Tiegen in helping the severely wounded and to reinforce the defensive positions of Paronto, Silva and Benton.

FALSE FINDING #6:
POLITICIANS IN WASHINGTON, D.C. CLAIM:

Page 16, Paragraph 2 states: "At the Annex, only one DS agent participated in the defense of the Annex, but he was in a defensive position on the roof of the Annex building #3 when it was hit with the mortar rounds and was severely injured. The other DS agents remained in a secure area with the CIA case officers and support staff."

FROM THE CIA CONTRACTORS ON THE GROUND:

SHOULD THIS READ THEY WERE IN DEFENSIVE POSITIONS?

Again, this is incorrect. We did not state to Mike Rogers and his committee that three DS agents were located at defensive positions with one on Building B, one on Building C, and one on Building D.

We all were in defensive positions; we're not sure why the Rogers report focused on how this DS agent was the only one in a defensive position.

FALSE FINDING #7:
POLITICIANS IN WASHINGTON, D.C. CLAIM:

Page 19, Paragraph 3 reads: "Specifically, upon receiving the first call of an attack from an assistant Regional Security Officer at 9:42 p.m., the Annex security team leader gathered the five other available security officers that were at the Annex, and he told them what he knew."

FROM THE CIA CONTRACTORS ON THE GROUND:

Wrong. The first call to the GRS team in Benghazi to muster due to the attack on the Temporary Mission Facility was at 9:32 p.m. This was stated to Mike Rogers and his committee.

FALSE FINDING #8:
POLITICIANS IN WASHINGTON, D.C. CLAIM:

Page 20, Paragraph 1 reads: "The CIA security team chief (GRS Staff Team Leader) in Benghazi, in consultation with the Chief of Base, made the decision to organize the rescue mission and to commence the operation."

FROM THE CIA CONTRACTORS ON THE GROUND:

This is incorrect. The chief of base "Bob" and GRS Staff Team Leader never commenced the rescue operation to save the State Department personnel. Further, the GRS contract security team disobeyed orders to "wait" and "stand down" taking it upon themselves to depart the Annex and come to the aid of the DS agents.

It's also important to note that Paronto was antagonized by a committee staff member while Mike Rogers and his fellow congressmen were in session. The young committee staff member asked Paronto about his military background and went on to continually ask for several minutes if it was normal for Rangers to disobey direct orders since it was not proper to disobey orders when he, the staff member, served in the Navy. If the Chief of Base "Bob" and GRS Staff Team Leader commenced the rescue operation immediately, the exchange between Paronto and that committee staff member would never have occurred.

FALSE FINDING #9:
POLITICIANS IN WASHINGTON, D.C. CLAIM:

Page 20, Paragraph 2 reads: "Although some security officers voiced a greater urgency to depart for the TMF, no officer at the CIA was ever told to stand down. The evidence from eyewitness testimony, ISR video footage, closed-circuit television recordings and other sources provides no support for the allegation that there was any stand-down order."

FROM THE CIA CONTRACTORS ON THE GROUND:

This statement is grossly incorrect. Paronto stated to Mike Rogers and his committee, looking Rogers directly in the eye, that he was delayed and was told to wait twice. Paronto also stated to Mike Rogers and his committee that the "27" minute delay and his team waiting was a severe military tactical mistake made by leadership figures who had little to no military training or experience in combat operations, and the delay cost the lives of Ambassador Stevens and Sean Smith due to them dying from smoke inhalation—something that takes time.

It should also be noted that the exact words "**STAND DOWN**" were used by the Chief of Base "Bob" to Tiegen approximately 15 minutes after the initial "help" call from the DS agents on the radio at the facility under attack. Tiegan did not testify with his fellow team-mates, Kris "Tanto" Paronto, Mark "Oz" Geist or Jack Silva. Tiegen testified alongside the CIA GRS staff team leader. This was a tactical maneuver by the Committee and the CIA since Tiegen was still employed by the CIA and scheduled to deploy shortly thereafter. This put immense pressure on Tiegen to testify in line with the CIA and Mike Rogers "cover up" agenda. It should be noted as well that Tiegen was not asked by Mike Rogers or the committee if he was told to "stand down" during his testimony. That question was directed, by the committee, to the GRS staff team leader only.

The video footage from the Annex show the GRS security contractors getting in and out of their vehicles and approaching the CIA Chief of Base "Bob" and GRS Staff Team Leader several times within the 27 minutes delay. This was due to the GRS security contractors continually requesting to "Bob" and Team Leader to leave the Annex to save the lives of the DS agents who were under attack and burning.

It is also important to note that the excuse for the delay by the CIA Base Chief "Bob" and GRS staff Team Leader was their *ALLEGED* effort to gather intelligence of the situation and obtain gun trucks with heavier weapons to assist in the rescue operation. Neither of these "excuses" by "Bob" or the Team Leader was realized once the GRS security contractors left the Annex without orders. The GRS security contractors still went in to the rescue, 27 minutes after the first DS request for help, without any new intelligence or information and without gun trucks or heavy weapons.

The delay departing the Annex allowed Ansar Al Sharia to reinforce the avenues of approach to the Temporary Mission Facility with AK-47s and RPG's. This caused the GRS security contractors to dismount their vehicles to suppress enemy fire and tactically move the remaining 350-400 meters, approximately, on foot over several 8-foot concrete walls and backyards through "deadspace" adding an additional 20 minute delay to the 27 minutes delay from the Annex.

FALSE FINDING #9:
POLITICIANS IN WASHINGTON, D.C. CLAIM:

Page 20, Paragraph 3 reads: "The 21 minute period between the time the Annex personnel first learned of the attack and when they departed reflects the time the Team needed to put on gear and the time during which the Chief of Base in Benghazi tried to secure local militias to assist in the mission."

FROM THE CIA CONTRACTORS ON THE GROUND:

This is also incorrect because, as stated to the Mike Rogers and the committee by the GRS security contractors, it was at a minimum of a 27 minute delay.

FALSE FINDING #10:
POLITICIANS IN WASHINGTON, D.C. CLAIM:

Page 21, Paragraph 1 states: "He (Deputy Director Morrell) also said: 'It has occurred to me that the Benghazi senior intelligence official sent them the moment they were ready to at that 15 minute mark.'"

FROM THE CIA CONTRACTORS ON THE GROUND:

This is false. Regarding Deputy Director Morrell, this inaccurate testimony shows that he is unclear of what happened on the ground in Benghazi 09/11/2012 to 09/12/2012 and that he failed to speak to the GRS security contractors, purposely or by accident, after the attack. This also shows a greater reliance on the CIA staff testimony, the majority of which is incorrect, rather than the GRS security contractors who were on the ground that night.

FALSE FINDING #11:
POLITICIANS IN WASHINGTON, D.C. CLAIM:

Page 21, Paragraph 2 reads: "Testimony from an Active CIA official who has personal experience in crisis situations provided a detailed validation of Morrell's assessment."

FROM THE CIA CONTRACTORS ON THE GROUND:

Since when does an outside source that was neither involved with the fighting in Benghazi or decisions made that night into the following morning, good or bad, play a vital role in a House Intelligence Committee's report? Then CIA Deputy Director Mike Morrell has no on the ground combat experience so his assessment is a guess at best based upon reading Intel cables, seeing video footage or talking in offices with those physically carrying out the combat operations. This entire section should have played no part in Mike Rogers and the committee's report.

Another point worth making is that the GRS security contractors on the ground did have actual combat experience in Iraq, Pakistan and Afghanistan theaters, and had been through multiple crises and combat situations. We represented all branches of service, specifically the Army's 75th Ranger Regiment, the Navy Seals and the Marine Corps'

Recon and Infantry. We were non-commissioned and commissioned officers as well.

There is also one more important fact: We were all on the ground fighting, trying to save lives and dying. We knew the continually changing situation and based all of our decisions on the "flow" of battle. We knew that minutes were costing lives where analysts and politicians sitting in D.C, all with little to no combat experience, did not. As such, to claim that Morrell's response was "validated" by an "active, senior CIA official" is incorrect. When combat starts, as it did that night in Benghazi, you have a few minutes to make decisions, and then you have to trust in your training and trust the man next to you. CIA analysts, particularly Morrell, obviously, do not understand this.

Therefore we knew the repercussions of leaving the base to aid the DS agents, but to say the Annex was left unprotected is entirely and completely inaccurate. The Annex had two Base Security Personnel with the primary responsibility of protecting the Annex from physical attack. Mark "Oz" Geist and one Case Officer with combat experience in Iraq were on site at the Annex. Also, all other CIA staff members at the Annex (approximately 20) were weapons qualified and knew how to operate their respective rifle and pistol weapons systems although none of them came up to the roofs during the attack on the Annex.

FALSE FINDING #12:
POLITICIANS IN WASHINGTON, D.C. CLAIM:

Page 23 Paragraph 3 states: "A member of the security team who served in Tripoli four months earlier had inquired about the availability of air assets and believed a Specter gunship was based and available in Sigonella, Italy. He assumed that it was still available that night, though he admitted that is was not his job to know whether it was available. Those officers who attended the emergency action committee meetings had discussed intimately what if any, US military resources were in the area. Those officers knew exactly what was and were not in the area and they understood there was not air support or any other assets in the general area."

FROM THE CIA CONTRACTORS ON THE GROUND:

This was either an intelligence failure or a misrepresentation of the facts. Paronto asked for an ISR (Drone) and an AC-130 Specter Gunship at 9:37 p.m, again at approximately 12:00 a.m., and again at approximately 2:30 a.m. He did so via his personal ICOM radio, something that the entire Annex personnel team uses. He was told by the GRS staff team leader and GRS deputy Chief of Base over the ICOM radio system that they were "working on obtaining both." Paronto received no response at 2:30 a.m. from his base leadership. At no time did the Annex leadership state over the ICOM radio system that the Specter gunship or air assets were unavailable. This was told to Mike Rogers and his committee by the GRS security contractors.

What is unclear is who "those officers" were in Mike Rogers and the Committee's report and why this crucial information was not passed on to the GRS Security Team in Benghazi. If what those anonymous "officers" told the committee is true—and the way their testimony was represented in this report was accurate—then that would be an intelligence failure. It's unheard of for such crucial information to be withheld from a security team. But, given Rogers' and his committee's other inaccuracies throughout this report, it wouldn't surprise us in the least if this section is entirely wrong—either misleading testimony from those "officers" or misrepresentation of their testimony by the committee. It was never communicated to us that we had no backup if attacked in Benghazi.

Another important note is that the 31st Fighter Wing consisting of the 555th and 510th Fighter Squadron located in Aviano Air Base is within range of Benghazi and could refuel in Sigonella Naval Air Station of Souda Bay Greece. Souda Bay Naval Base also supports F15/16s. Sigonella also supported a Marine FAST Company which was not used to assist the GRS security contractors on 09/11/2012 to 09/12/2012. It's possible to verify the above by examining the Global Command and Control System (GCCS). This system shows where all US assets are in the world from Major – Commands to Individual – C130 Specter Gunship. We do not believe this was examined by Mike Rogers or his committee based upon the references shown at the bottom of each page of this report. This system in classified, but portions can be declassified or examined by those with the proper clearance in order to verify US assets location on 09/11/2012 to 09/12/2012.

FALSE FINDING #13:
POLITICIANS IN WASHINGTON, D.C. CLAIM:

Page 31, Paragraph 6: "CIA did not intimidate or prevent any officer from speaking to Congress or otherwise telling his story."

FROM THE CIA CONTRACTORS ON THE GROUND:

This is incorrect as Paronto knows specifically of a CIA employee that was poorly treated while in Tripoli due to disagreeing with the story that was being fabricated by the CIA Benghazi Base Chief "Bob," CIA Station Chief and GRS Team Leader, who were briefing CIA Director Petraeus. The CIA employee also filed a complaint with the CIA Inspector General which either was never investigated or dismissed due to the fact it contradicted the fabricated report.

All GRS security contractors' were asked to sign multiple non-disclosure agreements after the event as well. This is important since a contractor will not be allowed deploy without signing non-disclosures put in front of them prior to a deployment. At the time GRS contractors were given little time to review the non-disclosure agreement and were not allowed to have an attorney of their choice review the non-disclosure agreement to ensure its fairness for both the contractors and the government.

Per Mike Rogers and the committee's central issue of there being no intelligence failures prior to the 09/11/2012 – 09/12/2012 attack we'd like to advise the committee to read page 51 of <u>13 Hours, The Inside Account of What Really Happened in Benghazi.</u>

This was taken from a "BOLO" (be on the lookout) report provided the GRS Security Team by the CIA staff approximately 2weeks prior to the 09/11/2012 attack on the TMF

"Be advised, we have reports from locals that a Western facility or US Embassy/Consulate/Government target will be attacked in the next week ... As a precaution, the operators moved their body armor,

long guns, ammunition, night-vision goggles, and other tactical gear
into their bedrooms, so they could more quickly "jock up," as they
called preparing for battle. Discussions had been under way for some
time about "co-locating" the Compound and the Annex on the same
property, so Bob the Annex chief suggested a trial run. He urged the
Diplomatic Security team to move to the Annex during the ambassador's visit, for added layers of protection. The offer was declined ... "

The GRS security contractor's consistent testimony and book, <u>13
Hours, "The Inside Account of What Really Happened in Benghazi"</u>,
written by Mitchell Zuckoff are the factual accounts of what took
place on the ground in Benghazi on 09/11/2012 to 09/12/2012. Over
the past two years, the mainstream media generally, have not once
pointed out the heroism displayed by the GRS security contractors
over 13 hours of hell even though it was stated several times in Mike
Rogers and his committee's report.

However, they are quick to jump on a false and misguided report,
written by those who have may have a conflict of interest, something
to lose, an agenda to protect, or a President and Secretary of State to
absolve, by calling us liars.

It's okay though. We have continually attempted to take the "high
road" and not delve into the political weeds, until we were once again
called liars by the same government we had sworn to protect. We never
did what we did that night into the following morning to support
agendas, political parties or presidencies. We did what we did that
night to save the lives of fellow Americans and defend American soil.
We disobeyed orders and went to help the DS agents and our friends
because they were under attack by terrorists and were on the brink of
death. Now it's our turn once again to set the record straight, show
integrity and tell the truth. It's a pity though that the truth is something
that's not very popular in today's society.

Acknowledgments

I would like to give a special thanks to the following people.

All the men whom I served with, you continue to inspire me. Never doubt the greatness you can achieve in whatever endeavor you choose to pursue after you leave teams, just as you achieved greatness on the inside.

Also, to all the men and women in OPSEC, you know who you are. Continue to fight for our brothers and sisters in arms, your work is important.

Thanks to David Freddoso for his help. And to the men and women at Regnery, I shall forever be grateful for the opportunity.

And, of course, to my family, extended family, and "Big Brother" Andy. Your support and love give me strength.

Notes

CHAPTER TWO: DISHONORABLE DISCLOSURES

1. "Bill Clinton Said the Day before 9/11 He Could Have Killed Bin Laden," *Time*, August 1, 2014. http://time.com/3070889/bill-clinton-bin-laden/.

2. "Biden Opposed bin Laden Raid," Daily Beast, January 31, 2012, http://www.thedailybeast.com/cheats/2012/01/31/biden-opposed-bin-laden-raid.html.

3. Brian Montopoli, "Who Deserves Credit for Bin Laden's Killing?" CBS News, May 3, 2011, http://www.cbsnews.com/news/who-deserves-credit-for-bin-ladens-killing/.

4. Aisha Chowdry, "Pakistani Anger Lingers a Year after Raid Killed bin Laden," *USA Today*, May 1, 2012, http://usatoday30.usatoday.com/news/world/story/2012-05-01/osama-bin-laden-pakistan-raid/54662824/1.

5. "Obama: Bin Laden Will Not Walk This Earth Again," CBS *60 Minutes*, May 5, 2011.

6. Ibid.

7. "Osama bin Laden Is Dead," White House transcript, May 2, 2011, http://www.whitehouse.gov/blog/2011/05/02/osama-bin-laden-dead.

8. Jackie Calmes "Bin Laden Killing Now Part of Obama Stump Speech," *New York Times*, May 10, 2011, http://thecaucus.blogs.nytimes.com/2011/05/10/bin-laden-killing-now-part-of-obama-stump-speech/?_r=0.

9. "Osama bin Laden is dead," White House transcript, May 2, 2011, http://www.whitehouse.gov/blog/2011/05/02/osama-bin-laden-dead.

10. Toby Harnden, "Joe Biden Opens His Mouth about US Navy SEALs," *Telegraph*, May 4, 2011, http://blogs.telegraph.co.uk/news/tobyharnden/100086416/joe-biden-opens-his-mouth-about-us-navy-seals/.

11. Ibid.

12. Greg Miller and Peter Finn, "New Osama bin Laden documents released," *Washington Post*, May 3, 2012, http://www.washingtonpost.com/world/national-security/new-bin-laden-documents-released/2012/05/03/gIQAYOcnyT_story.html.

13. Richard Tomkins, "'Loose Lips' Warning Still True," Human Events, May 29, 2011, http://humanevents.com/2011/05/31/loose-lips-warning-still-true/.

14. Jennifer Epstein and Charles Hoskinson, "Robert Gates: Raid Details Are Dangerous," *Politico*, May 18, 2011, http://www.politico.com/news/stories/0511/55229.html.

15. Daniel Halper, "Gates to National Security Team on Osama Raid: 'Shut the F--- Up'" *Weekly Standard*, June 6, 2012, https://www.weeklystandard.com/blogs/gates-national-security-team-osama-raid-shut-f_646731.html.

16. Greg Miller and Peter Finn, "New Osama bin Laden documents released," *Washington Post*, May 3, 2012, http://www.washingtonpost.com/world/national-security/new-bin-laden-documents-released/2012/05/03/gIQAYOcnyT_story.html.

17. Bryan Bender, "Troves of Files on JFK Assassination Remain Secret," *Boston Globe*, November 25, 2013, http://www.bostonglobe.com/2013/11/25/government-still-withholding-thousands-documents-jfk-assassination/PvBM2PCgW1H11vadQ4Wp4H/story.html.

18. Glenn Greenwald, "Selective bin Laden leaking," Salon, April 27, 2012, http://www.salon.com/2012/04/27/selective_bin_laden_leaking/.

19. David A. Graham, "The SEALs' Big-Screen Moment," Daily Beast, September 4, 2011, http://www.thedailybeast.com/articles/2011/09/04/targeting-bin-laden-history-channel-doc-relives-bin-laden-raid.html.

20. "Bush OKs US Raids into Pakistan," *APS Diplomat Redrawing the Islamic Map* 56 (208), issue 3.

21. Stephanie Condon, "Documents Show Filmmakers Were Granted Unique Access to bin Laden Raid Info," CBS News, May 23, 2012, http://www.cbsnews.com/news/documents-show-filmmakers-were-granted-unique-access-to-bin-laden-raid-info/.

22. Josh Gerstein, "Pentagon, CIA, White House Opened Up to Hollywood on bin Laden Raid," *Politico*, May 23, 2012, http://www.politico.com/blogs/under-the-radar/2012/05/pentagon-cia-white-house-opened-up-to-hollywood-on-124293.html.

23. Ibid.

24. "Judicial Watch Obtains DOD and CIA Records Detailing Meetings with bin Laden Raid Filmmakers," Judicial Watch, May 22, 2012, http://www.judicialwatch.org/press-room/press-releases/13421/.

25. Jim Miklaszewski, "Obama Aides Gave Classified Information on bin Laden Raid for Film, Watchdog Says," NBC News, May 12, 2012, http://usnews.nbcnews.com/_news/2012/05/22/11816421-obama-aides-gave-classified-information-on-bin-laden-raid-for-film-watchdog-says.

26. Gerstein, "Pentagon, CIA, White House Opened Up to Hollywood."

27. J. Hoberman, "Zero Dark Thirty: The US Election Vehicle That Came Off the Rails," *Guardian*, January 18, 2013, http://www.theguardian.com/film/2013/jan/18/zero-dark-thirty-us-election.

28. "Biden: OBL Raid Most Audacious Military Plan in 500 Years," Hot Air, March, 20, 2012, http://hotair.com/archives/2012/03/20/biden-obl-raid-most-audacious-military-plan-in-500-years/.

29. Remarks by President Obama to the Troops in Afghanistan, May 2, 2011, http://www.whitehouse.gov/photos-and-video/video/2012/05/01/president-obama-speaks-troops-bagram-air-base#transcript.

30. John Rossomando, "Obama Spikes the Football in Afghanistan Speech, Touts bin Laden Killing," Red Alert Politics, May 1, 2012, http://redalertpolitics.com/2012/05/01/obama-spikes-the-football-in-afghanistan-speech/.

31. Dylan Byers and Josh Gerstein, "Obama Talks bin Laden in Rare Sit Room Interview," *Politico*, April 27, 2012, http://www.politico.com/blogs/media/2012/04/obama-holds-bin-laden-interview-in-situation-room-121873.html.

32. Ed Morrissey, "Mullen: Hey, Maybe We Shouldn't Be Making the bin Laden Mission a Political Football," Hot Air, May 1, 2012, http://hotair.com/archives/2012/05/01/mullen-hey-maybe-we-shouldnt-be-making-the-bin-laden-mission-a-political-football/.

33. BarackObama.com, "One Chance," YouTube, https://www.youtube.com/watch?v=BD75KOoNR9k.

34. Lauren Fox, "New Obama Video Attempts to Make Mitt Romney Look Weak on Foreign Policy," *U.S. News and World Report*, April 27, 2012, http://www.usnews.com/news/blogs/washington-whispers/2012/04/27/new-obama-video-attempts-to-make-mitt-romney-look-weak-on-foreign-policy.

35. Katrina Trinko, "Obama Uses Bin Laden to Attack Romney," *National Review Online*, April 27, 2012, http://www.nationalreview.com/corner/297133/obama-uses-bin-laden-attack-romney-katrina-trinko.

36. Ibid.

37. James Joyner, "Obama Spikes Football on bin Laden Killing," Outside the Beltway, April 28, 2012, http://www.outsidethebeltway.com/obama-spikes-football-on-bin-laden-killing/.

38. Toby Harnden, "SEALs Slam Obama for Using Them as 'Ammunition' in Bid to Take Credit for bin Laden Killing during Election Campaign," *Daily Mail*, April 30, 2012, http://www.dailymail.co.uk/news/article-2137636/Osama-bin-Laden-death-SEALs-slam-Obama-using-ammunition-bid-credit.html.

39. "Obama Defends bin Laden Ad, Denies Using Anniversary for 'Excessive Celebration,'" Fox News, April 30, 2012, http://www.foxnews.com/politics/2012/04/30/romney-course-would-have-ordered-bin-laden-raid/.

40. Natalie Evans, "'Spoiler Alert: We Got Bin Laden!' Obama and Romney Trade Jokes at Charity Dinner Ahead of Third Presidential Debate," *Daily Mirror*, October 19, 2012, http://www.mirror.co.uk/news/world-news/obama-and-romney-poke-fun-at-each-1386716.

41. Obama's tweet is available online at https://twitter.com/BarackObama/status/265594411751178240.

42. "First Leads on bin Laden Gathered at CIA Prison," Associated Press, May 2, 2011, http://www.cbsnews.com/news/first-leads-on-bin-laden-gathered-at-cia-prison/.

43. "Phone Call to Kuwaiti Courier Led to Bin Laden," Associated Press, May 6, 2011, http://www.washingtonpost.com/world/national-security/death-of-osama-bin-laden-phone-call-pointed-us-to-compound—and-to-the-pacer/2011/05/06/AFnSVaCG_story.html.

44. Ibid.

45. Thomas M. Defrank, "Bush Feels Obama Ignoring ex-President's Role in Osama Bin Laden Strike for 'Victory Lap': Source," *New York Daily News*, May 4, 2011, http://www.nydailynews.com/news/politics/bush-feels-obama-ignoring-ex-president-role-osama-bin-laden-strike-victory-lap-source-article-1.140080.

46. James Dao and Dalia Sussman, "For Obama, Big Rise in Poll Numbers after Bin Laden Raid," *New York Times*, May 4, 2011, http://www.nytimes.com/2011/05/05/us/politics/05poll.html.

47. "President Obama Job Approval: Foreign Policy," Real Clear Politics, http://www.realclearpolitics.com/epolls/other/president_obama_job_approval_foreign_policy-2821.html#polls.

48. "Exit Polls 2012: How the Vote Has Shifted," *Washington Post*, November 6, 2012, http://www.washingtonpost.com/wp-srv/special/politics/2012-exit-polls/table.html.

49. "President Obama Job Approval."

50. Jo Becker and Scott Shane, "Secret 'Kill List' Proves a Test of Obama's Principles and Will," *New York Times*, May 29, 2012, http://www.nytimes.com/2012/05/29/world/obamas-leadership-in-war-on-al-qaeda.html?pagewanted=all.

51. Ibid.

52. Ibid.

53. Ibid.

54. Ibid.

55. Ibid.

56. Scott Wilson and Jon Cohen, "Poll Finds Broad Support for Obama's Counterterrorism Policies," *Washington Post*, February 8, 2012, http://www.washingtonpost.com/politics/poll-finds-broad-support-for-obamas-counterterrorism-policies/2012/02/07/gIQAFrSEyQ_story.html.

57. Janine Zacharia, "In Arab States' Fears, Israel Sees Impetus for Action against Iran," *Washington Post*, November 30, 2010, http://www.washingtonpost.com/wp-dyn/content/article/2010/11/29/AR2010112906276.html.

58. Ibid.

59. David E. Sanger, "Obama Order Sped Up Wave of Cyberattacks against Iran," *New York Times*, June 1, 2012, http://www.nytimes.com/2012/06/01/world/middleeast/obama-ordered-wave-of-cyberattacks-against-iran.html?pagewanted=all.

60. David E. Sanger, "Obama order sped up wave of cyberattacks against Iran."

61. David Ignatius, "Anatomy of a Leak," *Washington Post*, June 22, 2012, http://www.washingtonpost.com/opinions/david-ignatius-anatomy-of-a-leak/2012/06/22/gJQAuvq2vV_story.html.

62. John Cook, "White House Didn't Ask New York Times Not to Publish Classified Information," Gawker, June 1, 2012, http://gawker.com/5915026/white-house-didnt-ask-new-york-times-not-to-publish-classified-information.

63. Evan Perez and Adam Entous, "FBI Probes Leaks on Iran Cyberattack," *Wall Street Journal*, June 5, 2012, http://online.wsj.com/articles/SB10001424052702303506404577448563517340188.

64. CNN Wire Staff, "FBI looks into possible White House leaks." CNN Wire, June 6, 2012, http://www.cnn.com/2012/06/06/politics/white-house-leaks/.

65. Ibid.

66. "The Obama Administration 'Willfully Leaked the Existence of STUXNET (a Computer Worm Used against Iran), allowing our enemies to learn more of our secrets and of our operations,'" Politifact.com, August 24, 2012, http://www.politifact.com/truth-o-meter/statements/2012/aug/24/special-operations-opsec-education-fund/group-says-obama-administration-willfully-leaked-e/.

67. Siobhan Gorman and Julian E. Barnes, "Cyber Combat: Act of War: Pentagon Sets Stage for U.S. to Respond to Computer Sabotage with Military Force," *Wall Street Journal*, May 31, 2011, http://online.wsj.com/articles/SB10001424052702304563104576355623135782718.

68. "International Strategy for Cyberspace: Prosperity, Security, and Openness in a Networked World," White House, May 2011, http://www.whitehouse. gov/sites/default/files/rss_viewer/international_strategy_for_cyberspace. pdf.

69. Uri Friedman, "Good Leak, Bad Leak," *Foreign Policy*, June 8, 2012, http:// www.foreignpolicy.com/articles/2012/06/07/good_leak_bad_leak.

70. Charlie Savage, "Secret U.S. Memo Made Legal Case to Kill a Citizen," *New York Times*, October 8, 2011, http://www.nytimes.com/2011/10/09/ world/middleeast/secret-us-memo-made-legal-case-to-kill-a-citizen. html?pagewanted=all&_r=0.

71. Ibid.

72. Ibid.

73. Jack Goldsmith, "Fire When Ready," *Foreign Policy*, March 19, 2012, http://www.foreignpolicy.com/articles/2012/03/19/fire_when_ready.

74. Benjamin Weiser, "U.S. Ordered to Release Memo in Awlaki Killing," *New York Times*, April 21, 2014, http://www.nytimes.com/2014/04/22/nyregion/ panel-orders-release-of-document-in-targeted-killing-of-anwar-al-awlaki.html.

75. Richard Silverstein, "Obama's Virus Wars: Mutually Assured Cyber-Destruction," *Guardian*, June 8, 2012, http://www.theguardian.com/ commentisfree/2012/jun/08/obama-virus-wars-mutually-assured-cyberdestruction.

76. Ibid.

77. David Sirota, "Humanity's Oldest Story," Creators.com Syndicate, June 19, 2013, http://www.creators.com/liberal/david-sirota/humanity-s-oldest-story.html.

78. Mollie Reilly, "Obama Told Aides He's 'Really Good at Killing People,' New Book 'Double Down' Claims," Huffington Post, November 4, 2013, http://www.huffingtonpost.com/2013/11/03/obama-drones-double-down_n_4208815.html.

79. Katrina Vanden Heuvel, "Obama's 'Kill list' is Unchecked Presidential Power," *Washington Post*, June 12, 2012, http://www.washingtonpost. com/opinions/obamas-kill-list-is-unchecked-presidential-power/2012/06/11/ gJQAHw05WV_story.html.

80. David Sirota "Actually, Obama Does Support 'Perpetual War," Salon, January 25, 2013, http://www.salon.com/2013/01/25/actually_obama_ does_advocate_perpetual_war/.

81. Becker and Shane, "Secret 'Kill List.'"

82. Matt Sledge, "The Toll of 5 Years of Drone Strikes: 2,400 dead," Huffington Post, January 23, 2014, http://www.huffingtonpost.com/2014/01/23/obama-drone-program-anniversary_n_4654825.html.

83. "Global Opposition to U.S. Surveillance and Drones, but Limited Harm to America's Image," Pew Research Global Attitudes Project, July 14, 2014,

http://www.pewglobal.org/2014/07/14/global-opposition-to-u-s-surveillance-and-drones-but-limited-harm-to-americas-image/.

84. Michael S. Schmidt and Eric Schmitt, "U.S. Officials Say Libya Approved Commando Raids," *New York Times*, October 9, 2013, http://www.nytimes.com/2013/10/09/world/africa/us-officials-say-libya-approved-commando-raids.html?pagewanted=all.

85. Ibid.

86. Carlotta Gall, "Show of Power by Libya Militia in Kidnapping," *New York Times*, October 10, 2013, http://www.nytimes.com/2013/10/11/world/africa/libya.html?pagewanted=all.

87. Marc Thiessen, "Kidnapped Libyan Prime Minister Pays the Price for an Obama Leak," *Washington Post*, November 10, 2013, http://www.washingtonpost.com/opinions/marc-thiessen-the-consequences-of-an-obama-administration-leak/2013/10/10/cfd5b43c-31ad-11e3-8627-c5d7de0a046b_story.html.

88. Schmidt and Schmitt, "U.S. Officials Say Libya Approved."

89. Adam Goldman and Karen DeYoung, "U.S. Staged Secret Operation into Syria in Failed Bid to Rescue Americans," *Washington Post*, Aug. 20, 2014, http://www.washingtonpost.com/world/national-security/us-weighs-response-to-apparent-execution-of-american-by-islamic-state/2014/08/20/e33558a8-287d-11e4-8593-da634b334390_story.html.

90. Michael D. Shear and Eric Schmitt, "In Raid to Save Foley and Other Hostages, U.S. Found None," *New York Times*, August 20, 2014, http://www.nytimes.com/2014/08/21/world/middleeast/us-commandos-tried-to-rescue-foley-and-other-hostages.html.

91. Ibid.

CHAPTER THREE: CALL OF DUTY

1. Jeffrey M. Jones, "Views of Obama on International Matters Little Changed," Gallup Politics, August 1, 2008, http://www.gallup.com/poll/109189/Views-Obama-International-Matters-Little-Changed.aspx.

2. David Paul Kuhn, "Exit Polls: Economy Top Issue," *Politico*, November 5, 2008, http://www.politico.com/news/stories/1108/15270.html.

3. "President Barack Obama's Inaugural Address," January 21, 2009. http://www.whitehouse.gov/blog/inaugural-address.

4. Charlie Savage, "Accused 9/11 Mastermind to Face Civilian Trial in N.Y.," *New York Times*, November 13, 2009, http://www.nytimes.com/2009/11/14/us/14terror.html?pagewanted=all&_r=0.

5. Scott Shane and Benjamin Weiser, "U.S. Drops Plan for a 9/11 Trial in New York City," *New York Times*, January 29, 2010, http://www.nytimes.com/2010/01/30/nyregion/30trial.html?pagewanted=all.

6. Reid J. Epstein, "Hill Leaders Blast W.H. on Leaks," *Politico*, June 7, 2012, http://www.politico.com/news/stories/0612/77171.html.

7. Ibid.

8. Chris McGreal, "Senators Plan Legal Crackdown on Obama Administration Leaks," *Guardian*, June 7, 2012, http://www.theguardian.com/world/2012/jun/07/congressional-committee-legislation-leaks.

9. Donna Cassata, "McCain Says Classified Leaks Done to Boost Obama," Associated Press, June 5, 2012, http://www.bigstory.ap.org/article/mccain-says-classified-leaks-done-boost-obama.

10. Charles Krauthammer, "Barack Obama: Drone Warrior," *Washington Post*, May 31, 2014, http://www.washingtonpost.com/opinions/barack-obama-drone-warrior/2012/05/31/gJQAr6zQ5U_story.html.

11. Richard Cohen, "Obama loses veneer of deniability with intelligence leaks," *Washington Post*, June 11, 2012, http://www.washingtonpost.com/opinions/obama-loses-veneer-of-deniabilty-with-intelligence-leaks/2012/06/11/gJQA8lAoVV_story.html.

12. Debra J. Saunders, "Feinstein Takes On Culture of Leaks," *San Francisco Chronicle*, June 14, 2012, http://www.sfgate.com/opinion/saunders/article/Too-much-information-too-little-intelligence-3632441.php.

13. Uri Friedman, "Good Leak, Bad Leak," *Foreign Policy*, June 8, 2012. http://www.foreignpolicy.com/articles/2012/06/07/good_leak_bad_leak.

14. "Obama Leaks Risk National Security for Political Gain," *Investor's Business Daily*, June 5, 2012, http://news.investors.com/ibd-editorials/060412-613662-obama-leaks-war-on-terror-secrets.htm?ntt=can't%20white%20house%20keep%20a%20secret.

15. Josh Gerstein, "The 'Leak' Wars," *Politico*, June 8, 2012, http://www.politico.com/news/stories/0612/77194.html.

16. Laura Matthews, "Sen Lieberman: White House Leaks 'Worst in a Long Time,'" *International Business Times*, June 18, 2012, http://www.ibtimes.com/sen-lieberman-white-house-leaks-worst-long-time-703269.

17. Suzanne Kelly, "Feinstein: 'Avalanche of Leaks,'" CNN, June 6, 2012, http://security.blogs.cnn.com/2012/06/06/feinstein-avalanche-of-leaks/.

18. Saunders, "Feinstein Takes on Culture of Leaks."

19. Jack Kelly, "Who's Responsible for Security Leaks?" *Pittsburgh Post-Gazette*, July 31, 2012, http://www.post-gazette.com/opinion/jack-kelly/2012/07/31/Who-s-responsible-for-security-leaks/stories/201207310203.

20. Patrick Brennan, "Kerry Questions Obama Leaks and *Times* Stories," *National Review Online*, June 7, 2012, http://www.nationalreview.com/corner/302077/kerry-questions-obama-leaks-and-itimesi-stories-patrick-brennan.

21. Scott Shane, "Inquiry of Leaks Is Casting a Chill over Coverage," *New York Times*, August 1, 2012, http://www.nytimes.com/2012/08/02/us/national-security-leaks-lead-to-fbi-hunt-and-news-chill.html?pagewanted=all.

22. Josh Gerstein, "Senate Panel Nixes anti-Leak measures," *Politico*, December 22, 2012, http://www.politico.com/blogs/under-the-radar/2012/12/senate-panel-nixes-antileak-measures-152684.html.

23. M. J. Lee, "Lawmakers: Leakers Go to Jail," *Politico*, June 8, 2012, http://www.politico.com/news/stories/0612/77206.html.

24. "Holder Assigns Prosecutors to Investigate Alleged Leaks," CNN Wire, June 8, 2012, http://www.cnn.com/2012/06/08/politics/white-house-leaks/.

25. Charlie Savage, "2 Inquiries Set to Track Down Paths of Leaks," *New York Times*, June 9, 2012, http://www.nytimes.com/2012/06/09/us/politics/holder-directs-us-attorneys-to-investigate-leaks.html?gwh=06C6CAA075242FBB9D0AC4FFFD944CBF&gwt=pay.

26. Ibid.

27. Ibid.

28. Duane Lester, "Holder Appoints Obama Donor to Investigate White House Leaks," All American Blogger, June 12, 2012, http://allamericanblogger.com/blog/21973/holder-appoints-obama-donor-to-investigate-white-house-leaks/.

29. "Dishonorable Disclosures," YouTube, http://www.youtube.com/watch?v=X-Xfti7qtT0.

30. Jason Ryan, "FBI Investigates Media Leaks in Yemen Bomb Plot," ABC News, May 16, 2012, http://abcnews.go.com/blogs/politics/2012/05/fbi-investigates-media-leaks-in-yemen-bomb-plot/.

31. Rowan Scarborough, "Hollywood Endangers U.S. Special Forces by Revealing Tactics to Islamic Extremists," *Washington Times*, December 17, 2014, http://www.washingtontimes.com/news/2014/dec/17/special-operations-forces-tactics-compromised-by-h/.

32. Ibid.

33. Scott Shane, "Inquiry of Leaks."

34. "Dishonorable Disclosures."

35. Scott Change, "Ex-Officers Attack Obama over Leaks on Bin Laden Raid," *New York Times*, August 15, 2012, http://www.nytimes.com/2012/08/16/us/politics/ex-military-and-cia-officers-attack-obama-over-bin-laden-leaks.html.

36. Byron Tau, "Kerry Defends Obama against Vets' Attack," *Politico*, August 17, 2012, http://www.politico.com/politico44/2012/08/kerry-defends-obama-against-vets-attack-132451.html.

37. Jeremy Herb, "Senate Democrats Blast National Security Leak about Cyberattack against Iran," The Hill, June 6, 2012, http://thehill.com/policy/defense/230985-senate-dems-blast-leaks-about-iranian-cyberattacks.

38. Kate Wiltrout, "Obama Calls for Compromise to Avoid Military Cuts,"
     Virginian-Pilot, August 21, 2012, http://hamptonroads.com/2012/08/
     obama-calls-compromise-avoid-military-cuts.

39. Drew DeSilver, "Most Members of Congress Have Little Direct Military
     Experience," Pew Research Center, September 4, 2013, http://www.
     pewresearch.org/fact-tank/2013/09/04/members-of-congress-have-little-
     direct-military-experience/.

40. Kristen A. Lee, "Joint Chiefs Chairman Gen. Martin Dempsey Scolds
     Veterans over anti-Obama Documentary," *New York Daily News*, August
     22, 2012, http://www.nydailynews.com/news/politics/joint-chiefs-chairman-
     gen-martin-dempsey-scolds-veterans-anti-obama-documentary-
     article-1.1141768.

41. "Leakgate: Obama's Unspinnable Scandal," *Investor's Business Daily*,
     August 23, 2012, http://news.investors.com/ibd-editorials/082312-623334-
     joint-chiefs-chairmans-attack-on-ex-seals-unjustified.htm.

42. *On the Record with Greta Van Susteren*, Fox News Network, August 21,
     2012.

43. Daniel Politi, "Obama Has Charged More Under Espionage Act Than All
     Other Presidents Combined," *Slate*, June 22, 2013, http://www.slate.com/
     blogs/the_slatest/2013/06/22/edward_snowden_is_eighth_person_obama_
     has_pursued_under_espionage_act.html.

44. Gerstein, "The 'Leak' Wars."

45. Marisa Taylor and Jonathan S. Landay, "'Zero Dark Thirty' Leak
     Investigators Now Target of Leak Probe," McClatchy, December 20, 2013,
     http://www.mcclatchydc.com/2013/12/20/212378/zero-dark-thirty-leak-
     investigators.html.

46. Phil Stewart, "Pentagon Threatens Legal Action over bin Laden Book,"
     Reuters, August 30, 2012, http://www.reuters.com/article/2012/08/31/
     entertainment-us-usa-security-binladen-b-idUSBRE87U00F20120831.

47. Associated Press, "Seven SEALs from bin Laden Team Are Punished for
     Sharing Military Secrets with Creators of Video Game Medal of Honor,"
     Daily Mail, November 8, 2012, http://www.dailymail.co.uk/news/article-
     2230296/7-Navy-SEALs-team-6-punished-sharing-military-secrets-Medal-
     Honor-video-game-creators.html.

48. "OPSEC—Press release—Scott Taylor statement," August 31, 2012, http://
     www.standupamericaus.org/politics-washington-dc/opsec-press-release-
     scott-taylor-statement/.

49. David Wise, "Leaks and the Law: The Story of Thomas Drake," *Smithsonian*,
     August 2011, http://www.smithsonianmag.com/ist/?next=/history/leaks-
     and-the-law-the-story-of-thomas-drake-14796786/.

50. Ashley Fantz, "New massive release to put Iraq War and WikiLeaks in Spotlight" CNN.com, October 22, 2010, http://www.cnn.com/2010/US/10/22/wikileaks.iraq.documents/.

51. Apuzzo's tweet can be viewed at https://twitter.com/mattapuzzo/status/208557224371556352.

52. Dana Milbank, "In AP, Rosen Investigations, Government Makes Criminals of Reporters," *Washington Post*, May 21, 2013, http://www.washingtonpost.com/opinions/dana-milbank-in-ap-rosen-investigations-government-makes-criminals-of-reporters/2013/05/21/377af392-c24e-11e2-914f-a7aba60512a7_story.html.

53. Josh Gerstein, "The 'Leak' Wars."

CHAPTER FOUR: "LEADING FROM BEHIND"

1. Gregory N. Hicks, "Gregory Hicks: Benghazi and the Smearing of Chris Stevens," *Wall Street Journal*, January 22, 2014, http://online.wsj.com/news/articles/SB10001424052702304302704579332732276330284.

2. House Select Committee on Benghazi, "Implementation of the Accountability Review Board recommendations," September 17, 2014, http://benghazi.house.gov/hearings/hearing-1.

3. Tabassum Zakaria, Susan Cornwell, and Hadeel al Shalchi, "For Benghazi Diplomatic Security, U.S. Relied on Small British Firm," Reuters, October 17, 2012, http://www.reuters.com/article/2012/10/18/us-libya-usa-bluemountain-idUSBRE89G1TI20121018.

4. U.S. Senate Select Committee on Intelligence, "Review of the Terrorist Attacks on U.S. Facilities in Benghazi, Libya, September 11–12, 2012," January 15, 2014, http://www.intelligence.senate.gov/benghazi2014/benghazi.pdf.

5. Sharyl Attkisson, "Officials on Benghazi: We made mistakes, but without malice," CBS News, May 17, 2013, http://www.cbsnews.com/news/officials-on-benghazi-we-made-mistakes-but-without-malice/.

6. See Appendix A, July 16, 2014, letter to Scott Taylor from Representative Frank R. Wolf.

7. Terence P. Jeffrey, "Flashback—Obama: 'I Authorized' Intervention in Libyan Civil War Because 'Writ of International Community Must Be Enforced,'" CNS News, October 24, 2012, http://cnsnews.com/news/article/flashback-obama-i-authorized-intervention-libyan-civil-war-because-writ-international.

8. Gareth Evans, Proceedings of the Annual Meeting (American Society of International Law), vol. 98 (March 31–April 3, 2004): 78–89.

9. Colum Lynch, "The Libya Debate: How Fair Is Obama's New Claim That the U.S. Led from the Front?" *Foreign Policy*, Oct. 23, 2012, http://blog.

foreignpolicy.com/posts/2012/10/23/how_fair_is_obama_new_claim_that_the_us_lead_from_the_front_on_libya.

10. Ajnadin Mustafa, "ISIS to Launch TV Station Based in Sirte: report," *Libya Herald*, October 12, 2014, http://www.libyaherald.com/2014/10/12/isis-to-launch-tv-station-based-in-sirte/.

11. Paul Cruickshank, et al., "ISIS Comes to Libya," CNN, November 18, 2014, http://edition.cnn.com/2014/11/18/world/isis-libya/index.html.

12. Farai Sevenzo, "African Viewpoint: Colonel's Continent?" BBC, http://www.bbc.co.uk/news/world-africa-12585395.

13. Sam Dagher, "Libya City Torn by Tribal Feud," *Wall Street Journal*, June 21, 2011, http://online.wsj.com/news/articles/SB10001424052702304887904576395143328336026.

14. Omar Almosmari and Maggie Michael, "Libya's persecuted Tawergha people displaced for the 2nd time amid clashes that left 65 dead," Associated Press, October 20, 2014, http://bigstory.ap.org/article/b7847b9422fb4e58ae23966b013d3151/death-toll-hits-65-libyas-eastern-strife.

15. Jeremy Binnie, "Libya's anti-Islamist offensive suffers setback," IHS Jane's 360, http://www.janes.com/article/41155/libya-s-anti-islamist-offensive-suffers-setback.

16. Reuters, "Who is bombing Libya? U.S. says it's Egypt, UAE," August 25, 2014, http://www.newsweek.com/who-bombing-libya-us-says-its-egypt-uae-266599.

17. Mitchell Zuckoff with the Annex Security Team, *13 Hours: The Inside Account of What Really Happened in Benghazi* (New York: Twelve, 2014).

18. "13 Hours at Benghazi: The Inside Story," Fox News, September 5, 2014, http://video.foxnews.com/v/3793874919001/13-hours-at-benghazi-the-inside-story/#sp=show-clips.

19. Nic Robertson, Paul Cruickshank, and Tim Lister, "Pro-al Qaeda Group Seen behind Deadly Benghazi Attack," CNN, September 12, 2012, http://www.cnn.com/2012/09/12/world/africa/libya-attack-jihadists/.

20. Daniel Halper, "Father of Slain SEAL: Who Made the Decision Not to Save My Son?" *Weekly Standard*, October 25, 2012, http://www.weeklystandard.com/blogs/father-slain-seal-who-made-decision-not-save-my-son_657782.html#.

21. U.S. House of Representatives Permanent Select Committee on Intelligence, "Investigative Report on the Terrorist Attacks on U.S. Facilities in Benghazi, Libya, September 11–12, 2012," U.S. House of Representatives, 113th Congress, November 21, 2014, http://intelligence.house.gov/sites/intelligence.house.gov/files/documents/Benghazi%20Report.pdf.

22. Mollie Hemingway at the Federalist argues that "the executive summary of the report is not well supported by the contents." See Mollie Hemingway, "20 Ways Media Completely Misread Congress' Weak-Sauce Benghazi

Report," The Federalist, November 24, 2014, http://thefederalist. com/2014/11/24/20-ways-media-completely-misread-congress-weak-sauce-benghazi-report/.

23.   "Benghazi Debunked," *Washington Post*, http://www.washingtonpost. com/opinions/benghazi-debunked/2014/11/29/876ff67e-751f-11e4-bd1b-03009bd3e984_story.html.

24.   Ibid.

25.   John "Tig" Tiegen and Kris "Tanto" Paronto, "The CIA Global Response Contractors' Public Response to the November 21, 2014 House Intelligence Committee Report about the September 11 and 12, 2012 Benghazi Attacks: Michael Roger's House Intelligence Report Is Full of Inaccuracies." See Appendix B to this book for the full text.

26.   Hemingway, "20 Ways."

27.   Stephen F. Hayes and Thomas Joscelyn, "The Benghazi Report: An Ongoing Intelligence Failure," *Weekly Standard*, December 15, 2014, http://www. weeklystandard.com/articles/benghazi-report_820665.html.

28.   Ibid., 8.

29.   Ibid., 2.

30.   Ibid., 6.

31.   Ibid., 7.

32.   Committee on Intelligence, "Investigative Report," 21.

33.   Ibid.

34.   Ibid.

35.   Tiegen and Paronto, "The CIA Global Response Contractors' Public Response," 8.

36.   Committee on Intelligence, "Investigative Report," 20.

37.   Zuckoff, *13 Hours*, 111

38.   Tiegen and Paronto, "The CIA Global Response Contractors' Public Response," 6.

39.   Ibid.

40.   Ibid., 5.

41.   Committee on Intelligence, "Investigative Report," 20.

42.   Tiegen and Paronto, "The CIA Global Response Contractors' Public Response," 5–6.

43.   Committee on Intelligence, "Investigative Report," 23.

44.   Tiegen and Paronto, "The CIA Global Response Contractors' Public Response," 9.

CHAPTER FIVE: WHO LOST IRAQ?

1.   "Clinton Hits Obama on Foreign Relations Experience," CNN Politics, November 20, 2007, http://politicalticker.blogs.cnn.com/2007/11/20/ clinton-hits-obama-on-foreign-relations-experience/.

2.   Ibid.

3.   Patrick Healy, "Most Experience or Enough Experience?" *New York Times*, November 25, 2007, http://www.nytimes.com/2007/11/25/weekinreview/25healy. html?_r=0.

4.   The ad can be viewed on YouTube at: https://www.youtube.com/watch?v=aZ_ z9Tpdl9A.

5.   David Remnick, "Going the Distance: On and Off the Road with Barack Obama," *New Yorker*, January 27, 2014, http://www.newyorker.com/ magazine/2014/01/27/going-the-distance-2?currentPage=all.

6.   Josh Gerstein, "Obama's 'Strategy' Misfire," *Politico*, August 31, 2014, http://www.politico.com/story/2014/08/obama-no-strategy-isil-110435. html.

7.   Catherine Herridge, "Source: Obama Given Detailed Intelligence for a Year about Rise of ISIS," Fox News, September 2, 2014, http://www.foxnews. com/politics/2014/09/02/source-obama-given-detailed-intelligence-about- rise-isis-for-year/.

8.   See "ISIS Militants Carry Out Apparent Mass Execution in Syria," CBS, August 28, 2014, http://www.cbsnews.com/news/isis-militants-execute- dozens-of-captured-syrian-soldiers-activists-say/, and Aryn Baker, "ISIS Claims Massacre of 1,700 Iraqi Soldiers," *Time*, June 15, 2014, http://time. com/2878718/isis-claims-massacre-of-1700-iraqis/ for just two gruesome examples of many.

9.   Joel Gehrke, "Terrorists' Handbook: In Rhetoric and Tactics, ISIS Sounds a Lot Like an al-Qaeda Manual," August 29, 2014, http://www. nationalreview.com/article/386728/terrorists-handbook-joel-gehrke.

10.   Statement by the President, The White House, August 28, 2014, http:// www.whitehouse.gov/the-press-office/2014/08/28/statement-president.

11.   B. H. Liddell Hart, ed. *The Rommel Papers* (New York: Da Capo, 1982), 328.

12.   "Energy Security, America's Best Defense: A study of increasing dependence on fossil fuels in wartime and its contribution to ever higher casualty rates," Deloitte, May 2010.

13.   "Petroleum in the Near East," March 16, 1943, cited in Barry Rubin, *The Great Powers in the Middle East 1941–1947: The Road to the Cold War* (London: Frank Cass and Company, 1980), 11.

14.   Thomas W. Lippman, "The Day FDR Met Saudi Arabia's Ibn Saud," *The Link* 38, vol. 2 (April–May 2005): 1–12, http://www.ameu.org/ getattachment/51ee4866-95c1-4603-b0dd-e16d2d49fcbc/The-Day-FDR- Met-Saudi-Arabia-Ibn-Saud.aspx.

15.   David von Drehle and R. Jeffrey Smith, "U.S. Strikes Iraq for Plot to Kill Bush, *Washington Post*, June 27, 1993, http://www.washingtonpost.com/ wp-srv/inatl/longterm/iraq/timeline/062793.htm.

16. Michael R. Gordon and Bernard E. Trainor, "Even As U.S. Invaded, Hussein Saw Iraqi Unrest as Top Threat," *New York Times*, March 12, 2006, http://www.nytimes.com/2006/03/12/international/middleeast/12saddam.html?pagewanted=all.

17. Barack Obama, "Transcript: Obama's [October 2, 2002] Speech against the Iraq War," NPR, January 20, 2009, http://www.npr.org/templates/story/story.php?storyId=99591469.

18. Josh Voorhees, "Obama Just Sent 130 More 'Military Advisers' to Iraq. Is a Rescue Operation Next?," *Slate*, August 13, 2014, http://www.slate.com/blogs/the_world_/2014/08/13/u_s_military_advisers_in_iraq_obama_sends_in_another_130_troops_as_talk.html.

19. John F. Kerry, "We Still Have a Choice on Iraq," *New York Times*, September 6, 2002.

20. Angie Drobnic Holan, "Obama Sticks to His Iraq Plan," FactCheck.org, *Tampa Bay Times*, August 12, 2008, http://www.politifact.com/truth-o-meter/statements/2008/aug/12/barack-obama/obama-sticks-to-his-iraq-plan/.

21. Kate Brannen, "Top Marine Commander: Iraq Chaos Shows Costs of U.S. Withdrawal," *Foreign Policy*, July 15, 2014, http://complex.foreignpolicy.com/posts/2014/07/15/amos_afghanistan_iraq.

22. "Leon Panetta: How the White House Misplayed Iraqi Troop Talks," *Time*, October 1, 2014.

23. Ibid.

24. PBS Frontline, "Losing Iraq," July 29, 2014, http://www.pbs.org/wgbh/pages/frontline/losing-iraq/.

25. Fox News Sunday, October 5, 2014.

26. White House press conference, June 19, 2014, http://www.whitehouse.gov/the-press-office/2014/06/19/remarks-president-situation-iraq.

27. Michael R. Gordon, "Iran Supplying Syrian Military via Iraqi Airspace," *New York Times*, September 4, 2012, http://www.nytimes.com/2012/09/05/world/middleeast/iran-supplying-syrian-military-via-iraq-airspace.html.

28. PBS Frontline, "Losing Iraq," July 29, 2014.

29. Ben van Heuvelen, "The Man Who Would Be King," *Foreign Policy*, June 13, 2011, http://www.foreignpolicy.com/articles/2011/06/13/the_man_who_would_be_king.

30. Patrick Cockburn, "Iraq Regime Tries to Silence Corruption Whistleblowers," *Independent*, September 29, 2011, http://www.independent.co.uk/news/world/middle-east/iraq-regime-tries-to-silence-corruption-whistleblowers-2362637.html.

31. Zaid Al-Ali, "How Maliki Ruined Iraq," *Foreign Policy*, June 19, 2014, http://www.foreignpolicy.com/articles/2014/06/19/how_maliki_ruined_iraq_armed_forces_isis.

32. "Iraq's Maliki Accuses Kurds of Hosting ISIS," *Al-Arabiya News*, July 9, 2014, http://english.alarabiya.net/en/News/middle-east/2014/07/09/Iraq-s-Maliki-accuses-Kurds-of-hosting-ISIS.html.

33. PBS Frontline, "Losing Iraq," July 29, 2014.

34. Gordon, "Iran Supplying Syria."

35. Eli Lake, "Why Obama Can't Say His Spies Underestimated ISIS," Daily Beast, September 28, 2014, http://www.thedailybeast.com/articles/2014/09/28/why-obama-can-t-say-his-spies-underestimated-isis.html.

36. "Annual Threat Assessment: Statement before the Senate Armed Services Committee," February 11, 2014, http://www.armed-services.senate.gov/imo/media/doc/Flynn_02-11-14.pdf.

CHAPTER SIX: "CHICKENSH*T DIPLOMACY"

1. Jeffrey Goldberg, "Obama on Zionism and Hamas," *The Atlantic*, May 12, 2008, http://www.theatlantic.com/international/archive/2008/05/obama-on-zionism-and-hamas/8318/.

2. Jeffrey Goldberg, "The Crisis in U.S.-Israel Relations Is Officially Here," *The Atlantic*, October 28, 2014, http://www.theatlantic.com/international/archive/2014/10/the-crisis-in-us-israel-relations-is-officially-here/382031/.

3. David Maraniss, *Barack Obama: The Story* (New York: Simon & Schuster Kindle edition, 2012), 354.

4. Ibid, 355.

5. David Freddoso, *The Case Against Barack Obama: The Unlikely Rise and Unexamined Agenda of the Media's Favorite Candidate* (Washington, DC: Regnery, 2008), 165.

6. Nazila Fathi, "Wipe Israel 'Off the Map' Iranian says," *New York Times*, October 27, 2005, http://www.nytimes.com/2005/10/26/world/africa/26iht-iran.html.

7. Seth Mandel "Obama's Telling Comment About Likud," *Commentary*, September 9, 2011, http://www.commentarymagazine.com/2011/09/19/obama-likud-netanyahu/.

8. Richard Miniter, *Leading from Behind: The Reluctant President and the Advisors Who Decide for Him* (New York: St. Martin's Press Kindle edition, 2013), 173.

9. Larry Rohter, "On McCain, Obama and a Hamas Link," *New York Times*, May 10, 2008, http://www.nytimes.com/2008/05/10/us/politics/10mccain.html.

10. Roni Sofer, "Poll: Israel votes McCain in US elections," ynetnews.com, October 27, 2008, http://www.ynetnews.com/articles/0,7340,L-3613689,00.html.

11. John Heilemann, "The Tsuris," *New York*, September 18, 2011, http://nymag.com/news/politics/israel-2011-9/.

12. James Traub, "The New Israel Lobby," *New York Times Magazine*, September 9, 2009, http://www.nytimes.com/2009/09/13/magazine/13JStreet-t.html?pagewanted=all.

13. Michael E. O'Hanlon, et al., *Bending History: Barack Obama's Foreign Policy* (Washington, DC: Brookings Kindle edition, 2012), 117.

14. Press Availability with Egyptian Foreign Minister Ahmed Ali Aboul Gheit, May 27, 2009, http://www.state.gov/secretary/20092013clinton/rm/2009a/05/124009.htm.

15. Chris McGreal and Rory McCarthy, "Obama: Halt to New Israeli settlements Is in America's Security Interests," *Guardian*, May 29, 2009, http://www.theguardian.com/world/2009/may/28/barack-obama-jewish-settlements-israel-palestine-relations.

16. "President Obama's Speech in Cairo: A New Beginning" http://www.whitehouse.gov/blog/NewBeginning/transcripts.

17. "Full text of Netanyahu's Foreign Policy Speech at Bar Ilan," Haaretz.com, June 14, 2009, http://www.haaretz.com/news/full-text-of-netanyahu-s-foreign-policy-speech-at-bar-ilan-1.277922.

18. O'Hanlon, et al., *Bending History*.

19. Ibid.

20. Joe Klein, "Q&A: Obama on His First Year in Office," *Time*, January 21, 2010.

21. Ethan Bronner, "As Biden Visits, Israel Unveils Plan for New Settlements," *New York Times*, March 9, 2010, http://www.nytimes.com/2010/03/10/world/middleeast/10biden.html.

22. Miniter, *Leading from Behind*, 177.

23. Ibid.

24. Adrian Blomfield, "Obama Snubbed Netanyahu for Dinner with Michelle and the Girls, Israelis Claim," *Telegraph*, March 25, 2010, http://www.telegraph.co.uk/news/worldnews/barackobama/7521220/Obama-snubbed-Netanyahu-for-dinner-with-Michelle-and-the-girls-Israelis-claim.html.

25. Ibid.

26. Joseph Park, "At Summit, Equatorial Guinea's President Looks to Soften Image," *Georgetowner*, August 4, 2014, http://www.georgetowner.com/articles/2014/aug/04/summit-equatorial-guineas-president-looks-soften-image/.

27. David E. Sanger, *Confront and Conceal: Obama's Secret Wars and Surprising Use of American Power* (New York: Random House Kindle edition, 2012), 227.

28. Richard Wolffe, *Revival: The Struggle for Survival Inside the Obama White House* (New York: Crown, 2011), 267.

29. "Palestinian Leader Mahmoud Abbas's Frustration with Obama," *Newsweek*, April 24, 2011, http://www.newsweek.com/palestinian-leader-mahmoud-abbass-frustration-obama-66509.

30. Hillary Rodham Clinton, *Hard Choices* (New York: Simon & Schuster Kindle edition, 2010), 315–16.

31. Mark Landler, "Netanyahu Sees Arab Alliance Aiding Mideast Peace," *New York Times*, October 1, 2014, http://www.nytimes.com/2014/10/02/world/middleeast/obama-netanyahu-israel-white-house.html.

32. Carol Morello and William Booth, "White House: Israel Faces Estrangement from Allies If Settlement Building Proceeds," *Washington Post*, October 1, 2014, http://www.washingtonpost.com/world/national-security/white-house-israel-faces-estrangement-from-allies-if-settlement-building-proceeds/2014/10/01/cd2680d6-4999-11e4-b72e-d60a9229cc10_story.html.

33. "Remarks by the President on the Middle East and North Africa," May 19, 2011, http://www.whitehouse.gov/the-press-office/2011/05/19/remarks-president-middle-east-and-north-africa%20.

34. Miniter, *Leading from Behind*.

35. Ibid., 183.

36. Ibid., 187.

37. "Remarks by the President at the AIPAC Policy Conference 2011," http://www.whitehouse.gov/the-press-office/2011/05/22/remarks-president-aipac-policy-conference-2011, May 22, 2011.

38. Rebecca Shabad, "New Tensions for Obama, Israel," The Hill, June 8, 2014, http://thehill.com/policy/international/208552-new-tensions-for-obama-israel.

39. Josef Federman, "Kerry Plays Down Spat with Israeli Defense Chief," Associated Press, January 15, 2014, http://bigstory.ap.org/article/kerry-plays-down-spat-israeli-defense-chief.

40. Josh Rogin, "Exclusive: Kerry Warns Israel Could Become 'An Apartheid State," Daily Beast, April 27, 2014, http://www.thedailybeast.com/articles/2014/04/27/exclusive-kerry-warns-israel-could-become-an-apartheid-state.html.

41. Karl Vick, "Obama Approval Rating Dives in Israel," *Time*, February 7, 2014.

42. Vick, "Obama Approval Rating Dives."

43. Gil Hoffman, "Poll finds Israelis don't trust Obama, Abbas," *Jerusalem Post*, October 2, 2014, http://new.jpost.com/Israel-News/Poll-finds-Israelis-dont-trust-Obama-Abbas-377936.

44. "The Covenant of Hamas—Main Points," Information Division, Israel Foreign Ministry, no date, http://fas.org/irp/world/para/docs/880818a.htm.

45. "Israel & the US: The Delusions of Our Diplomacy," *New York Review of Books*, October 9, 2014.

46. John Cassidy, "Hamas Snatches Disaster from the Jaws of Victory," *New Yorker*, August 2, 2014, http://www.newyorker.com/news/john-cassidy/hamas-snatches-disaster-jaws-victory.

47. "Brian Williams Interviews Netanyahu on Israel-Gaza Conflict," NBC *Nightly News*, http://www.nbcnews.com/storyline/middle-east-unrest/brian-williams-interviews-netanyahu-israel-gaza-conflict-n161276.

48. Leon Wieseltier, "Israel and Gaza, A Just and Unjust War," *New Republic*, August 6, 2014, http://www.newrepublic.com/article/118986/leon-wieseltier-israel-and-gaza-just-and-unjust-war.

49. Mudar Zahran, "Gazans Speak Out: Hamas War Crimes," Gatestone Institute, September 19, 2014, http://www.gatestoneinstitute.org/4706/gazan-hamas-war-crimes.

50. Michael Hausam, "Netanyahu on Hamas: Terrorists 'Using Their Civilians To Protect Their Missiles,'" IJReview, July 1, 2014, http://www.ijreview.com/2014/07/156651-netanyahu-hamas-theyre-using-civilians-protect-missiles/.

51. Jeff Mason, "White House Pressures Israel Over Civilian Deaths in Gaza," Reuters, July 21, 2014, http://www.reuters.com/article/2014/07/21/us-palestinians-israel-obama-idUSKBN0FQ22T20140721.

52. Adam Kredo, "Obama's 'Unprecedented' Support of Israel Includes Blocking Arms," *Washington Free Beacon*, August 15, 2014, http://freebeacon.com/national-security/obamas-unprecedented-support-of-israel-includes-blocking-arms/.

53. Adam Entous, "Gaza Crisis: Israel Outflanks the White House on Strategy," *Wall Street Journal*, August 14, 2014.

54. Noah Pollak, "Why Did the State Department Announce a Travel Warning for Israel?" *Weekly Standard*, July 22, 2014, http://www.weeklystandard.com/blogs/why-did-state-department-announce-travel-warning-israel_797262.html.

55. Michael R. Gordon and Rick Gladstone, "Kerry Claims Progress Toward Gaza Truce, but Hamas Leader Is Defiant," *New York Times*, July 23, 2014, http://www.nytimes.com/2014/07/24/world/middleeast/israel-gaza-strip-casualties.html.

56. Michael R. Gordon, "Even Gaza Truce is Hard to Win, Kerry is Finding," *New York Times*, July 27, 2014, http://www.nytimes.com/2014/07/28/world/middleeast/kerry-finds-even-a-truce-in-gaza-is-hard-to-win-cease-fire-hamas.html.

57. Entous, "Gaza Crisis."

58. Ibid.

59. Ibid.

60. Raphael Ahren, "US Officials Warn Kerry Criticism Could Jeopardize Israel Ties," *Times of Israel*, July 28, 2014, http://www.timesofisrael.com/us-officials-warn-kerry-criticism-could-jeopardize-israel-ties/.

61. Michael Doran, "Reconciliation with Iran Helps Fuel Middle East Mayhem," Brookings Institution, August 13, 2014, http://www.brookings.edu/blogs/markaz/posts/2014/08/13-doran-obama-middle-east-policy-danger-to-allies.

62. Tom Rose, "Israeli Leader to Obama: 'Leave Us Alone Already,'" Breitbart, July 28, 2014, http://www.breitbart.com/Big-Peace/2014/07/28/Leave-Us-Alone-Already-Israeli-Leader-Tells-Obama.

63. Ibid.

64. Ibid.

65. Entous, "Gaza Crisis."

66. Adam Entous and Nicholas Casey, "Gaza Tension Stoked by Unlikely Alliance Between Israel and Egypt," *Wall Street Journal*, August 6, 2014, http://online.wsj.com/news/article_email/unlikely-alliance-between-israel-and-egypt-stoked-gaza-tension-1407379093-lMyQjAxMTA0MDAwNzEwNDcyWj.

67. Goldberg, "The Crisis."

68. Michael D. Shear, "Obama Tries Diplomatic Outreach to Israeli Public," *Washington Post*, July 9, 2010, http://www.washingtonpost.com/wp-dyn/content/article/2010/07/09/AR2010070901313.html.

69. Margaret Talev and Warren P. Strobel, "Obama Speaks to Iranian People in Video Message," McClatchy DC, March 19, 2009, http://www.mcclatchydc.com/2009/03/19/64434/obama-speaks-to-iranian-people.html.

70. Sanger, *Confront and Conceal*, 157.

71. Robert F. Worthy, "Dissidents Mass in Tehran to Subvert an Anti-U.S. Rally," *New York Times*, November 4, 2009, http://www.nytimes.com/2009/11/05/world/middleeast/05iran.html?_r=0&gwh=7CBF13FE997375322E6163A769162D2E&gwt=pay.

72. "Israel Concerned over U.S. 'Defensive Umbrella,'" Associated Press, July 23, 2009, http://www.realclearworld.com/news/ap/international/2009/Jul/23/israel_concerned_over_us__umbrella__on_iran.html.

73. Sanger, *Confront and Conceal*, 178.

74. William Booth, "Israel's Netanyahu calls Iran deal 'historic mistake,'" *Washington Post*, November 24, 2013, http://www.washingtonpost.com/world/israel-says-iran-deal-makes-world-more-dangerous/2013/11/24/e0e347de-54f9-11e3-bdbf-097ab2a3dc2b_story.html.

75. "Rohani's Outstretched Hand," *Economist*, October 4, 2014. http://www.economist.com/news/middle-east-and-africa/21621868-could-americas-fight-against-islamic-state-hasten-nuclear-deal-iran.

76. Michelle Moghtader and Fredrik Dahl, "Iran says centrifuge testing, but no violation of atom deal with powers," Reuters, Nov. 12, 2014, http://

www.reuters.com/article/2014/11/12/us-iran-nuclear-centrifuges-idUSKCN0IW11O20141112.

77.   Lee Smith, "Appeasing Iran," *Weekly Standard*, October 13, 2014, http://www.weeklystandard.com/articles/appeasing-iran_808497.html.

78.   David Frum, "How Iran Scammed America Out of a Nuclear Deal," *The Atlantic*, October 1, 2014, http://www.theatlantic.com/international/archive/2014/10/how-iran-scammed-the-us-out-of-a-nuclear-deal/381014/.

79.   David Remnick, "Going the Distance," *New Yorker*, January 27, 2014, http://www.newyorker.com/magazine/2014/01/27/going-the-distance-2.

CHAPTER SEVEN: WHO LOST EGYPT?

1.   David E. Sanger, "As Mubarak Digs In, U.S. Policy in Egypt Is Complicated," *New York Times*, February 5, 2011, http://www.nytimes.com/2011/02/06/world/middleeast/06policy.html?pagewanted=all.

2.   "Egypt Crisis: 17 Days of Fluctuating US messages," *Telegraph*, February 11, 2011, http://www.telegraph.co.uk/news/worldnews/africaandindianocean/egypt/8318329/Egypt-crisis-17-days-of-fluctuating-US-messages.html.

3.   Matt Spetalnick and David Alexander, "Obama Ratchets Up Pressure on Egypt's Mubarak," Reuters, January 27, 2011, http://www.reuters.com/article/2011/01/27/us-egypt-protest-usa-idUSTRE70Q7XQ20110127.

4.   "Press Briefing by Press Secretary Robert Gibbs, 1/27/2011," January 27, 2011, http://www.whitehouse.gov/the-press-office/2011/01/27/press-briefing-press-secretary-robert-gibbs-1272011.

5.   Dan Murphy, "Joe Biden Says Egypt's Mubarak No Dictator, He Shouldn't Step Down … ," *Christian Science Monitor*, January 27, 2011, http://www.csmonitor.com/World/Backchannels/2011/0127/Joe-Biden-says-Egypt-s-Mubarak-no-dictator-he-shouldn-t-step-down.

6.   Glenn Thrush, "Hillary Clinton Plays Key Role in Dance with Hosni Mubarak," *Politico*, February 2, 2011, http://www.politico.com/news/stories/0211/48658.html.

7.   "Secretary Clinton in 2009: 'I Really Consider President and Mrs. Mubarak to Be Friends of my Family,'" ABC News, January 31, 2011, http://abcnews.go.com/blogs/politics/2011/01/secretary-clinton-in-2009-i-really-consider-president-and-mrs-mubarak-to-be-friends-of-my-family/.

8.   "U.S. to Reconsider Aid to Egypt As It Eyes Mubarak's Response to Protests," Associated Press, January 28, 2011, http://www.haaretz.com/news/world/u-s-to-reconsider-aid-to-egypt-as-it-eyes-mubarak-s-response-to-protests-1.339833.

9.   M. J. Lee, "Gibbs Misses the mark on Clinton," *Politico*, February 2, 2011, http://www.politico.com/politico44/perm/0211/read_the_transcripts_b4f1ecfe-4c02-49ba-8105-13457741e2c3.html.

10.   Sanger, "As Mubarak Digs In."

11. Mary Beth Sheridan and Michael Birnbaum, "Clinton Urges Egyptians to Support Government-led Reform Process," *Washington Post*, February 5, 2011, http://www.washingtonpost.com/wp-dyn/content/article/2011/02/05/AR2011020501459.html.

12. Sanger, "As Mubarak Digs In."

13. Marc Thiessen, "How Obama Lost the Egyptian People," *Washington Post*, February 15, 2011, http://www.washingtonpost.com/wp-dyn/content/article/2011/02/14/AR2011021403059.html.

14. Edmund Sanders, "Egyptians Angry at U.S. for Not Backing Protests," *Los Angeles Times*, February 1, 2011, http://articles.latimes.com/2011/feb/01/world/la-fg-egypt-anti-american-20110201.

15. Sanders, "Egyptians Angry at U.S."

16. David Corn, *Showdown: The Inside Story of How Obama Fought Back Against Boehner, Cantor, and the Tea Party* (New York: Harper Collins Kindle edition, 2012), 229.

17. David E. Sanger, *Confront and Conceal: Obama's Secret Wars and Surprising Use of American Power* (New York: Random House Kindle edition, 2012).

18. Ibid.

19. Ibid.

20. Vali Nasr, *The Dispensable Nation: American Foreign Policy in Retreat* (New York: Knopf Doubleday Kindle edition, 2013).

21. Helene Cooper, "For U.S., Risks in Pressing Egypt to Speed Civilian Rule," *New York Times*, November 25, 2011, http://www.nytimes.com/2011/11/26/world/middleeast/us-urges-egypt-to-let-civilians-govern-quickly.html?pagewanted=all.

22. Ibid.

23. Ibid.

24. David D. Kirkpatrick, "Islamists Win 70% of Seats in the Egyptian Parliament," *New York Times*, January 21, 2012, http://www.nytimes.com/2012/01/22/world/middleeast/muslim-brotherhood-wins-47-of-egypt-assembly-seats.html.

25. Yitzhak Benhorin, "'Muslim Brotherhood Pledged to Honor Israel Peace Treaty,'" ynetnews.com, January 6, 2012, http://www.ynetnews.com/articles/0,7340,L-4172048,00.html.

26. Elhanan Miller, "Egyptian Parliament Demands to Cut Ties with Israel over Gaza," *Times of Israel*, March 12, 2012, http://www.timesofisrael.com/egyptian-parliament-demands-to-cut-ties-with-israel-over-gaza/.

27. Ibid.

28. Spencer Case, "How Obama Sided with the Muslim Brotherhood," *National Review Online*, July 3, 2014, http://www.nationalreview.com/article/381947/how-obama-sided-muslim-brotherhood-spencer-case.

29. Ibid.

30. David D. Kirkpatrick, "Named Egypt's Winner, Islamist Makes History," *New York Times*, June 24, 2012, http://www.nytimes.com/2012/06/25/world/middleeast/mohamed-morsi-of-muslim-brotherhood-declared-as-egypts-president.html?pagewanted=all.

31. Patrick Goodenough, "In Egypt, Clinton Fends off Allegations of U.S. Support for Muslim Brotherhood," CNS News, July 16, 2012, http://cnsnews.com/news/article/egypt-clinton-fends-allegations-us-support-muslim-brotherhood.

32. "Egypt's Morsi Assumes Sweeping 'Final' Powers," France24.com, November 22, 2012, http://www.france24.com/en/20121122-egypt-morsi-sweeping-final-powers-presidency-appeal/.

33. Kristen Chick, "New Egypt NGO law could expand Morsi's control," *Christian Science Monitor*, May 30, 2013, http://www.csmonitor.com/World/Middle-East/2013/0530/New-Egypt-NGO-law-could-expand-Morsi-s-control.

34. "Egypt Opinion Polls Reveal Dissatisfaction with Morsi," *Ahram Online*, July 2, 2013, http://english.ahram.org.eg/NewsContent/1/152/75491/Egypt/Morsi,-one-year-on/Egypt-opinion-polls-reveal-dissatisfaction-with-Mo.aspx.

35. John Hudson, "Knives Come Out for U.S. Ambassador to Egypt Anne Patterson," *Foreign Policy*, July 3, 2013, http://foreignpolicy.com/2013/07/03/knives-come-out-for-u-s-ambassador-to-egypt-anne-patterson/.

36. Marc Thiessen, "Obama Blew it in Egypt—Again," *Washington Post*, July 8, 2013, http://www.washingtonpost.com/opinions/marc-thiessen-obama-blew-it-in-egypt—again/2013/07/08/c0a394e8-e7c5-11e2-a301-ea5a8116d211_story.html.

37. Eric Trager, "Obama Just Made a Terrible Mistake on Egypt," *New Republic*, October 9, 2013, http://www.newrepublic.com/article/115115/obama-cuts-egypt-aid-why-hell-regret-it.

38. Sarah Lynch, "Egypt's Christians under Attack Since Morsi's Ouster," *USA Today*, August 15, 2013, http://www.usatoday.com/story/news/world/2013/08/15/egypt-coptic-church-islamists/2640419/.

39. David D. Kirkpatrick, Peter Baker, and Michael R. Gordon, "How American Hopes for a Deal in Egypt Were Undercut," *New York Times*, August 17, 2013, http://www.nytimes.com/2013/08/18/world/middleeast/pressure-by-us-failed-to-sway-egypts-leaders.html?pagewanted=all.

40. Jay Newton-Small, "Does Obama Support the Muslim Brotherhood in Egypt?" *Time*, August 23, 2013.

41. Nicole Gaouette and John Walcott, "Obama Call for Muslim Brotherhood Role Overtaken in Egypt," Bloomberg, July 7, 2013, http://www.bloomberg.com/news/2013-07-05/obama-call-for-muslim-brotherhood-role-overtaken-in-egypt.html.

42. "US Cutting Military Aid, Hundreds of Millions in Cash Assistance to Egypt," Fox News, October 10, 2013, http://www.foxnews.com/politics/2013/10/10/us-cutting-hundreds-millions-in-aid-to-egypt/.

43. Bill Gertz, "Obama Administration Rejects Appeal from Egypt to Deliver Helicopters," Fox News, March 12, 2014, http://www.foxnews.com/politics/2014/03/12/obama-administration-rejects-appeal-from-egypt-to-deliver-helicopters/.

44. Andrew Jarnigan, "How to Lose Friends and Alienate People: Obama in Egypt," *Georgia Political Review*, August 25, 2013, http://georgiapoliticalreview.com/how-to-lose-friends-and-alienate-people-obama-in-egypt/.

45. Patrick Howley, "Obama Accused of Crimes Against Humanity in International Court," Daily Caller, November 9, 2013, http://dailycaller.com/2013/11/09/obama-accused-of-crimes-against-humanity-in-international-court/.

46. Marc Lynch, "They Hate Us, They Really Hate Us," *Foreign Policy*, July 19, 2013, http://foreignpolicy.com/2013/07/19/they-hate-us-they-really-hate-us/.

47. "Report: By Supporting Muslim Brotherhood, Obama Drove Egypt to Russia, China," World Tribune, September 25, 2013, http://www.worldtribune.com/2013/09/25/report-by-supporting-muslim-brotherhood-obama-drove-egypt-to-russia-china/.

48. Lynch, "They Hate Us."

49. Josh Rogin, "How Obama Lost His Influence in Egypt," Daily Beast, August 16, 2013, http://www.thedailybeast.com/articles/2013/08/16/how-obama-lost-his-influence-in-egypt.html.

50. Ibid.

51. Ibid.

52. Adam Kredo, "Russia, Egypt Ink $2 Billion Weapons Deal," *Washington Free Beacon*, December 16, 2013, http://freebeacon.com/national-security/russia-egypt-ink-2-billion-weapons-deal/.

53. Barbara Salvin, "Fahmy: Egypt will 'Diversify' Foreign Policy with Closer Ties to Russia," Al-Monitor, April 15, 2014, http://www.al-monitor.com/pulse/tr/originals/2014/04/egypt-russia-foreign-policy-diversify-washington.html#.

54. Ibid.

55. Kredo, "Russia, Egypt Ink $2 Billion Weapons Deal."

56. "Report: By Supporting Muslim Brotherhood."

57. Adam Entous and Nicholas Casey, "Gaza Tension Stoked by Unlikely Alliance Between Israel and Egypt," *Wall Street Journal*, August 6, 2014, http://online.wsj.com/articles/unlikely-alliance-between-israel-and-egypt-stoked-gaza-tension-1407379093.

58. "Kerry, Aides Checked by Security at Egyptian Presidential Palace," Reuters, July 22, 2014, http://www.reuters.com/article/2014/07/22/us-egypt-usa-kerry-security-idUSKBN0FR15V20140722.

59. Entous and Casey, "Gaza Tension Stoked."

60. Ibid.

61. Barak Ravid and Jack Khoury, "Behind the Scenes of the Short-Lived Cease-Fire," Haaretz, July 16, 2014, http://www.haaretz.com/news/diplomacy-defense/1.605363.

62. Thomas Rose, "Egypt/Israel to John Kerry's Mediation Offer—'Please God, No!'" Breitbart, July 20, 2014, http://www.breitbart.com/Big-Peace/2014/07/18/Egypt-Israel-To-John-Kerry-s-Mediation-Offer-Please-God-NO.

63. Danny Danon, "Obama's Wrong Choices on Israel," *Washington Times*, August 25, 2014, http://www.washingtontimes.com/news/2014/aug/25/danon-obamas-wrong-choices-on-israel/.

64. Aaron David Miller, "Who won the Gaza War?" *Foreign Policy*, August 6, 2014, http://foreignpolicy.com/2014/08/06/who-won-the-gaza-war/.

65. Shoshanna Solomon, "Israel Nears Gas Sales to Egypt as Mideast Unrest Flares," Bloomberg, August 21, 2014, http://www.bloomberg.com/news/2014-08-20/israeli-gas-to-reach-global-market-via-pipelines-to-egypt.html.

CHAPTER EIGHT: THE CURRENT MESS—AND SOLUTIONS MOVING FORWARD

1. David S. Cloud, "Wrong Red Button" *Politico*, March 6, 2009, http://www.politico.com/news/stories/0309/19719.html.

2. In 168 B.C., the Roman envoy Gaius Popillius Laenas confronted the Seleucid Emperor Antiochus IV in Egypt to demand, on behalf of the Roman Senate, that he stop his invasion of Egypt. In an impertinent and dramatic gesture, Gaius drew a line around the emperor in the sand and demanded an answer before he stepped out of the circle. The emperor agreed and withdrew his army to Syria.

3. "Remarks by the President to the White House Press Corps," White House Office of the Press Secretary, August 20, 2012, http://www.whitehouse.gov/the-press-office/2012/08/20/remarks-president-white-house-press-corps.

4. Peter Baker, et al., "Off-the-Cuff Obama Line Put U.S. in Bind on Syria," *New York Times*, May 4, 2013, http://www.nytimes.com/2013/05/05/world/middleeast/obamas-vow-on-chemical-weapons-puts-him-in-tough-spot.html.

5. "Report of the United Nations Mission to Investigate Allegations of the Use of Chemical Weapons in the Syrian Arab Republic on the Alleged Use

of Chemical Weapons in the Ghouta Area of Damascus on 21 August 2013," United Nations, September 16, 2013, http://www.un.org/disarmament/content/slideshow/Secretary_General_Report_of_CW_Investigation.pdf.

6.   Jonathan Karl, "John Kerry Promises 'Unbelievably Small' U.S. Strike Against Syria," ABC News, September 9, 2013, http://abcnews.go.com/blogs/politics/2013/09/john-kerry-promises-unbelievably-small-u-s-strike-against-syria/.

7.   Arshad Mohammed and Andrew Osborn, "Kerry: Syrian Surrender of Chemical Arms Could Stop U.S. attack," Reuters, September 9, 2013, http://www.reuters.com/article/2013/09/09/us-syria-crisis-kerry-idUSBRE9880BV20130909.

8.   "Kerry Speaking Rhetorically over Syria Turning in Weapons: State Department," September 19, 2013, http://www.reuters.com/article/2013/09/09/us-syria-crisis-weapons-idUSBRE9880GE20130909.

9.   Cara Anna, "UN: Syria Declares Another 4 Chemical Facilities," Associated Press, October 7, 2014, http://abcnews.go.com/International/wireStory/syria-declares-chemical-facilities-26021611.

10. "One-on-one with Mitt Romney," CNN's Situation Room with Wolf Blitzer, January 19, 2012.

11. Josh Voorhees, "Obama Says Russia Is weak and Romney was Wrong," *Slate*, March 25, 2014, http://www.slate.com/blogs/the_slatest/2014/03/25/obama_nuclear_presser_president_takes_a_shot_at_vladimir_putin_s_ego_by.html

12. R. James Woolsey, "Old Problems with New Start," *Wall Street Journal*, November, 15, 2010.

13. Luke Harding and Ian Traynor, "Obama Abandons Missile Defence Shield in Europe," *Guardian* (UK), September 17, 2014, http://www.theguardian.com/world/2009/sep/17/missile-defence-shield-barack-obama.

14. Patrick Goodenough, "Top Polish Politician Quoted As Saying Alliance With U.S. Is 'Worthless'," CNS News, June 23, 2014, http://www.cnsnews.com/news/article/patrick-goodenough/top-polish-politician-quoted-saying-alliance-us-worthless.

15. Will Dunham, "Kerry condemns Russia's 'Incredible Act of Aggression' in Ukraine," Reuters, March 2, 2014, http://www.reuters.com/article/2014/03/02/us-ukraine-crisis-usa-kerry-idUSBREA210DG20140302.

16. Adrian Karatnycky, "Obama Can't Admit that Romney Was Right: Russia Is Our 'Top Geopolitical Threat,'" *New Republic*, September 17, 2014, http://www.newrepublic.com/article/119472/russias-geopolitical-threat-and-obamas-meeting-poroshenko.

17. Bennett Ramberg, "Why the U.S. Has an Obligation to Help Ukraine Defend Itself," *Los Angeles Times*, November 19, 2014, http://www.latimes.com/opinion/op-ed/la-oe-1120-ramberg-arm-ukraine-20141120-story.html.

18. Adam Kredo, "Top Iranian Official: Obama Is 'the Weakest of U.S. Presidents,'" *Washington Free Beacon*, October 23, 2014, http://freebeacon. com/national-security/top-iranian-official-obama-is-the-weakest-of-u-s-presidents/.

19. "Rohani's Outstretched Hand," *Economist*, October 4, 2014.

20. "Iran Makes the Rules," *Wall Street Journal*, September 29, 2014.

21. Ibid.

22. Parisa Hafezi and Louis Charbonneau, "Exclusive—Iran Seeks Give and Take on Islamic State Militants, Nuclear Programme," Reuters, September 22, 2014, http://uk.reuters.com/article/2014/09/21/uk-iran-nuclear-idUKKBN0HG0YD20140921.

23. "Iran Makes the Rules."

24. "Gas injection into IR-5 centrifuges has not stopped: Iran," PressTV.ir, November 12, 2014, http://www.presstv.ir/detail/2014/11/12/385700/ iran-feeding-gas-into-ir5-centrifuges/. Press TV is a news organ of the Iranian regime.

25. David Frum, "How Iran Scammed America Out of a Nuclear Deal," *The Atlantic*, October 1, 2014, http://www.theatlantic.com/international/ archive/2014/10/how-iran-scammed-the-us-out-of-a-nuclear-deal/381014/.

26. Paul Richter and Ramin Mostaghim, "Report Says U.S. May OK More Centrifuges in Iran Nuclear Talks," *Los Angeles Times*, October 20, 2014, http://www.latimes.com/world/middleeast/la-fg-iran-nuclear-20141021-story.html.

27. Lee Smith, "Appeasing Iran," *Weekly Standard*, October 13, 2014, http:// www.weeklystandard.com/articles/appeasing-iran_808497.html.

28. David Remnick, "Going the Distance," *New Yorker*, January 27, 2014, http://www.newyorker.com/magazine/2014/01/27/going-the-distance-2.

29. Howard LaFranchi, "Iran Nuclear Talks Extended, So Congress Might Turn Up the Heat (+Video)," *Christian Science Monitor*, November 24, 2014, http://www.csmonitor.com/USA/Foreign-Policy/2014/1124/Iran-nuclear-talks-extended-so-Congress-might-turn-up-the-heat-video.

30. "Obama Mustn't Bypass Congress with Iran deal," *Washington Examiner*, October 21, 2014, http://www.washingtonexaminer.com/obama-mustnt-bypass-congress-with-iran-deal/article/2555057.

31. David E. Sanger, "Obama Sees an Iran Deal That Could Avoid Congress," *New York Times*, October 19, 2014.

32. Plato, *Republic*, 1.347bf.

33. George Friedman, "Principle, Rigor and Execution Matter in U.S. Foreign Policy," Stratfor Global Intelligence, October 28, 2014, http://www.stratfor. com/weekly/principle-rigor-and-execution-matter-us-foreign-policy #axzz3K75whyei.

34.   Mike Allen, "'Don't Do Stupid Sh—' (stuff)," *Politico*, June 1, 2014, http://
       www.politico.com/story/2014/06/dont-do-stupid-shit-president-obama-
       white-house-107293.html.
35.   "State Department Memo Reveals Possible Cover-Ups, Halted Investigations,"
       CBS News, June 10, 2013.

Index

conflict with Netanyahu, 133, 139–45, 154

cultural chauvinism of, 129

cynicism of, 118

Egypt and, 159–78, 201

foreign policy failures of, 3, 14, 71, 80–81, 85, 153, 179, 196–98, 200–1

foreign policy guiding principle, 84–87

and ISIS, 43–45, 85, 100–5, 118, 120, 123–26, 143, 157, 179–85, 191–92

"jayvee team" comments of, 100–2, 123–24, 157

and the kill list, 33–35, 41, 51

lack of foreign policy experience of, 47, 100, 106, 129, 195

and the "Muslim world," 48, 154

"A New Beginning" speech, 87, 138

opposition to Iraq War, 84, 115–17

opposition to torture, 31–33

OPSEC and, 4–5, 45, 55–59, 63–64, 66

"red line" for Syria, 182–84

reelection campaign, 18, 32–33, 48, 53, 58, 185–86. *See also* Obama, Barack: subordination of security to politics

relationship with Iran, 155–58, 190–94, 202

relationship with Israel, 134–47, 149–53, 155, 158, 175–78, 201

Russia and, 181–90, 202

and security leaks, 3, 17–19, 21–25, 35–37, 42–45, 48–55, 57, 59, 62–71, 82, 85, 179

and settlements in the West Bank, 136–43, 146, 154

and spiking the football, 21, 143

and the Stuxnet computer virus, 18, 36

and subordination of security to politics, 14, 18–19, 22, 25–31, 53, 61, 198–99, 205

support of Muslim Brotherhood by, 82, 87, 160–74

Twitter account of, 31

victory lap on assassination of bin Laden by, 28–29

weak negotiations with Iran by, 40, 190–94

and withdrawal of troops from Iraq, 106, 116–26, 201

Occidental College, 133–34

O'Hanlon, Michael, 139

oil

importance to world powers, 107–14, 190, 198–99

in Libya, 84

in the Middle East, 103–4, 106–14, 122, 126–27, 131, 174, 190, 194

U.S. production of, 198–99

oilfields, 104, 122

Ollivant, Douglas, 119

"One Chance," 30

O'Neill, Robert, 66

On the Record with Greta Van Susteren, 63–64

operational security, 3–4, 14, 18, 42, 55, 69. *See also* OPSEC

Operation Neptune Spear, 20

Operation Olympic Games, 36

Operation Overlord, 28

Operation Protective Edge, 147–50

OPSEC

group, 3–5, 14, 45, 56–63, 66, 69, 77, 93, 202

military meaning of the term, 3–4, 55–56

Oren, Michael, 152

Ottoman Empire, 107

Overseas Security Policy Board, 74–75

Owen, Mark. *See* Bissonnette, Matt

P

Pace, Julie, 119

Pakistan, 19–21, 26, 32–33, 41, 91, 218

Palestine

1948 invasions of, 110–11

peace talks with Israel, 73, 128, 137–38, 142–46, 175, 178, 201

relationship with Israel, 128, 130, 134, 136–40, 145, 147–48, 164, 166, 201

Palestinian Authority, 152–53

Panama, 10

Panetta, Leon, 21, 36, 65, 118–19, 125

Paronto, Kris, 89, 93–94, 96–98, 209, 213–16, 220–21

Patterson, Anne, 166, 171–73

PBS *Frontline,* 119–20

peace

America in the 1990s, 10

Libya and, 80–81

Middle East and, 113, 125, 133, 136, 156–57, 159, 161–62, 178, 184, 193, 195–96, 198, 200–1

peace talks, 73, 128, 133–34, 137–46, 152, 154, 162, 165–66, 175, 178, 201

Pentagon, the, 24, 40, 44–45, 63, 65, 124, 203

Petraeus, David, 120–21, 221

Plato, 196

plausible deniability, 35–36, 52

Poland, 32, 187–88